THE RO[...]

❋   ❋   ❋

WALKING IN THE PATHS

OF THE GYPSIES

❋

Roger Moreau

KEY PORTER BOOKS

Copyright © 1995

Canadian Cataloguing in Publiction Data

Moreau, Roger (Roger C.)
    The Rom : walking in the path of the Gypsies

ISBN 1-55013-635-6

1. Gypsies – Origin.   2. Gypsies – Migrations.
3. Moreau, Roger (Roger C.) – Journeys.   4. Voyages
and travels.   I. Title.

DX135.M67   1995   909'.0491497   C95-930426-6

The publisher gratefully acknowledges the assistance of the Canada
Council, the Ontario Arts Council and the Ontario Publishing Centre.

Key Porter Books
70 The Esplanade
Toronto, Ontario
Canada M5E 1R2

Design: Scott Richardson
Endpaper illustration: Leah Gryfe

Printed and bound in Canada

95 96 97 98 99   5 4 3 2 1

TO MEREDITH

WHO KEPT THE FLAME BURNING

Acknowledgments

✻ ✻ ✻

A work of this nature necessarily involves the collaboration of a large number of people. Among those whose contribution is far greater than I can ever thank them for is my dear friend Bibi Anisa, secretary general of the West European Romany Kris: Shriji Arvin Singh Mewar, whose charm and aristocracy of manner are exceeded only by the warmth of his Rajput generosity of spirit: Dr. G.N. Sharma, who despite his eighty years has not forgotten a line of Indian history and who serves as an example to us all on how to grow young gracefully. And dear Johnnie Pathania, way up there in Jammu who, without a pinch of the *kalo rat* – the dark Gypsy blood – in his protoplasm, is without doubt one of the finest Rom I know.

And my most sincere thanks to the Gypsiologists, scholars and Rom I was fortunate to meet and count as friends during all that time of travel in India, Asia Minor and Europe.

✻ ✻ ✻

Contents

✳   ✳   ✳

Prologue

✻   ✻   ✻

Ever since I can remember the Gypsies have fascinated me. They attracted my mother too. There was a kinship there. A lure courted and desired, a spell cast and caught. Come spring they'd turn up at the house with sachets of lavender, clothes pegs, and odds and ends and mutter away darkly with all the panache and authority of Nostradamus forecasting the return of the Ice Age. A fortune telling – palm or teacup – cost half a crown, and the CinemaScope version, including a full range of dramatic pauses, stealthy whispers and accompanying sidelong glances plus an emotional choke or two deep in the larynx, a whole five shillings. No matter what they predicted, only half of it was ever accurate, but that was the half my mother remembered.

Years later, when the velvet-eyed, leather-skinned women in the ankle-length skirts and impossibly kitsch earrings ceased to call, I recall my mother reading my teacup and warning me to beware of injury in a place surrounded by lions. Not very likely in deepest Wimbledon, I thought at the time. But the portent returned to haunt me the next week when – surprise, surprise – I found myself despatched by the company to darkest West Africa: heading for Brazzaville, the capital of what was then the French Congo. I steered very clear of the jungle and avoided the zoo just in case.

The accident happened some three months later in Manchester, northern England, of all places when, slipping on a greasy patch in the City Square, I broke my ankle and, lying prostrate on the ground, found myself being sneered at by a pride of disdainful stone lions.

I once asked my mother where our Gypsies came from.

"St. Albans way, they tell me."

"No, before that. Back in history."

"Egypt, they do say. That's why they're called Gypsies."

"Do you think I could ever find out one day?" I persisted, conjuring up a past full of mystery and great adventures.

"I shouldn't try if I were you. You'd never get to the bottom of it. They're a feckless lot."

My mother said
I never should
Play with Gypsies
in the wood.

I sang it all the way to school the next day.

Some years later, there was a Gypsy girl in the Vale of Evesham, emerging from the damp woods carrying a dead rabbit by the ears. I stopped the car to give her a lift. She was soaked to the skin, a whisker away from pneumonia, or so her sneezes implied. I drove her to a patch of open land where her people had their caravans parked. Making conversation, I asked her which country she thought the Travellers had come from way back in the past.

"Somewhere far away. Wales maybe."

"Not India?"

"Now, do I look Indian?" she answered all cross, tossing her dark ringlets, teeth startling white in the dusky face. Very Punjabi indeed.

After I'd dropped her off, I discovered that in return for leaving behind one underprivileged, very poached rabbit and an untamed aroma of greasy wood smoke that never quite left the car, she had – quite unthinkingly, I'm sure – taken my silver

St. Christopher. Maybe he'd adapt just as well protecting a horse-drawn caravan as my six-cylinder Ford.

Sure, I missed him, but it was worth it for the sight, the indelible recollection of that child of nature coming through the wet trees holding lunch by the ears.

For many years the idea of finding out from where these people had originated and why they had come so far to sell clothes pegs to my mother lay dormant. It wasn't until I met a German landscape painter in Papeete, Tahiti, of all places and – for no particular reason – the conversation turned to Gypsies, that my interest was rekindled. He told me he had traveled around Europe with a *Kumpania* (caravan train) of the Rom for two years before the Belgian police found him and sent him back to his parents in Goslar in the Harz mountains.

"*Ja,*" he said, "according to our [German] Gypsiologists the Romani peoples originated in northern India – in the Punjab/Rajasthan area. The linguistics prove it. It is that no man to this day has been able to discover from which tribe they came. Also the reason why and the year they left India. Also the route they followed to come to Europe. Also, why they took five hundred years for a journey which should have lasted *nur zwanzig Jahren.* Also, why they never tried to return to the Fatherland."

Quite a salvo of "alzos" to assimilate at one seance, but it hooked me. And when this young painter, whose name now eludes me, added that the Gypsy migration represented one of the world's last unsolved mysteries even after close to two hundred years of intensive research, I was doubly enmeshed in the challenge of it.

He must have become aware of my burgeoning resolve. "You will undertake it, *ja*? I see you have determined it. *Ich warne dich,* it is a hard mountain to climb. It may take a lifetime."

The drinks at his one-man showing in Papeete's leading art

gallery were beginning to run low but they had performed their function with devastating power. The room was weaving in a peculiarly Tahitian way.

"I should make the point," I said through compressed lips, "that I have absolutely no knowledge of the Gypsies, even less of India; no expertise whatever in the craft of the historian or indeed the slightest cognizance of the undoubtedly essential areas of linguistics and anthropology."

"*Schon gut*," he replied. "No problem. You sound just right to me, *Junge*."

I went back to the hotel that night, but not to sleep. The thought wouldn't go away that, however ephemerally, I'd just been offered a window of opportunity that most middle-aged men yearn for – albeit by a sozzled German painter. The one chance to leave a footprint, however faint, in the annals by cracking something no one else had. And in a world fast running out of mysteries.

Was that the reason or was it simply mid-life crisis? Or was it the spell of Tahiti, which had previously demonstrated on at least one singular occasion the power to transform a mature and successfully settled Parisian stockbroker into a wild, bohemian painter of tragic genius?

But all the time I knew it went deeper than that. Far deeper. It went back to a childhood studded with superstitions and do's and dont's, during which I'd naively assumed that everyone in the world went around with eyes averted on the night of the full moon for fear of seeing it through a glass window. Cutting your hair or fingernails on Friday was akin to committing hara-kiri. These taboos were imposed by a mother and were set in stone, every bit as immutable as the rites of the masses I attended at Catholic boarding school.

It wasn't just a Don Quixote romantic fancy to tilt at windmills before the world ran out of them but a deep-down, driving compulsion – hitherto firmly suppressed if and when it ever surfaced – to find out more about a people who were in my blood and bone from the moment I first drew breath.

"Of course, you know you're quite, quite, bonkers," said my wife, Meredith, in her usual forthright Australian way. "You realize it would mean throwing away everything we've built up: career, home, friends, way of life, not to mention the Russian Blue, to launch into the unknown and with no experience to speak of behind you."

I nodded dumbly. That was that, I thought. *Finis.*

She poured coffee. The sun was slanting into the hotel room. Outside, coconuts being picked by a small boy were falling to earth with a regular thud, thud, thud from forty feet up. I wished I were up there with him.

"Well? Say something, Roger."

"I read you."

"Good. Sounds like a real challenge. Of course, I know you can do it. The month after next might be a good time to start. What do you say?"

Crunch time. Was I actually going to go through with this lunacy or had I just been fooling myself? Slowly, ever so slowly, I said those fateful words: "Who have you in mind to take care of the cat?"

And that's how the great adventure started. As simply and as mundanely as that.

"BRING ME THE HEAD OF A GYPSY BOY"

Hyg.-bakt. Unters.-Stelle
der Waffen-SS, Südost
Auschwitz O3., am 29. Juni 1944.

Anliegend wird übersandt:

Material: Kopf einer Leiche (12-jähriges Kind)
entnommen am
zu untersuchen auf Histologische Schnitte
Name, Vorname:
Dienstgrad, Einheit: siehe Anlage
Klinische Diagnose:

Anschrift der einsendenden Dienststelle: H.-Krankenbau
Zigeunerlager Auschwitz II, B II e
Bemerkungen:

Der 1.Lagerarzt
K.L.Auschw.tz II

SS-Hauptsturmführer.
(Stempel Unterschrift)

Copy of memorandum dated Auschwitz 29 June 1944 from SS-Hauptsturmführer Josef Mengele, signed by him and addressed to Hospital Building H, Gypsy Camp, Auschwitz II, B II O, asking that the head of a twelve-year-old Gypsy boy be brought to him.

B O O K O N E

✳ ✳ ✳

Before the creation of man, heaven and earth dwelt as a married couple and lived together in peace.

They had five sons: Mist King, Fire King, Wind King, Moon King and Sun King.

The Rom ascribe their wandering habits to the constant movements of the planets. The sun — the glorious Cham — was originally a Gypsy king eternally seeking to seduce Shion, his lovely sister, the moon.

— *OLD ROM LEGEND*

1. A Small Town in Rajasthan

THERE IS A SAYING THAT UPON EXAMINING THE HEAD OF A SLAIN
SERPENT, A PRECIOUS STONE WILL BE REVEALED.

— *OLD HINDU BELIEF*

Goduli is Hindi for twilight. Literally, it means "cowdust," the fine powder raised by cattle as they sway back to the village at eventide.

In such a soft blue and gold evening, I stood in the marketplace of Balotra, western Rajasthan, waiting for the four-wheel-drive to be fixed, intensely aware of a group of luminously saried women drifting from stall to stall, bantering; their silver laughter filling the sound spaces between the tinkling of ankle bells. Oil lamps came alive one by one like a long, low ripple of piano keys, faces of dark, brooding sensuality caught in the sudden spurts and flickering surges of light. Pausing, the women turned to gaze at the white intruder daring to blemish the purity of Shiva's night. They drifted toward me as if on cushions of air: a cloud of predatory butterflies. They begged silently with open palms, looking up with slow, contemptuous, veiled eyes.

"Kanjar women," said my Rajasthan Tourist Office guide and interpreter, Gopi Lal, drawing his eyebrows together and staring critically at a petrol pump.

I stood there with my heart pumping hard and my legs gone

rubbery. "*Yashwan bhava*" – "be lucky," as they say in Rajasthan. I couldn't believe I had caught up with what I had been searching for all this time. I couldn't take my eyes from them. There was no doubt in my mind. The million-to-one shot had come up, the missing piece of the jigsaw puzzle rising from the floor to smack one in the eye. "Yashwan bhava," I said again out loud.

It was an intensely dramatic moment. And the reason for this inner turmoil? Not, as one might imagine, love at first sight with one of the Kanjar maidens but something altogether different.

To begin with, let me summarize what I had learned about the Gypsies – the Children of the Wind, as they like to call themselves – after spending many long hours poring over books in the Reading Room of the British Museum and at the Gypsy Lore Society in Liverpool and studying them at first hand in North Wales.

All that had been established for certain was that a people (undefined) migrated from northern India at some period between the eighth and thirteenth centuries, motivated by either plague, famine, bad weather or foreign conquest and turned up in Greece in the first quarter or thereabouts of the fourteenth century – from which point they eventually spread over the planet like Coca-Cola or measles, depending how you view them.

It was not, however, until 1782 that a German, J.C. Rudiger, published his discoveries on the Indian origins of the Rom. The following year, in a massive flow of erudition, H.M.S. Grellman etched the fact in Teutonic granite that northern India had been their cradle: Rajasthan and/or the Punjab. All this was based purely on linguistic comparisons.

Since then research has continued mainly on this philological basis: establishing similarities between the Romani *chib* (language) and various Indian dialects in an endeavor to determine which of them had exercised the greatest influence on Romanes and, in consequence, which existing Indian tribe out of many might rightfully call itself the true rootstock of the Rom.

Present-day Romanes, I knew, was composed of a 50 percent Indian "core," with admixtures principally of Persian and Greek – the languages, in fact, of the countries through which the Rom had traveled on their way to Europe. The fact that Romanes seemed to be related to not one but several north Indian dialects led me to believe that the Gypsies could have been a nomadic people *before* they left India, but this view tended to be in the minority among Gypsiologists.

All in all, I had very little to go on except a general agreement that they came from northern India; also, my gut feeling was that they were of nomadic ancestry as opposed to landowning or peasant stock. As my German painter friend had said, there wasn't the slightest clue as to which tribe, caste or segment of Indian society had sired them. Or why they had left India and when. Or the circumstances of their trek to Europe, which could have taken anywhere between one hundred and six hundred years, depending on when the actual exodus took place. Or why they never sought to return. And, perhaps most perplexing of all, why they had retained their language but jettisoned something (normally) even more fundamental and ingrained in the human psyche, their faith – the Hindu religion. That was totally unexplainable. The Jews, too, had been driven out of their homeland and similarly scattered over the earth but had held on tenaciously to the thing that made them unique and set apart: their Judaism.

Certainly, over the past two centuries there had been theories a-plenty but none that stood up to close scrutiny. One of the most popular in recent decades ascribes an aristocratic

Rajput origin to the Gypsies. Pared down to its essentials, the theory had it that after the Battle of Tarain (near Delhi) in A.D. 1192, which saw the Afghan-Turks under Shihabuddin Muhammud Ghuri defeat the Rajput confederacy and establish the first ever foreign dynasty in India, the ruling aristocracy fled west toward Europe. Adopting the nomadic way of life — smithying, horse-trading, tinkering — they became the ancestors of those Gypsies who, during the early fourteenth century, swarmed into Greece and Eastern Europe.

This hypothesis had the signal benefit of providing not only the rationale for the migration — the why — but also a very cogent reason for their never having attempted to return to their homeland: ancestral fear of the Moslem conqueror.

But however hard I tried, I couldn't accept the theorem. It required a great deal more imagination than I possessed to picture a high-caste Rajput warrior (equivalent in noble deportment and pride of chivalry to, say, the Anglo-Norman knight of the twelfth century) selling firewood door to door to village housewives or mending cook-pots as he trudged through rural India and Persia en route to Constantinople. Additionally, why flee west, in the very direction from which the invaders had come? No born and bred military caste would ever be guilty of such unprofessional not to say suicidal behavior.

When it came right down to it, I had to find my own truth, not one necessarily that would stand up to expert testing and analysis — as the recorded facts simply weren't there to back it up — but one that because of its obvious, simple veracity and sheer rightness cried out to be accepted as being as close as we would ever get to the whys and wherefores of those elusive Romany roots.

To complicate the business of locating the ancestral stock, an idea had come into my head that it might be possible for the

Gypsies to have sprung from not one tribe but a racial mélange of two, three, four or even five. I had floated the idea to Agnes Vranckx, "Bibi Anisa," the highly knowledgeable and multi-talented Romni (Gypsy woman) who was general secretary of the West European Romani Kris (Gypsy Council), headquartered in Alicante, Spain.

"And what if there were two or more tribes in India contributing to the genetic make-up of the Rom, Agnes? Putting the picture together could take a lifetime, and a roomful of computers."

"Highly doubtful," she replied. "Not impossible, of course, but nearly so. Indian tribes *cannot* intermarry. Caste and religious reasons prohibit it. In modern-day Rom terms, it would be like a Lovari marrying a Kalderash or a Sinti or a Manush. 'Not done', as you English say."

"Therefore they could intermarry only by foreswearing caste and religion? Is that right?"

"Yes, but if you knew India, you would know there could never have been any circumstances that would allow miscegenation. The Hindus would prefer to forfeit life on earth rather than become what you might call the People of the Taboo. They would be putting at risk the whole of their cosmic existence. And on top of that there's the physical revulsion a tribe or caste has for another that has been bred into them ever since the Aryans conquered India four thousand years ago."

"Like me and a Congolese pygmy of the female gender, you mean, Agnes?"

"No, much, much stronger, Ruzo. More like you and a female baboon."

That seemed to settle that.

So here I was many months later, a long way from Alicante, in a small town in Rajasthan watching the Kanjar women melt away into the night and going over in my mind the events that had combined to lead to this one sublime moment when the matrix of an entire people's history suddenly took form and substance.

On arriving in India some months before, I had confined my search for the ancestors of the Rom to the nomadic tribes of Rajasthan and the Punjab. From whichever way I looked at the problem, it seemed the most practical method of tackling it, bearing in mind the theories formed from book study and discussion with Gypsiologists. Pragmatically, too, checking out *all* the tribes for possible Gypsy antecedents would have been madness. Even so, it meant covering thousands of miles to track down and interview the candidate tribes. The criteria were:

- They had to be ancestrally nomadic.
- They had to earn their livelihood from one of the three traditional occupations of the Rom, the skills they brought with them into Eastern Europe in the fourteenth century and which enabled them to survive. These were: the metalsmith's calling – working in iron, copper and bronze; animal husbandry – horse doctors, farriers and dealers in livestock (bullocks and camels in India, horses in Europe); the art of the entertainer – singers and dancers, conjurers, magicians, jugglers, fortune tellers and acrobats.

To my astonishment, rapidly leading to chargrin, then despair, it became apparent that no one individual tribe embodying all three skills existed as such. There just wasn't one ancestral tribe of the Rom in existence today and neither, I was absolutely certain, could there have been one at any time during the past 4,000 years of Aryan occupation of the Indian subcontinent.

To explain the situation in greater depth, there were tribes possessing one accomplishment and still practicing it, moving from village to village and town to town across Rajasthan and the neighboring states in time-honored ritual. But each of these nomadic tribes kept to its own specialty. You were a smith and that was what you were and nothing but. Not one of them would have conceived the idea of piggybacking another's occupation onto his own. To requote Bibi Anisa, "it simply wasn't done."

Fundamentally, it was something far greater than just earning a living, this craft of theirs. It was integral to their form of worship, the Gods they petitioned. One had only to talk to them to be aware of the fierce pride in the craft that was their id; it was their claim to recognition in Hindu society, their way of distinguishing themselves from other castes and tribes – in short, their uniqueness under the eye of heaven. Whether they were traveling smiths or nomadic snake charmers, theirs was a God-given, obstinately protected, inviolable individuality that allowed of no dilution.

Those were the hard facts of life. In accordance with Hindu tradition it was not possible now – and even less a thousand years ago, when it was thought the Gypsy migration took place and when, if anything, the rules were more draconian – to have had one tribe exercising all three professions. India, Hinduism and society as a whole simply wouldn't have tolerated it.

Inescapably, logically, as night follows day, miscegenation *had* to be the answer. Three tribes – each possessing one of the traditional Gypsy skills – had intermingled to produce the Romani race as we know it today. And so, with the greatest possible forethought and premeditation, I was now proposing to go off half-cocked and pursue a line of research that not one

Gypsiologist of note had even toyed with. Crazy or not, I decided I would find those three nomadic tribes who together constituted the matrix of the Rom. Then, and only then, would I tackle what seemed the insoluble problem of how – under what singular or miraculous conditions – they had melded together.

And then followed what must rank as among the most frustrating weeks stretching into months I could ever remember. Every tribe I came into contact with failed miserably to fit the bill. Yes, they were nomadic, the first criterion. But from that point onward it was all downhill. Put simply, delving into their history, studying them at close quarters to discern anything that resembled what I had absorbed about Gypsy characteristics and, above all, by employing every ounce of *Fingersptizengefühl* – intuition – in me, I left them, saddened and dejected.

Once, after solidly tracking across the length and breadth of Rajasthan and Gujarat and interviewing the Bhils, the Meenas, the Bhats, the Mairs and the Sodas et al., I thought I had struck gold. Far off the beaten track, I chanced on the Kalanders.

It was a small community: not more than a hundred people, who hid indoors fearing we were from the Health Department, they told us later. Finally, Abaad Khan, the chief, was coaxed from his hut by the simple expedient of rattling a handful of coins together. By the side of the hut, a large brown bear with sad woman's eyes was tethered to a post, and a couple of young monkeys to another. Horses and donkeys grazed on nonexistent grass. Dogs roused from their afternoon torpor raced madly toward us, barking hungrily.

Through my interpreter, Abaad first made the point crystal clear that the Kalanders should never be confused with inferior castes such as the Bajigars, Jadugars and Nats. "They beg and do every wicked thing."

The Kalanders were in the entertainment business – bear

and monkey acts — while the horses and donkeys we saw were kept as pack animals to transport their goods and chattels from village to village, town to town, even as far as Delhi, where the pickings were good but food expensive. Traditionally, only the men put on the entertainment, being loath to display their women to the public gaze.

Abaad had one of the entertainers bring out his show equipment. There was a *dug-dugi*, a small hand drum to attract attention as he walked down the street to draw an audience; then a chair; another, larger drum; a *topa*, (colored cap); an iron hoop for the male monkey to jump through; and a *gahagharia* (festive skirt) for the female monkey. There was also a toy pistol that served to control the monkeys, and a long stick and some *gur* (molasses) to give to them as a reward after the performance.

They put on a show for me. In the act I most remember, the male monkey sat on a small chair looking disdainfully regal while the female danced before him for his entertainment. It was very well done, most enjoyable I thought, and accompanied by a tremendous feeling of adolescent "kids at the circus" vitality. It seemed, on the surface at least, that the Kalanders might just be what I was looking for. But the faces had a solidity about them, the eyes a little narrow with no trace of that unique velvety look that is so indicative of the Rom.

I spent all day and the next morning with them, learning about their way of life and customs. They were Moslems, although none prayed the traditional five times a day. "We're too busy earning enough to eat," said Abaad. He was anxious to be with me and away from his wives. He said all the Kalander women were quarrelsome, always trying to stir the men up against one another. For my part, all I could see was that they were very kindhearted to strangers and incredibly loving with their children.

A little girl sang me a tale about a louse. You don't hear many of those nowadays. The translation went like this:

> O louse, O louse,
> where do you go?
> I go to fill my belly and find a husband.
> On the way she met a pipal tree
> and clasping it tightly, she fell asleep.

She caroled with great verve, eyes shining and every inch of her body moving in rhythm with her small brothers on their tinny toy drums.

It was an either-or situation. Either they were one of the original roots of the Rom or they weren't. I had to decide. And I couldn't.

Before leaving the next day and after a breakfast of dhal and brushing my teeth with charcoal powder, I had a final conversation with Abaad. After all, I thought to myself, they are entertainers very much in the mode of those in Eastern Europe, it just might be. . . .

I had realized at an early stage by the chief's withering contempt for the other nomadic tribes to which he referred always with the most biting sarcasm that miscegenation between tribes could not possibly figure on the discussion agenda, so I contented myself with enquiring into the history of the Kalanders. It was then the whole thing fell apart.

"Truly it is said that our ancestors came from Agra where they worked as servants to the Moslems. From Agra we migrated to various places: Bhopal, Ahmedabad, Jaipur and many others, always following the occupation of dancing bears and performing monkeys, and this for some ten generations. . . ."

"Is that all?" I could not help blurting out. Obviously if true, and I had no reason to doubt the statement, it made their nomadic experience of much too recent an origin for my purposes.

Toward noon, I said good-by. As we left, the whole community turned out with their *dug-dugi* to give us a farewell chorus. Despite my disappointment, it was a moving moment and one I will always look back on with great warmth. How was it that a people so desperately poor could be so happy, I couldn't help thinking time and time again.

The last words Abaad said to me were: "Tomorrow if we do not leave the officers come to move us on."

Udaipur, a week later. There is no more romantic city on earth with its fairy-tale palaces, hilltop fortresses and beautiful lakes and forests. Medieval chivalry and deeds of great valor and daring surround one at every turn. It's a city made for the conjuring up of great adventures, except that mine wasn't turning out that way at all. The plot was all there but I couldn't get the script right.

Outside the Tourist Office where I'd gone to pick up a map, I was accosted by a slim young man in his early twenties who, after introducing himself as one Gopi Lal, without further preamble asked me the purpose of my visit to Rajasthan. I could see no harm in telling him and so I did, standing in the hot sun with half my mind on the cold beer awaiting me by the hotel pool.

"It is within my power to help you, honored sir. Without the slightest reservation, I take upon myself the privilege of being your guide. I work only for the honor and very cheap rates. My people, the Banjara, are the true Gypsies you are seeking. It is an established fact during the whole time of creation and even before. Everyone, honored sir, knows that established fact. Per se," he added winningly.

Of course I had heard of the Banjara. There were too many of them — 20 million or so I'd been told — not to be aware of them. However, somewhat perversely, I had been saving them for last after I'd exhausted all the other possible candidates. Also, on my way back from my encounter with the Kalanders, I'd picked up a smattering of information about an interesting nomadic tribe called the Lohar and to connect up with them was a matter of priority.

"Yes, Gopi Lal, I'm sure you're right, but it's first stop the Lohar tomorrow if you want to come aboard. Crack of dawn departure from the Shiv Niwas Hotel suit you? Splendid. Oh, and try to find out in the meantime just where we can meet up with these Lohars, if you wouldn't mind. Apparently there's a group camping right now just outside the city on the road to Jaipur."

It was my first encounter in life with a voice that said "yes," while the totality of the physical structure implied "no, not on your life." I didn't think our relationship — Gopi Lal's and mine — would survive more than a day. In fact, anything past lunchtime might be considered well in the St. Francis of Assisi class when it came to a test of my forbearance.

Twenty families or so of the Gaduliya Lohar (literally, traveling blacksmiths), to give them their full name, were camped by the side of the road, the sun glinting on their distinctive, boat-shaped carts; the bronze plating and iron studding were indicative of the family name.

A slip of a girl stood barefoot before a steel anvil, wielding a ten-pound sledgehammer — the *ganga*. Finely sculptured features, her eyes heavy lidded, on her chest a peacock tattoo, symbol of her devotion to her lifetime's partner. Barely sixteen (we found out later), her slender figure was clothed in a long skirt of brightly printed cotton together with the traditional red and blue brassiere. Her 'Odhani' was draped loosely around her. On her arms, forty-six ivory bangles proclaimed her married state.

From October to the commencement of the monsoon season in June, the Gaduliya Lohar traveled Rajasthan in time-honored circuits: making and repairing farm implements, tin kitchen utensils, housewares, bangles and amulets.

We talked at length, the old chief and I, via the interpreting skills of Gopi Lal, whose native Banjara dialect was very similar to that of the Lohar. Nathu Ji Lohar, for such was his name, had married recently for the fourth time and presented a cart and two fine bullocks to his new bride. She had not ceased showing her gratitude in the variety of ways – mainly physical – and it was obvious we were in the presence of a man truly at peace with the world. We sipped a home brew, containing no fewer than twenty-six ingredients, he averred. It had a pleasant, fruity taste and a wicked tendency to make one's eyes leave their sockets the moment it barged into the blood stream.

Nathu Ji Lohar, speaking as if it had happened yesterday instead of A.D. 1568, closed his rheumy, wordly-wise eyes and related how his people fell from grace during the siege of Chittorgarh – the fort of Chittor.

"At that time we Lohars were weapon makers to the Rajputs and enjoyed the many privileges accorded to our elevated status. For months we had been brave under siege although short of food and water. However, when it became clear that Chittorgarh would fall to the devil Mogul emperor, Akbar, we escaped by a secret way. It was then we swore never to return to Chittorgarh until it was free again. Scorned as cowards and deprived of our noble calling, we were condemned to wander the face of the earth in fulfillment of our Karma."

He went on to recall the time when Nehru, then prime minister, invited the Gaduliya Lohar back to Chittor in 1955 (eight years after India's independence from the British). "Only a few thousand Lohar dared accept the summons and all the way from the old railway station up to the fort, lining the road, our women were wailing and carrying on and beseeching Ram Deo and Kali to spare their menfolk for having broken the vow." He chuckled throatily but later let slip he wasn't one of the Lohar who turned up at Chittor that day. Not he.

As we left, he shouted out his free man's defiance of all things bureaucratic: "Those ghee-fed, soft-bellied turds in Tribal* want to tidy us up and make us sleep in houses so's we can be killed when the roofs fall in. Well, we won't and you can tell them what they can do with their houses . . . five-foot chimneys and all. Especially the chimneys. . . ."

As Gypsy as they come were Nathu Ji Lohar, his wives, family and clan. Looks, voices, gestures, everything about them positively screamed kinship with their European cousins, including that determination amounting to a mania to remain free at all costs, despite every inducement from the government to settle them permanently.

At Gopi Lal's insistence, the Banjara had been next and together we visited a Banjara *tanda* (village).

Nomadic carriers from time immemorial, Banjara traders often measured their wealth in tens of thousands of bullocks, on the backs of which they transported salt, grain and spices along the 7,500-mile-long Silk Road from China in the east to

---

* Department of Tribal Affairs.

Constantinople in the west. An unrivaled, first-hand knowledge of India and its princes, together with a highly developed expertise in securing supplies of pack animals/beef on the hoof/grain supplies had raised them to unprecedented heights of wealth and position in the new Moslem India created by Babur, the first of the Mogul emperors, in the mid-sixteenth century.

On the occasion of our visit, the *Naik* (Banjara chief) gave us a potted history of his tribe while Gopi Lal and I squatted in the gloom of the mud brick hut.

"We Banjara," said the *Naik*, speaking with deep, slow authority, "continued to prosper until the British Raj came with its railways. Overnight we became destitute. What use were our bullocks without goods to transport? The Banjara died, a tear from every eye, watching their cattle waste away to skin and bone. We who had the spring of travel in our blood and eyes accustomed to fresh landscapes no longer followed the road as our forefathers had done ever since bullock worked for man. The wings of the falcon of the world had been torn off forever by an alien hand."

It was the authentic voice of the Gypsy we had heard that blazing hot afternoon. Their love of animals, their expertise (they bred, bought and sold camels now in lieu of bullocks) was so much in the tradition of the Rom. But it was the women who convinced with their brooding ways giving way to fierce passion – that indefinable aura-scent of the jungle, of the wild wood from whence the Banjara originated, according to legend.

I was in no doubt that I had struck it lucky again and that these Banjara together with the Lohar I had previously encountered made up two-thirds of the matrix I was seeking. But just that and no more. Neither possessed to any marked degree that gift, that elusive panache, that charisma that makes the born entertainer. Not just the talent, but the driving, compulsive desire to exercise it, that strutting, exhibitionist lust to perform, to flaunt voice, face, eyes, body and personality to be devoured whole by a rapt audience.

There had to be another nomadic tribe out there, a race of wandering entertainers. The problem was that nobody had heard of any such tribe. They didn't exist, it seemed. Collapse of theory.

Or was it?

One day, with that side of the triangle still obstinately missing, in the Udaipur museum I happened to come across a collection of three-foot-tall wooden figurines – man and wife couples dressed in traditional costume – representing the wild tribes of Rajasthan. There they were, the Bhils and the Meenas, the Kalanders, Bhats, Mairs and Sodas, all of whom I had met up with and crossed off my "eligible" list. And tucked away in an alcove gathering dust, a pair of real desperados, fierce and predatory of mien, savage of eye, but both with an unmistakable Gypsy air about them, accentuated by the gaudy clothing and barbaric jewelry the artist had lavished upon them that not even the cobwebs could hide.

"Who are these people?" I asked the museum attendant.

"Very bad mens and womens, Sahib. Kanjar peoples. All day drink spirits, steal chickens, kill the folks." Then adding the worst thing he could say about anybody: "Eat cow." Wrinkling his nose and joining his fingertips in salutation, he quickly walked away as if from a bad smell.

I went back to the museum the next day with Gopi Lal to find out more about these turbaned Robin Hoods. Frankly, although they intrigued me, they puzzled me even more. If all they did was drink and steal, why bother to dress in such a rich manner? It made no sense unless . . . unless (could I be that lucky?) they were somehow in the entertainment business.

Initially, Gopi Lal wasn't much help. In fact, I detected a distinct aversion to my Kanjar theory. To be precise, a distinct aversion to the Kanjars per se, to use his favorite expression. Nonetheless, he questioned the attendant at length and afterward checked studiously through the museum library. Later, at tea at a nearby restaurant, he summed up his findings.

"It is, as I said concerning the description of them, the habits of the Kanjar are entirely foul. In the past, before television, they earned the honest portion of their income going from village to village, juggling, dancing on stilts, singing, dancing, performing with dancing bears and monkeys. Their women practiced fortune telling – 'casting the stones,' we say – also tattooing and other things that my upbringing will not permit me to impart to your ears."

"Anything else, Gopi Lal?"

"They spend their rupees on drink and clothes and turn away from food in preference to the dance."

Now I was getting really excited. "Can we find some of these Kanjar, Gopi Lal? And if we do, are you able to converse with them?"

"Finding them, Uncle?* Certainly. For sure. Maybe. If we are lucky. I try."

He paused to scratch his twenty-three-year-old head. "Speaking to them? *Aaccha*."** He paused again but more meaningfully this time. "As well as Kanjar tongue they speak secret language of the road."

"You speak this secret language, do you, Gopi Lal?"

"Of course not, Uncle. It would not be secret then. But do not worry, I find driver who can."

---

* A term of respect in India.

** *Aaccha* translates straightforwardly as "okay," but as used by Gopi Lal could also mean "maybe" or even "definitely not." When enunciated in a positive, forthright manner and accompanied by a quick flash of his intelligent eyes, it signified "I don't understand the question."

* * *

So here we were in this small town in Western Rajasthan, a couple of hundred miles due west of Udaipur, and I had just seen my first Kanjars (apart from Patsi, our one-armed driver, that is, and he was on board only because Gopi Lal had not been successful in locating a driver of his own Banjara tribe who spoke Kanjar).

As the women disappeared into the darkness, I began to experience that tingling sensation. It was all coming together.

We tried everything the next morning, but there was no finding the Kanjar encampment. True to form everyone – police included – sent us off in totally wrong directions time and time again. It was hopeless. I was forced to the conclusion that the entire Kanjar community, which we had been told amounted to well over a hundred people, had folded their tents and melted away to wherever Kanjars go to escape the attentions of amateur Gypsiologists.

I was bitterly disappointed, but not for long. An inspired piece of driving by Patsi led to an impressively built, silk-suited Indian dusting himself down in the middle of Balotra High Street. Of all people, we had run into – literally – the GP who treated the Kanjars. After checking himself for broken bones and keeping a wary eye on Patsi, Dr. Joshi magnanimously offered to guide us to their settlement.

On the way, he confirmed that these particular Kanjars had, to all intents and purposes, ceased their nomadic way of life. The settlement we were about to visit had been established seven years ago. Men and women worked as casual laborers on nearby building sites, from which they contracted respiratory diseases such as asthma and bronchitis. There were approximately 250 of them in the settlement, half of whom were under the age of ten, Dr. Joshi continued. Forty percent of the adults had VD and a third had TB. "Civilization, the sedentary life, is slowly murdering them," he concluded as Patsi drove into the camp with his knee on the horn.

Hunkering down with the Kanjar chief, whose name was Baburam, and his wife, Kalali, and their six children, I asked him why he and his people had opted for the settled life.

"It was this way," Dr. Joshi translated. "Up until seven years ago we led the life of traveling entertainers, the same as our forefathers and their forefathers. The women sang and danced in the towns and villages, begged, and sold their bodies when times were hard and even when they weren't. We men made papier-mâché horses, staged cock fights, robbed on occasion, got drunk and ambushed the odd policeman or two. A wholesome, manly sort of life, you might say."

"What on earth persuaded him to give it up?" I asked Dr. Joshi. "It sounds like the sort of existence that could grow on a man."

Baburam's reply, expressed volubly and with much piteous rolling of eyes, went something like this: "Business was going down the drain. Tastes are different now, it's all television dung and five-piece bands. The villagers don't want to see our famous stilt dances any more." He pointed to a pair of fifteen-foot-long wooden stilts gathering dust and goat excreta by the side of the hut. "It was all over for us. Then we discovered that by breaking large bricks into smaller bricks we could eat once a day." He spread his arms out wide, crooking both forefingers. "Sometimes twice." But he looked sideways at us and there was guilt in his eyes, nabbed (that favorite media word in India) in the act of selling his birthright for a mess of dhal.

The women put on a song-and-dance show for us while the men accompanied them on sitar and kettle drums. They sang about a Kanjar maiden by the sweet Gypsy name of Mauti and

ended the performance with the up-and-down trills and appog-
giatura of "The Myrtle Tree." Their faces — among the most daz-
zlingly beautiful of any tribe in India — looked to the heavens in
mock-tender supplication: shoulders, arms drooping and folding
like stricken swans.

They were Gypsy, Gypsy, Gypsy, the heart and soul of the
Rom, part of the original die stamp that made up the Romani
race. On the evidence of my own eyes, it was impossible to
doubt it.

The Lohar.   The Banjara.   The Kanjar.

A combination, a melding of the three made up the race that
swept into Europe in the mid-fourteenth century. I just knew it.

I was cock-a-hoop and not a little puffed up with myself.
But steady on — the mountain still had to be climbed. Just how
had this mingling of the blood happened? Under which circumstances had the impossible been made possible? What the
heck, just look at the way Gopi Lal and Patsi reacted toward
each other. There were thousands of years of enmity, fear and
loathing between them, topped up by a caste system that pre-
cluded them even sitting side by side.

A tough one that. The more I thought of it, the more it
seemed to boil down to locating an event, a set of circumstances
in Indian history during which the three streams *could* have
become a river: simply, naturally and inevitably. Or, pushed a
little further, *had* to have become a river.

So that was the task now. To find that one, singular hap-
penstance that had produced a race, even if it took a lifetime
and then some. Per se.

2. Udaipur – The Palace

From Colonel James Tod's *Annals and Antiquities of Rajasthan*, Volume I:

To

HIS MOST GRACIOUS MAJESTY
GEORGE THE FOURTH

Sir,

The gracious permission accorded me, to lay at the foot of the Throne the fruit of my labours, allows me to propitiate Your Majesty's consideration towards the object of this work, the prosecution of which I have made a paramount duty.

The Rajpoot princes, happily rescued, by the triumph of the British arms, from the yoke of lawless oppression, are now the most remote tributaries to Your Majesty's extensive empire; and their admirer and annalist may, perhaps, be permitted to hope, that the sighs of this ancient and interesting race for the restoration of their former independence, which it would suit our wisest policy to grant, may be deemed not undeserving Your Majesty's regard.

With entire loyalty and devotion, I subscribe myself,

Your Majesty's

Most faithful subject and servant,

JAMES TOD

Bird Hurst, Croydon
20th June 1829

U d a i p u r ,   M e w a r ,   R a j a s t h a n

Two personages dominate the enchanted lake city of Udaipur. In chronological order, Lieutenant Colonel James Tod, one-time political agent for the Western Rajput states. A superb administrator, this remarkable man of Anglo-American parentage not only reformed Mewar's finances and made the state solvent but also dedicated himself over a period of eighteen years to the 1,260 pages and hundreds of footnotes and charts contained in his *Annals and Antiquities of Rajasthan* (1829).

At a time when the world was swept up in a frenzy of expansion and commercial activity, when so much that was old and rare was being lost or discarded, Colonel Tod lived out his love affair with Rajasthan, unearthing, collating and recording for posterity the archival records and the verbal treasures of bardic accounts passed down through the centuries by word of mouth.

Under British rule the old state of Mewar was one of twenty-two that made up Rajasthan ("the place of kings") or rather Rajputana ("the home of the Rajputs") as it was known under the Raj. Roughly the size of Switzerland, Mewar's original capital, Chittor, was abandoned in 1559 in favor of the present capital, Udaipur – one of the most ethereally beautiful places in the world and the most perfect locale imaginable in which to take time off from the world. Everyone should go there at least once in a lifetime to bathe his or her soul.

I was there to ask a favor and so, traveling forward to the present time, let me introduce our second personage, Shriji Arvind Singh Mewar, the end product of nearly 2,000 years of breeding and seventy-five generations of personal rule, whose ancestors styled themselves "Maharana" and, until the India Parliament Act of 1971, represented the longest surviving dynasty on earth. Deprived of his title and position as head of state he may be, but nonetheless he is responsible for a major portion of the philanthropic work carried out in Udaipur by financing schools, libraries and hospitals from the profits of his real estate and hotel holdings. What makes his position so strong with his millions of erstwhile subjects is that he is seen as being above politics and totally incorruptible in a land where politics have replaced big business as a means of getting rich quick.

"It's a case of 'you can take away the form but not the function,' if you see what I mean," he explains. "My role takes in all the duties and cares of office but none of its prerogatives or, indeed, the recognition. What one might call responsibility without power. Not a bad thing, though, in this day and age."

But under the charm and ease of manner one senses an implacable devotion to the welfare of a people he still considers his and who reciprocate the feeling totally – the solemn obligation of the Hindu ruler to guard and serve his subjects. "I suppose by this time, it could be in the blood, eh?" he adds. India: part fable, part fate. Only on the surface does it change.

Arvind Singh generously granted me permission to make use of the Maharana of Mewar's Research Institute facilities, including considerable chunks of the time of Dr. Gopinath N. Sharma, a leading historian in his own right, and principal in charge and responsible for the enormous task of indexing the records produced over the centuries relating to the history of Mewar. He is also a wise and venerable man of great culture and penetrating insight who gave me some of my most uplifting and abiding memories of India.

To find the Maharana of Mewar's Research Institute is not the easiest of tasks. One way is to come up from the super-luxury Shiv Niwas Palace Hotel, past the polo field and the garage housing twelve Mercedes and the venerable 1947 Rolls-Royce kept for state occasions, and go through the wrought iron gates to the granite and marble of the Old Palace built on the eastern bank of Lake Pichola.

Alternatively, approaching from the City end, you walk along the *chowk* (street market) and through the massive, three-portal Tripolia Gate with its cruel, spike-studded doors designed to repulse elephant charges. The market has its own unique brand of heat. Even the photographs you take of it appear to swim as they take in the dust and the odor of goat and bullock urine, and the teeming thousands of store keepers and shoppers and herbivores. Those myriad bright colors, the sheer vibrancy and drama sweep you up and away and leave you bewildered, topsy-turvy and achingly thirsty. It's too much at first, all this movement and vitality. You have to take it in small doses until you establish landmarks for yourself.

From out of the melee you plunge into the cool of the Old Palace with its courtyards connected by narrow stairways, its carved pillars and marble pools. The eye is caught and entranced by walls decorated with inlaid semiprecious stones, miniature paintings and mirrored mosaics of exquisite green, blue and gold beauty.

It's quite tangible, this feeling that every stone in this illogical labyrinth of corridors, rooms and courtyards is stained irrevocably with the romance of history, of bloody sieges and of a queen's undying, tragic love for her lord: the romantic passion of Lady Tara Bae and the Prince Rajendra. This is one of the most tender, beautifully poignant tales ever told in any culture and, to give you an idea of the plot, it's almost a dead ringer for Shakespeare's *Othello*.

A series of high-ceilinged chambers crammed with books and folios and odorous of that special grace that falls on those who wear the mantle of serene scholarship; walls ten feet thick; the smell of old parchment; a mild dryness of air as in a Byzantine chapel – Tod must have written his *Annals* in one of these rooms, speaking in an acquired language, having to deal with the sinuosities of Brahmin thought, they who were his mentors in the mores and manners of Mewar. One can imagine him, eating strange, highly spiced food, depriving himself of port wine and claret and tobacco in deference to his hosts, a sexless, friendless, totally cerebral existence. Only the flame of scholarly research and the passionate desire to set down on paper all the romance, epic chivalry and reckless courage epitomized by the word "Rajput" to keep him going through his years of residency.

You find yourself envying Tod. These high chambers produce an urge to slip back into another, more innocent age in which honor was deemed more important than wealth or power. For there was only honor a man could take with him to the next life while leaving it behind as well.

It was within those cool stone walls that a picture gradually emerged. Dr. Sharma's quiet, precise voice wove a backdrop of the history of Rajasthan against which the historical antecedents of the Rom begin to stand out and take on flesh.

"It was the poets and the bards, stretching from the immortal Vyasu all the way to Beni-dasa, the chronicler of Mewar at the time of the arrival of your compatriot, James Tod, in Udaipur in 1817, who were the historians of India.

"Unfortunately, bardic accounts were primarily concerned with the martial exploits of the great: the *rung-rin bhom*, or field of slaughter. Civil matters, normal everyday pursuits, the simple joy of following the path of duty were of no interest to the bard. Idealized, highly emotive romance and the noble deeds of war were the core and essence of his calling.

"But to answer your question, there is nothing in our history – the little we do have recorded – or in any of Tod's writings that refers in any way to an exodus of Indian peoples or tribes to the west. It is generally understood that the history of our country is rather the opposite – a great number of people *coming* in. You British, for instance? I fear you are talking to the wrong person. You should address yourself to the Department of Tribal Affairs. If anyone knows anything about your Banjara, Kanjar and Lohar tribes it should be they."

But I had been down that road before, to no avail. I asked Dr. Sharma to let me have his thoughts on the future of the three tribes. After quite some hesitation, he said he didn't really know anyone who could help and I left it at that as, changing tack, I asked him about the incidence over the centuries of Hindus having been taken prisoner in battle or on raiding expeditions and marched westward as slaves: to Persia . . . Anatolia . . . Byzantium even. Increasingly, the proposition was taking shape in my mind that disparate tribes might conceivably have been confined together in an early form of concentration camp, under which conditions they might well have interbred and produced a race we now call the Rom.

Dr. Sharma frowned a little at this, miscegenation not being a choice topic of conversation in polite Indian society.

"Well," he said eventually, "might I suggest you start with the Arab invasions of northern India in the eighth century. Many, many slaves would have been required to transport booty back to Kabul – the springboard for their annual assaults. Tradition-ally, as you are aware, the Arabs encouraged their slaves to mate and thereby produce or reinforce desired physical characteris-tics. Yes, I suggest you start with the Arabs."

A servant, turbaned and wearing a white dhoti, padded silently into the small chamber to take away the teacups. I rose to leave. As I did, Dr. Sharma remarked very quietly, almost under his breath: "There is nothing in Indian history that can help you, I fear. You see, those whose duty it should have been to record historical events – the Brahmins – chose not to, believing all life to be *maya* [illusion]. A dreadful indictment of a nation, is it not, that it was left to a British officer – Colonel Tod – to salvage what he could of our past."

And he smiled that sweetest, most gentle of smiles and sighed and pressed his hands together in the age-old Hindu gesture of farewell.

As I turned to make for the door, I caught my first glimpse of the Sacred Thread – the distinguishing mark of the Brahmin – he wore under his arm. It occurred to me as I passed through the courtyard that, for all I knew, our conversation might have been *maya* too.

The Arabs and the Conquest of the Sindh

According to R.C. Majumdar in his splendid work *Ancient India* (first published in 1927), the early history of the Aryan Gurjara clan is unclear, but it seems they first entered northern India – along with the Huns – toward the end of the fifth century A.D. Cities and districts bearing their name denote their advance through the Punjab to Jodhpur.

Occupying Rajasthan, they brought peace and prosperity to the land. Under their rule, villages produced a superabundance of food, the mines yielded great riches of precious stones and ores, and the quarries, beautifully toned marble. The nomadic tribes moved about the countryside in their age-old fashion in an atmosphere of unparalleled peace and plenitude.

The Gurjara had been settled for over 150 years when the Arabs made their first incursions from the west. Up to that time the followers of Mahomet had carried all before them. Syria and Egypt had been conquered within six years of the Prophet's death. The northern coast of Africa, and Persia and Spain had fallen in quick succession. Before a century had passed, the empire of the Caliphs extended from the Loire in the heart of France to the Oxus and Kabul rivers.

This fierce and formidably competent people, filled with religious fervor and an unquenchable desire for slaves and treasure, now cast covetous eyes on the fertile plains and rich cities of India. They were the first would-be conquerors of any significance since Alexander the Great, circa 300 B.C., a whole millennium before.

In the event, the first Arab incursions lacked their usual irresistible élan. A series of plundering raids was undertaken but nothing of any consequence until A.D. 712 when the situation abruptly moved up several notches in intensity.

At that time, the king of Ceylon, anxious to ingratiate himself with Arab power, sent to Hajjaj, governor of Iraq, a number of women (twenty-four, according to most reports) who had been born in Ceylon of Moslem fathers now deceased. The women of that country, incidentally, had the reputation of being the most beauteous in the world. Unfortunately, the ship in which they traveled was captured by the pirates of Debal, a seaport of the Sindh (now Pakistan).

Hajjaj accordingly wrote to Dahar, king of the Sindh, asking for the release of these women, to which Dahar blandly replied he had no control whatever over the pirates who had captured them.

The outcome was inevitable. As far as Hajjaj was concerned, casus belli now existed. The Caliph of Baghdad, the overall potentate of the Moslem world, at first unwilling to sanction what he regarded as a risky expedition to unknown territory, finally gave his consent to Hajjaj to assemble an army for the invasion of the Sindh.

The dogs of war were unleashed. A train of events was now put into motion that would lead to the eventual Moslem domination of India. That the invading army did not sweep all before it at that time was due solely to the extraordinary defense put up by the Gurjara-Pratihara clan, and the Arabs had to be content with occupation of the Sindh and northern Gujarat. However, it did not require a great effort of imagination to foresee that sooner or later the Baghdad Caliphate would use this acquired territory as a springboard from which to conquer the rest of India. But it was not to be. A more ruthless invader waited in the wings.

The Invaders from the Kabul Valley

The Pala family, described as "Indianized foreigners," ruled in Kabul until the ninth century. Alberuni, the eleventh-century astrologer and chronicler (we shall come to him later), called them descendants of Kanishka, the second most powerful figure in ancient India after Asoka and who ruled not only over Afghanistan but the whole of northern India, including Kashmir. The dynasty endured until the Arab, Saffarid Yaqub ibn Layth, assumed power in A.D. 870. But increasingly the Caliphate's former Turkish slaves began to exert a powerful control over what is now Afghanistan. The situation clamored for clear-cut resolution.

It was not long in coming. In a few short years, the Turkish slaves assumed total power and thus Afghanistan gave birth to one of the greatest – and least reported – empires Asia has ever known. The provinces of Ghazni and later Ghur were to smash

India into a hundred million pieces. "He rendered the Hindus as atoms of dust," wrote Alberuni of the Sultan Mahmud of Ghazni.

Someone – I forget who – once remarked that history could be summarized as the impact of character on circumstance. This has always struck me as a most profound observation, but interestingly enough the story that I imagined to be taking shape was the very opposite – the effect of circumstance on character, circumstance that formed a race, its integrity, its persona, its charisma.

In its simplest form, my tentative feeling – one that would later become a positive conviction as more and more facts checked out – was that the Rom had started their existence in a slave holding pen in Afghanistan. Where else but in a slave labor camp could oil, water and vinegar have blended with no fear of retribution from on high, simply because according to Hindu tenets, as captives of the *Mleccha* (the impure ones) they were already polluted beyond redemption?

With a sinking feeling I realized the real challenge had only just begun. I now had to locate, somewhere in the vastness of Asia, the site of the world's first concentration camp. Where does one start?

Over the next few weeks, throwing reserve to the winds, I cajoled interviews, telephoned, sent telegrams and wrote letters to just about every Indian historian of note. The response was always the same. No one had ever heard of a long-term holding area or labor camp for Indian slaves. Not in northern India, nor Afghanistan, nor Persia nor anywhere. They did, however, concede the idea to be quite interesting. A people lost in history for hundreds of years? Frozen in a time capsule? Developing at their own rhythm like a tree in a forest? Yes, they liked that. Intriguing. But quite, quite dippy, of course.

As I was on the point of giving up on what seemed to be an

increasingly unrealizable hypothesis, I found myself one day brows-
ing through some old volumes in a public library. It was then I
came across Colonel Sir Thomas Holdich's *Gates of India*, published
by Macmillan & Co. in 1910. I quote now from the notes I took
at the time and that unfortunately, after a dunk in the Ganges,
may no longer be considered faithful to the original. However,
textual blurring aside, their meaning is clear, as bright and inspiring as it was to me when I first read those passages that gave such
support to my theory and, indeed, my battered self-confidence.

"Northern Afghanistan was to these Assyrian kings [circa
750 B.C.] the dumping ground for unconsidered numbers of
slaves; a bourn from which no captive ever returned. Did they
drift eastward for centuries from Syria, Armenia and Greece
carrying with them the rudiments of their art? It is impossible
to set a limit to the number and variety of people who, in these
early centuries either migrated or were deported from West to
East through Persia to Northern Afghanistan or who drifted
southwards into Baluchistan."

He continued, still describing these mass dislocations of
peoples: "We cannot understand India without a study of that
wide hinterland [Afghanistan, Persia and Baluchistan] through
which the great restless tide has ever been on the move: now
a weeping nation of captives led by soldiers to a land of exile;
now a band of merchants reaching forward to a land of the
golden purse; or, perhaps, an army of pilgrims walking with
their feet treading deep into ancient footings to the shrine of
forgotten saints."

And further on: "The outlying provinces of his [Tiglath
Pileser III (745-727 B.C.)] dominions were convenient dumping
grounds for such bodies of captives not required for public works
at home."

This was what I had been praying for. The fact that these

slaves of the Assyrians were being taken east toward India and not west and from it made no difference to the established fact that northern Afghanistan *had* been used as a dumping ground or holding pen for large numbers of slaves – and with a tradition dating back over 2,500 years.

If, for instance, an ideal area of internment – a natural geographical stockade requiring a minimum of guards – had been discovered by the Assyrians in Afghanistan, might it not also have served the same purpose right down the centuries for other conquerors bringing *in* slaves from India?

My researches showed that from circa A.D. 800 onward, Moslem invaders were returning to the west with great numbers of Indian slaves carrying booty pillaged from palaces and temples. And in the main the route they took led through northern Afghanistan.

Things were beginning to slot into place.

The obvious guess was a holding camp somewhere in the Kabul area (the first main center of civilization after leaving India and an ideal spot for some necessary R & R after tackling the murderous Khyber Pass). Adjacent, too, to the Silk Road for ready access to the thriving slave markets of Nishapur, Balkh and Herat.

With mounting excitement, I pored over a map of Afghanistan, tracing with my finger the route the raiders would have taken on their way back from India. There, a little to the west of a town called Ghazni, was a clearly defined plain some ninety miles square, on the edge of a vast, dried-up lake and ringed by high mountains on three sides while the unguarded west opened up to an inhospitable barrenness with the ominous name of the Desert of Death. It was a natural prison if there ever was one. No barbed wire or guard dogs were required. On the map it looked pretty escape proof.

The name of the place was Dasht i Nawar (Dasht means

desert). I had always nurtured a wish to learn Arabic, but as things were I had but two words in my repertoire. One was *Inshallah* and the other *Nawar*. *Inshallah* means "according to the will of God," which was what I was experiencing at that moment. *Nawar* is the Arab word for Gypsies. Translated, *Dasht i Nawar* means "Desert of the Gypsies."

My plan was to go to Delhi to find out all I could about this mysterious desert. I felt certain it could turn out to be the vital element I had been searching for.

I was due to fly out the following morning and that evening was enjoying one of those whimsical Indian films on the TV – all soft, languorous glances and blood-spattered decapitated heads rolling about on the marble tiles – when I saw a long buff-colored envelope slowly being pushed under the door. Intrigued enough to drag myself away from the scene in which the young couple are saved from the giant saw by Lord Krishna, who deposits them in the middle of a gaily flowered mountain meadow there to dance and sing a love duet, I took out a closely typewritten letter. In style, it was more of an official report. There was no signature, not the slightest clue as to who had sent it. Obviously not someone who was big on pride of authorship. As I read, it became apparent why. The Indian government is awfully sensitive about some things: *Sati* (ritual immolation of the surviving widow), for one; the extraordinarily high rate of female infant mortality; the sale of child brides to wealthy Gulf Emirs; the desperate plight of the Harijans (Untouchables) under the iniquitous caste system that makes serfs of many of them; the Indian Army's jack-booted occupation and suppression of human rights in Kashmir, Punjab and other places.

Starting off without any form of preamble, it read:

Sir,

    Since 1896 the Banjara, Kanjar and Lohar tribes have come under the classification of Criminal or Scheduled tribes. It is hard to determine how this came about in the first place. It is possible, of course that, to the British Raj, being nomadic automatically spelt felon: in the same way as they branded their own Gypsies in England. 'No visible means of support, constable? Why, put the fetters on the rogue this instant.'

    The case of the Banjara is especially tragic. Once they were respected pillars of Indian mercantile society. Astute traders owning large tracts of land and enormous herds of cattle – trusted by the Princes with confidential messages.

    As far as one can see, the future for the nomadic tribes is grim. Death at an early age is the only certainty. It is said truly that images of doom and suffering have the greatest impact as deep down we think it might happen to us. Well, here indeed is one such picture simply due to the fact that it is not considered in the corridors of power that nomadic societies have a role in modern India. They are an embarrassment to be swept under the carpet as quickly and – if necessary – as ruthlessly as possible. For thousands of years, thanks to their traditional skills they fulfilled a vital function in rural India. Now their inheritance serves no purpose. They have had their day. Plastic utensils have replaced the copper and bronze housewares they used to make and mend. Mercedes trucks, the bullock train. A colour television set does duty for travelling mummers and entertainers.

    One does not have to be versed in the science of economics to realise that the only occupations open to them will be of the unskilled, common labourer variety. Long hours, poor pay

and death in their twenties await them. Now, with a hugely
expanding population (we are nearly one billion people in
India and will certainly double that within the next 50 years
unless someone sees sense – which is unlikely) our resources,
especially food, will become scarcer. Inevitably, these erstwhile nomadic tribes will find themselves at the very bottom
of the nutritional/survival chain.

To our shame, and that of the human species, they will
succumb. Alcoholism, inadequate diet, lack of money to pay for
medical attention, unhygienic living conditions, disease and,
above all, too many babies at too early an age, will attend to that.

Reduced to its essentials, the Government in Delhi will
always have too many pressing problems to concern itself with
its Nomads. Ideally, they should be stuck in the middle of India
in the same way as millions of our Aboriginals are, and have
been ever since Independence. Tribes like the Muria, Marias,
Halba, Kamar, Abujhmaria, Gonds, Santal, Khasis and Bonda.
Termed the 'Adivasi' (first occupants), some 60 million of
them are sentenced to live like animals on land nobody wants
(yet) for the heinous crime of being non-Aryan. Living in
the manner of primitive man 50,000 years ago. Penned in
'Restricted Areas' so that no one can visit them and report on
their plight. Left to die out from disease as rapidly and, above
all, as inconspicuously as possible so that we Indians can get on
with our true vocation of acting as the conscience of the world
without the inconvenience of any visible skeletons rattling in
our own closet.

Aboriginals and Nomads. They are, and will remain, The
Untouchables, The Unmentionables, The Unspeakable, The
Unwanted. Buried in 'Restricted Areas' – the Indian Govern-
ment's euphemism for the Gulag, or classified as Criminal or
Scheduled Tribes. What sort of a country is this where up to

60 million people (the population of Britain) are unwanted . . . uncared for, swept under the carpet to rot and die? Where generations of Public Servants in New Delhi aspire only to wake up one morning and find they have all disappeared without a trace? Or, better still, left for Pakistan.

You see, dear Sir, they simply do not fit in to the bright, shiny-modern, nuclear power image India wishes of itself and that our masters are so desperate to project to the world.

I put down the letter. Certainly it filled valuable gaps in my knowledge but hadn't I got a bit more than I'd bargained for? Like asking someone to pat you on the back to cure your hiccups and being mowed down from behind by a four-ton truck.

I never did find out who the letter came from, even less what prompted its author to send it to me.

My initial reaction, I must confess, was a feeling of shame for India. That a people so intellectually gifted and so proud of a civilization that went back at least four thousand years should turn out to be perpetrating what amounted to the largest campaign of genocide in history, beside which Hitler and even Stalin, with the deaths of 20 million fellow citizens to his credit, ranked only in the second division.

The information it contained was to my mind absolute dynamite and I wondered if I shouldn't be doing something with it. Was that what the author had in mind? I went down to the pool and ordered a beer while I listened to the musicians and watched the lights dancing blue and green on the water. Now that the first effect of all the human misery the author had described was wearing off, I was thinking more rationally. The thought struck me forcibly that what the Indian government was doing, for instance, to its Aborigines, was not that different to what we in Europe were doing to our *Untermenschen* – the Rom.

How could I or anyone point the finger at India when technologically advanced and ultra-civilized Europe was in the process of killing off 8 million Gypsies by sheer bloody-minded callousness? At least in India the poor blighters weren't starving to death or dying of cold clutching cardboard suitcases on the platforms of East European railway stations with the women selling their bodies to feed their infants.

No, I thought, this is not a situation that calls for a holier-than-thou attitude. The Indian government may well be putting cockney grannie away in a terminal nursing home as it moves into the bright new world of suburbia, but Europe – west as well as east – is starving her to death and letting her die from hypothermia.

The Third Reich slaughtered close to 1 million Gypsies in World War Two and hadn't paid a cent in reparation. Surely one would have thought that the richest country in Europe would have felt a degree of noblesse oblige to help out in what is rapidly becoming a matter of life or death for the Rom as their plight grows worse as one terrible winter follows another. It was now becoming a very real question whether they can survive another decade unless something is done to help them.

I made the resolution there and then that the only thing I could do was to set down my quest – my adventure, call it what you will – in a book. If it were ever published and if only a few score people read it, then at least they would be aware of the antecedents of the Rom and, I hoped, knowing a little of their history, feel some sympathy and understanding for a race that has suffered like no other. It was only a little thing I was doing, but at least it was a first hopeful step toward conserving one of the most remarkable races on earth.

3. Alberuni's India

From: *Alberuni's India, An Accurate Description of All Categories of Hindu Thought, As well those which are admissible as those which must be rejected. Composed By Abu-Alraihan Muhammad Ibn Ahmad Alberuni:*

THE STRONGEST OF THE PILLARS [OF ISLAM], THE PATTERN OF A SULTAN, MAHMUD [OF GHAZNI]* THE LION OF THE WORLD AND THE RARITY OF THE AGE, MAY GOD'S MERCY BE WITH HIM.

HE UTTERLY RUINED THE PROSPERITY OF THE COUNTRY [INDIA], AND PERFORMED THOSE WONDERFUL EXPLOITS BY WHICH THE HINDUS BECAME LIKE ATOMS OF DUST SCATTERED IN ALL DIRECTIONS, AND LIKE A TALE OF OLD IN THE MOUTH OF THE PEOPLE.

In Delhi, with access to first-class information sources, I put the area around Dasht i Nawar under intensive scrutiny: reading everything I could about it, studying every map I could lay my hands on.

Dasht i Nawar lay some seventy miles to the southwest of Ghazni, the nearest urban center and itself some eighty-five miles south of Kabul. Now a melancholy, down-at-heel little town, inconceivably, nine centuries ago Ghazni had been one of the most magnificent capitals of the world, ranking with Constantinople and Rome and, militarily, with Byzantium, the leading power in Asia.

I sensed that Ghazni, on which Dasht i Nawar would have depended, could well be the key to the riddle of how the Gypsy

---

* Ghazni, Afghanistan. Ruled A.D. 997-1030.

race had come into existence. I had to pinpoint the one period in Ghazni's existence during which it was most likely that the birth of a race could have come about. That would give me the missing "when." With Dasht i Nawar, I had the feeling I had already found the "how" and "why."

The first question to be answered was how Ghazni, this God-forsaken, provincial little town set amidst an empty, rock-strewn landscape, had become the most gloriously embellished metropolis of its day. And who were these Afghan Turks – these former slaves of the Arab Caliphate who were to shake India and Persia to their very foundations and rise to become the most potent force in the Moslem world?

Back to the history books, then, for one of the most fascinating rags-to-riches tales ever told, a story straight out of *The Arabian Nights*. Scheherazade, with her golden-scented imagination, could not have improved upon it.

In A.D. 953 Alptigin, an erstwhile Turkish slave taking advantage of the waning power of the Baghdad Caliphate, had carved out an independent principality in the Soleiman hills around Ghazni in northern Afghanistan. In time, the kingdom passed to his son-in-law, Sabuktigin, another Turkish slave captured young who, by outstanding ability, had risen high in Alptigin's service.

By the time Sabuktigin died in A.D. 997 the River Kurram was running red with Indian blood as he fought his way to mastery over all the territories to the Sindhu. Not to be outdone, his son, Mahmud, now the inheritor of a kingdom stretching from the Sindh in India to the heart of Persia, launched a series of murderous incursions deep into northern India – a ruthless, systematic devastation of land, a barbarian desecration and looting of palaces and temples. Religious zeal and unholy greed fused together under the banner of a monstrous *jihad*.

The Persians called him *Butshikan*, the Iconoclast; The Hindus, *Ashoka*, the Impure.

A look at the map shows that India is bounded to the north by the Himalayas and to the south, east and west by the open sea. To the northeast and the northwest, hill ranges connect the main chain of the Himalayas with the sea.

Despite these formidable natural defenses, never has a country been so open to invasion. Even the forbidding Himalayas offer roads from Tibet through to Nepal that have brought in missionaries, merchants and warring armies in free-flowing numbers throughout the ages.

To the west there are several passes across the Hindu Kush. The pass most commonly used by invaders intent on plundering the riches of northern India was that which follows the valley of the Kabul River from northern Afghanistan and descends to Peshawar, via the Khyber Pass.

To the brave, the determined and the avaricious, India was a lure, a lodestone mine of gold and emeralds. Its 1.5 million square miles (equal to the whole of Europe minus Russia) was in A.D. 1000 incomparably the richest – and easiest – source of plunder in the world.

A total of seventeen expeditions against India were attributed to Sultan Mahmud, including the rape of the city of Nagarkot, which yielded, according to the scribe, "70,000 golden dinars, 700 mans* of gold and silver plate, 200 mans of pure gold ingots, 1,000 mans of various jewels including pearls, corals, diamonds and rubies." On another raid in A.D. 1018 on fair Mahalar, he brought back 2 million dinars of gold on the backs of 53,00 slaves and 350 elephants.

I gawked at the figure of 53,000 slaves. This was human

---

* Approximately one pound weight.

plundering on an industrial scale. And then, an astonishing discovery: in toto, during the course of his reign, Mahmud brought back no fewer than 750,000 slaves from India to transport his booty to Ghazni, there to lay it in the courtyard of his palace before the slaves were sold – if in any sort of condition – in the slave markets of Kandahar, Herat, Balkh, Kabul, Nishapur and Samarkand.

Actually, even though many Indian historians consider their effect as no more than transient, I think it certain that those seventeen raiding expeditions by Sultan Mahmud destroyed India. They drained the country of wealth, of men, of equipment, of morale, while the Ghaznivite occupation of the Punjab made it inevitable that the Gates of India would be opened wide enough to allow the Moslem hordes to claim formal possession of the empire less than two centuries later.

Such was the legacy of the Amir Mahmud.

It was Mahmud's life and times that held the key to the birth of the Gypsy race. I needed to concentrate on him, the Sultan, the Amir, the Emperor Mahmud. And by so doing, I hoped to comprehend just how the impossible had come to pass.

It all came back to my theory that circumstances had had an impact all the way along the line of the Rom. They hadn't transformed themselves into a race as a deliberate result of a planned exodus from India. No, circumstances beyond their control had done it for them. Always they were acted upon rather than instigating action.

Alberuni's writings were my chief source of research data. The great student of religion, astrology, philosophy, the physical sciences, optics, mechanics, mineralogy and geology had been taken from his native Kwarazim to be held hostage at the court of Ghazni most of his adult life. He had described the court in minute detail and with as much hidden malice as he could get away with, especially insofar as the physically repulsive, pederastic Amir Mahmud was concerned.

And what a court it was. In the eyes of the sophisticated who visited it, the most magnificent, the most ornate, the most richly perfumed of its age: filled to bursting with the treasures of Kwarazim, India and Persia. It was a court in which an army of poets, mingling with astrologers, astronomers, physicians and mathematicians, chanted their over-blown paeans of praise, "*kasidas,*" to the Sultan, his court officials and high-ranking military officers. Courtiers lounged in cool, high-ceilinged rooms on silken cushions, waited on by slaves from every province of Central Asia. Scholars walked sedately, white-gowned, serious, in deep discussion in the fragrant gardens and marble courtyards, their minds rich with the treasures of the libraries ransacked from Ray and Isfahan.

Even Alberuni could not entirely conceal his admiration for Mahmud despite the Sultan's faults of character and wanton life. A man at once poetic, inspired, cultured and cruel, he was without doubt the foremost military man of his age, a superb organizer and administrator. His terrifying raids on India laid the basis for the future conquest of that empire and the commencement of a dynasty that lasted until the arrival of the Moguls in the sixteenth century.

Traditionally, the Moslem raiding schedule was determined by the weather and followed the same inexorable pattern year after year. December through February were the cold months when it was best to gaze into the fire and dream of the riches and glory to come. March through May was sowing time in India — therefore poor pasture for the horses and little assistance from the overworked peasantry. June through August was the rainy season during which nothing could move. But September through November – now *that* was the raiding time: fine, balmy weather and lush grass.

Mahmud of Ghazni's father, the Amir Sabuktigin, had built roads in order to descend more rapidly onto the rich pasture-land of the Plain of Panipat in September, from whence to fan out in search of temples and palaces to plunder.

Incongruously, the idea of laying waste to that verdant plain at the onset of spring and thus denying fodder to the Moslem cavalry would have been considered unsporting by the Rajput who, secure in his own castle, however, felt not a frisson of chivalry when it came to helping out a kinsman under siege a bare fifty miles away. The concept of uniting in the defense of Hinduism and their common heritage simply did not occur. And it was this very absence of common cause more than any other factor that ultimately allowed the conqueror to plant the heel of his boot on India's neck.

Without a doubt, what made Mahmud of Ghazni's raids so different from those of the past was their vastness of scale; the massive bulk of treasure he brought back to embellish Ghazni; and the astronomical number of slaves, a large proportion of which he retained to assist in his ambitious programs of public works.

This was how I visualized the Dasht i Nawar operation working in the hands of this supremely competent man – the practical administrator par excellence. I was sure to be wrong on numerous points of detail but the core of it, I felt, would be valid.

As the crow flies, from central Rajasthan to Dasht i Nawar is approximately eight hundred miles. That bald statement conceals the fact that nearly half the distance is taken up by the aching immensity of the Thar Desert and the lung-bursting Khyber Pass. Death for the slaves would have taken many forms: thirst, malnutrition, internal hemorrhaging caused by beatings, and multiple rape on both men and women – their captors would not have been selective. Dying of backs that suddenly went "snap," dying with gray, exhausted, pain-racked faces, staring blindly at a Heaven that had ceased to listen to their pleas. And at each death the load on the surviving bearers increased with each step as they too grew weaker.

Many of the carrier-slaves who outlived the journey to Dasht i Nawar would have been left to die there: heaps of skin and bone, broken in mind and body, winded beyond succor. For the stronger ones, a period of rest would have been necessary before being despatched to the slave markets.

Some – apathetic, uncaring, lifeless – would have slid into an ad hoc form of permanent residence in the desert, rendering the occasional service to passing soldiery in return for a rusty knife, a piece of leather or a scrap of dried meat. In the normal course of events, babies would have been born and, such is the power of the human spirit, a small percentage survived to adolescence. But, reduced to its essentials, life would have been short, sharp and brutish for these permanent, hard-core residents.

The camp would have grown and expanded as Mahmud and his advisers realised the advantages it could offer and the many and varied purposes it could serve. It was just the right distance from Ghazni in case plague broke out or the slaves revolted. It was convenient, too, for receiving supplies from the capital. An additional attraction would have been the great lake. In those days it would have provided drinking water and fish, and vegetation would have sprouted along its banks, providing tree bark to satisfy gnawing hunger and to use for medicinal purposes.

One of the camp's evolving functions would have been to

act as a resting base for soldiers returning from the Indian front instead of their marching straight into Ghazni and creating the sort of mayhem that soldiers with gold in their pockets are normally disposed to. The artisanal slaves could repair their equipment; others, versed in animal husbandry, could doctor horses and camels. As a bonus, the troops could take their pick of the female slaves. And all this at no cost to the exchequer except for the provision of a bare minimum of food.

In synopsis, this was how I imagined the functions of the camp at Dasht i Nawar: part crematorium, part holding center against future programs of public works, part R & R camp for slaves coming in from India prior to sale in the main centers, and part equipment-repair center and brothel for the Sultan's troops returning from the Indian campaigns.

It all made perfect sense so far. But how, I asked myself, did the camp's facilities lead to the formation of the Gypsy race as an amalgam of three nomadic tribes? The answer came slowly, but come it did. The key lay in the place itself.

In winter, at 10,000 feet above sea level, the bitter wind at Dasht i Nawar would have sliced through skin tissue and turned calcium-deprived bones into brittle ice sticks. In summer the temperatures would have soared to above 50 degrees Celsius. As is known, the Hindus hold a large number of hells in their tradition, the total of which is 88,000 in ascending order of severity, according to Vishnu Parana. Doubtless to its inmates, Dasht i Nawar would have been at the very pinnacle of those Hindu Hades. Only the very, very toughest would have survived, those who were ancestrally tough, genetically tough.

Although admittedly having an axe to grind, I found it logical to suppose that it would have been the super-fit nomads who endured most successfully, with their inherent superior resistance to disease and malnutrition, and who furthermore — if you take the Lohar, Kanjar and Banjara as cases in point – had the specific skills to be of benefit to the camp and thus form the hard core of its resident population.

In fact, there was a valid case for postulating that it was precisely those nomadic tribes crisscrossing the Sindh River and northwest India who would have been primarily sought as carrier slaves by the Afghan-Turks. From the Moslem point of view, the nomad with twenty to thirty miles a day in his legs would have been a much better proposition than any soft, pot-bellied villager.

Year after year the slaves would have tottered in, more dead than alive, there to witness their fellow Hindus as prey to disease, robbery, brutality, sadism, rape, sodomy, murder and cannibalism. For the inmates of Dasht i Nawar, it was nothing less than a place where the living dead delayed the finality of interment for the briefest of time. But the mortality rate could be reduced simply by the slavers concentrating on a minimum number of nomadic tribes to bring back their booty from India. By doing so, they ensured that more of them survived in the camp to be eventually sold as slaves. The fewer the tribes the more chance there would be of their being taken in hand and protected by their own kith and kin on arrival, thus significantly reducing cannibalism.

In my excitement the thoughts spilled out. This was the reason no one had ever unlocked the secrets of the Rom and their origins. It was because Gypsiologists had always visualized – and still did – their leaving India as a mass migration, a voluntary, determined, premeditated act by one tribe.

It all began to make enormous sense. There just wasn't a Gypsy migration as popularly conceived, I was convinced of that now. After only a few months on the subcontinent, I couldn't imagine for a single moment the tribes destined to become the

Rom sitting down and declaring unanimously: "Next Wednesday week we go west." They simply weren't made that way.

In any case, if they had taken that totally out-of-character decision to move away from their ancestral habitat in Rajasthan/Punjab, it would have been toward safety in the south, where the original Dravidian population had fled from the advance of the Aryan invaders circa 2500 B.C. Never, ever had they gone to the north or west, from where all ills originated. No, they had been picked up on their traditional wanderings, and against their will, to end up in a hellhole of a place where conditions positively encouraged miscegenation between clan and tribe, caste and *gotra*.* They had become a race apart, divorced from their faith and origins.

The more I checked out the proposition, the more it became apparent there wasn't one hitherto unsolved enigma about the history of the Rom that Dasht i Nawar didn't answer. It felt so right it had to be true. The world's first concentration camp had acted as the crucible of a race. It was from its iron earth that those Romany roots had sprung.

The word in Romanes for foreigner or non-Gypsy is *Gaujo*. (pronounced "Gorgio" in the United Kingdom). It is the word that separates us from them. No Gypsiologist to date has satisfactorily explained how the word came into being. It is a complete mystery. My supposition is that it was minted in and around Ghazni. The slaves called the guards "Ghazni." In time Ghazni became corrupted to "Ghazzi" and then "Gauzo" and then ultimately, "Gaujo" or "Gadjo" or "Gorgio."

Dasht i Nawar polluted its inmates: Banjara, Lohar and

---

* A lineage segment within an Indian caste that prohibits intermarriage by virtue of the members' descent from a common mythical ancestor. An important factor in determining Hindu marriage alliances, the prohibition was intended to keep the *gotra* free from intended blemishes and to avoid the possibility of consanguinity.

Kanjar among them. It besmirched, defiled, rendered them Untouchable, first by forcing them into contact with the *Mleccha*, the "impure" Moslems but, above all, by creating conditions that made the unpardonable sin of miscegenation virtually inevitable – inter-tribal copulation. From that point onward, there was no amount of penance the Brahmins could impose that would allow them to re-enter society, to take their place again on the *chakra*, the wheel of life, death and rebirth. They had become lower than vermin, outside the pale of Universal Being forever. It was the core reason they could never return to Mother India – which answered another question that has puzzled Gypsiologists, namely, why they never tried at any stage of their wanderings to return, but always forged west.

Defilement also explained why the Gypsies discarded something as integral, as positively fundamental to human existence as their religion, while retaining the other talismans of their Indian origin, their language and way of dress. It explained, too, why, when arriving in Europe as an ostensibly homogeneous group, they lost no time in dividing up and going off in three separate directions. Unconsciously, the river was reverting to its original, pristine, elemental streams: Banjara, Lohar, Kanjar.

And would not the sin ensuing from the blending of tribe, caste and blood go a long way toward explaining the feeling the Rom have always had deep inside of being placed on earth to be punished? As scapegoats for the human race? The old Romany had a saying: "God punishes all, the Rom twice as hard."

There was a book waiting for me at New Delhi's main post office. Entitled *The Position of Romani in Indo Aryan*, it was written in 1927 by Ralph L. Turner, the noted Sanskrit scholar (of the School of Oriental Studies at London University). In simple, striking sentences it postulated double parenthood for the Gypsies: a north Indian background followed by a prolonged stay in Afghanistan. Well, it seemed that someone else had the germ of the same idea more than half a century ago – and a real heavyweight, at that. I had to admit that the sun was really shining on me that day.

In the courtyard of the Palace on an evening that gleamed pink and gold, the birds of Vishnu – the blue, intense green-within-green peacocks – strutted before the peahens as I sat to write down this torrent of thoughts teeming in my head.

The lady of the house, whose rank once entitled her to be addressed as Rani, passed soundlessly by on her way to tend the Shrine of the Lord Ganesh – the Elephant God – set in the stonework of the far wall. The lights of the city far below began to come on one by one. The temple monkeys ceased their chatter; wing after wing of bats passed overhead as the saga of the Rom took form and substance on the paper before me.

Ironic, I thought, that that other great exodus hadn't been chronicled, either. The ancient Egyptians who habitually recorded everything – not a detail being spared to give posterity the most accurate insight into life under the Pharaohs – made no mention of the flight of the Jews.

A spurt of fire glowed briefly in the dark retreat of the wall. The scent of jasmine hung in the air. All was forest quiet in the velvet blue eternity that is India.

It occurred to me how important it was from the very beginning to set my parameters and, above all, to get my format right. At this precise moment I had a theory and, I thought, a valid one, but unless I could prove it – and at this distance removed in time, compounded by a complete lack of recorded historical fact, it seemed unlikely – all I could do would be to weave in those facts that were definitely established with educated suppositions and present it as more or less a work of fiction: a romance. Anything else would be dishonest.

But despite everything, I desperately hoped I would get closer to the heart and soul, center and marrow, roots and origin of the Rom than anyone ever before.

Slowly stealing over me was the feeling that a deeply interred wish was about to be granted. I knew what I was about now, knew the why, when, how and wherefore of the birth of the Rom. It was an intensely exhilarating feeling, but humbling at the same time.

Some time ago I'd met a man in the terrace bar of the Rambagh Palace in Jaipur, the Pink City. He claimed he had been bathed in the light at the end of the rainbow where it met the ground one day in the Aravalli Hills in northern Rajasthan. He had never quite recovered from the experience. He saw the world differently now, in different terms, he said. "It was like stepping out of a prism of polished ice, old man. Everything was suddenly quite new and special."

For the first time since that odd encounter I knew fellowship with that man. I was on the point of unearthing something adamantine, which would change the way a people thought about themselves by informing them of their own history – alter, too, how the rest of the world saw them by stripping away the mystery, the false conjecture, the alien sound.

Tomorrow I would start planning the great trek. Beginning at Dasht i Nawar, I would follow the Silk Road its 4,000-mile length all the way to Istanbul, retracing the original footsteps taken by the Rom a millennium ago.

I couldn't undertake the trip alone, that was for sure. It meant assembling a team of experts, hard-driving, objective, totally committed professionals who felt the same way I did about the importance of the project. In fact, I thought I had the answer. I had recently made contact with three PhD Anthropology students at Jaipur University and felt confident they'd be keen to accompany me. It would be the trip of a lifetime for them. Happily, their holidays were coming up soon so the timing was perfect. I had three weeks to get the trip organized, shipshape and Bristol fashion. I really couldn't see it going wrong. It was simply a question of Planning One's Work and Working One's Plan, as an ex-advertising colleague used to say.

A bit of a hiccup intruded into this euphoria, causing me to wing my way out of Rajasthan on Air India to Delhi on the first plane available. Just one little thing that in all the excitement I had failed to take into account: Under no circumstances would I be allowed into Afghanistan.

In Delhi I tried everything, but to no avail. Mr. Khan at the British Embassy was especially understanding but the message was clear. "A simple in-and-out flip to Kabul alone, okay. That is, if you can get the Afghans to grant you a visa. But on your head be it. The Embassy takes no responsibility. And there is absolutely no question of your venturing outside Kabul. Certainly not to Ghazni. You'd be cut down before you'd traveled a mile, my dear sir. Not even a regiment of the SAS could guarantee your safety. Your visit to Ghazni and its environs is totally out of the question. But good luck and have a nice day."

At the Afghan Information Services, I explained in fine detail why going to Kabul was quite useless to me, as my purpose in wishing to visit the country was to stay in Ghazni and to explore the Dasht i Nawar area. I watched a harassed desk officer's attitude change from frankly uncaring to churlish as he told me to wait. After twenty minutes, he took me into another room and told me to wait some more. Another official came in fifteen minutes later and told me to wait. After an hour had passed, I was taken into a room full of bearded, baleful Afghans all desperate to return to their country and all clamoring to get the attention of the one official in charge. More pungent than anything was the smell of furniture polish, of rancid butter, of fruit gone too ripe, all mingled with this fantasy feeling of being caught up in a medieval play whose end was death.

Eventually it was my turn, and it was explained to me what I already knew. Yes, it was possible to acquire a short-term visa to visit Kabul but only that. No question of being allowed outside the city. For that matter, at this time of the year, the official chuckled, New York might be safer. Obviously he'd told that one before.

It was plain that I was not going to find anyone there to share my interest in Gypsies. To be fair, what they probably had on their mind was the not unimportant matter of their country tearing itself to pieces. And so it was past the chador-covered, transfixed women in the ante-chamber and out into the street.

Back in Udaipur I mulled over the idea of going in hidden in the merchandise of a big truck. "From what I've seen of the driving on the Trunk Road, you'll be lucky to be still alive twenty-five miles outside Delhi," said Meredith, gazing across at the Lake Palace seemingly floating on the water.

I would have to abort the project. I had come so far only to fall down at the final fence. It was intensely depressing. I had the formation of the Rom in the palm of my hand and was deprived of the opportunity of proving it. I went to bed sick at heart and cursing every single official I had ever met in my entire life and woke up next morning with a plan, or rather, a compromise course of action.

In Udaipur I would pick up my three PhDs and, leaving Meredith, we would drive up to the Khyber Pass, retracing the original route. I envisaged a roundabout route covering all the places the slave caravans would have stopped at from Chittor through the Thar Desert, up to Multan, then Peshawar. At Peshawar, within a few miles of the Khyber Pass, I would find out for myself just how practicable and safe it was to get into Afghanistan and down to Dasht i Nawar. Put another way, was there a sporting chance of *not* joining the Russian prisoners taken by the Mujahedeen and having to work as indentured field hands for the next twenty-five years?

Well, at least I would get as far as the Khyber, I told myself, endeavor to make the trip go like clockwork and try for some really interesting discoveries en route. But what if my researchers couldn't make it? Nonsense, of course, they'll come. They have to. What was the alternative? No — never that. No one but a raving idiot would saddle himself with traveling companions like Gopi Lal and Patsi — even as a very last resort. And I smiled to myself before laughing out loud in the cool of the sun-green courtyard at the sheer giddy absurdity of the idea. Wasn't it Victor Hugo who said that there is one thing stronger than all the armies in the world, and that is an idea whose time has come? The time had well and truly come. Not even India could stuff up all the Swiss-watch planning and preparation I was going to put behind this trip. And I gave another resonant laugh just for the simple joy of hearing it boomerang off the thousand-year-old limestone walls.

That night I dreamt of the Gypsy who would become a tree. He spoke partly in Romanes as he bade farewell to his bride. "Have no fear, my Moon, *nana bistrave tut* (I will never forget you). And when I hear the birds sing in my branches I will remember your breasts and all the night I will not sleep."

And she, the deserted wife, replying: "I have bloody tears

in my eyes. I am homesick for you. At first *augobashno* (cock-crow) you will be gone. My heart eats blows. Who will hold me in the spring when peacocks dance? Would I were a swallow on your branches, oh, iris of my eyes." And she began to sob uncontrollably and I felt a wetness on my cheeks as I woke up.

4. Jaisalmer – Seelya of the Lohar

THEY THAT HAVE THE KNOWLEDGE FOLLOW THE WESTERN PATH
OF THE SUN.

FIRE, LIGHT, AIR, DAY, THEY GO FORTH; THOSE WHO KNOW THE
ABSOLUTE GO TO THE ABSOLUTE.

THE LODESTONE LURE
BECKONS THE LOVER OF LIFE.

Some weeks later. En route from Jodhpur

So this was where the Thar Desert began. The daunting Great
Indian Desert, the natural barrier that had broken the spirit of
many an impetuous invader, moonstruck by tales of the fabled
riches of Rajasthan and the Punjab. In its unforgiving, desolate
wastes on his way back to Afghanistan after the rape of the Indian
holy city of Nagtacket, Mahmud of Ghazni, the self-styled
Hammer of the Hindus and Destroyer of Icons, became hopelessly lost (through the wily efforts of a vengeful Brahmin guide,
it was said) and survived only by the skin of his teeth and the
grace of Allah to flagellate Hinduism even more mercilessly.

Gopi Lal had located on the map what he called a lost city,
which he was very keen to visit. Call me cynical if you will, but
I had a chill feeling it would not be the only thing lost.

The four-wheel-drive was standing up well to Patsi; Gopi Lal
less so. One sensed a distinct *froideur* between them. The reasons
were varied and complex. Gopi Lal's tribe, the Banjara, with their
fair complexion, oval face, long, flowing silky hair and straight

nose, were undoubtedly the aristocrats of the nomadic world. Originally the word "Banjara" meant an inhabitant of the woods – or you could take your pick from the Persian "Biranjar," meaning rice carrier, or the Sanskrit "Vanijya," meaning trader. They referred to themselves royally as the "Gor Boli" – White People – and all others as the "Khor Boli," that is to say, Black People. It never did go down well with the other tribes.

If you add to that piece of upstaging the supreme position achieved by the Banjara in the seventeenth century when the invading Moguls found them indispensable to their conquest of the south – both for their insight into local affairs and the 250,000-odd bullocks they could make available day or night as pack animals or beef on the hoof – then you had an appreciation of just how superior, in caste terms, Gopi Lal thought himself to this scallywag of a Kanjar. Patsi's Kanjar tribe had no caste. They were as shunned by decent Hindu society as an Untouchable or a beefburger.

I won't bore you with how Gopi Lal and Patsi came to be deputizing for a trio of India's brightest PhDs who failed to show (call it sheer desperation on my part), but suffice to say the situation was not improved by the fact that for caste reasons, two of our three-man team couldn't sit around the same table, much less use the same eating utensils. The only bright aspect was that, willy-nilly, by some sort of divinely inspired providence, I had as traveling companions two-thirds of the Gypsy Trinity.

"Uncle (as Gopi Lal was now addressing me), why does this most important scientific research undertaking of the utmost magnitude require the services of a driver with only one arm to control his vehicle?" asked Gopi Lal in a sotto voce bellow. "Also it is most clear to me – and to most of Rajasthan by now, I am sure – that he cannot read road signs or interpret traffic indications." He paused for breath and tightened his grip on his marble effigy of the Lord Ganesh – The Remover of Obstacles – as Patsi took a curve wide, nearly shearing a goat.

It was decidedly peculiar at first being called "uncle" by a person not of one's own family let alone people, but like everything else in India, one got used to it in time. Gopi Lal also had a fondness for adding "ish" to words, as in "small-ish," "definitely-ish." And there was his trick of throwing in a totally unanticipated, uncalled for "per se" into his speech. He'd admired Basil Rathbone using it to great effect in a Sherlock Holmes movie.

Example: "What is that cow doing in the middle of the road? I'd say deadish, wouldn't you, Uncle? Per se, not one that Patsi got." Slight pause. "This time."

It was hard not to like him. He was India with all its faults and virtues, by turns merry and sullen, tight-fisted and generous, cowardly and brave, forthright and devious, obsequious and arrogant, petty-minded and magnanimous. It was difficult to remain cross with someone who placed you and your mission on the same level as Einstein's search for the Great Unifying Theory of the Universe.

I grew more tolerant as daily I began to understand the horrible Indian uncertainties and insecurities that racked him and simply thanked my lucky star I hadn't been born that way.

From what I gathered as the four-wheel-drive careered erratically over Rajasthan, his father was a bank manager and his uncle very high up in the Railways. He'd obtained a BA in Business Administration but it was obvious he hadn't the slightest aptitude for the hard-nosed commercial world – a disappointment to his father for, as a true Banjara, he should have been destined to be in trading or commerce or in transport like his uncle. While framing the momentous decision as to which career path to choose, he had got a job with the Tourist Office as a guide.

Actually, he didn't really have to work, he told me half-boast-ingly. He could, if that was his desire, live rent-free at home and write poetry all day or count the flowers in the garden. His mother had completed the negotiations for a sweet-natured bride: a gentle, obedient creature who adored him and who would give him many sons. Naturally she would live with him in the family home. But the truth of the matter was, as I came gradually to realize, that although bereft of any marked talent, there was inside of Gopi Lal a burning ambition to achieve some-thing in life, be someone. He didn't know what it was, he simply knew he would find it some day. He was absolutely certain of it. The Lord Ganesh had not actually told him this but it was definitely implied, so to speak.

We were on the main highway to Jaisalmer, the medieval fortress city to the west. We traveled mile after mile of fiercely hot desert and knew there was a lot more to come. Every now and again, we spied a village in the background, sited well away from the road. Butterfly women gathered loosely around the well, or strolled back to their mud-brick houses with that loose-limbed, flowing right arm, burnished copper pots on their heads glinting out bright-rayed messages to every corner of the uni-verse, tawny, red-orange of sari against a blind, blue sky that rarely cried.

Trees and shrubs by the side of the road were stripped bare of bark and foliage — passing camels take what goats, standing on their hind legs, cannot reach. Nothing goes to waste in India — there must be 50,000 uses for the *Times of India* the publisher never thought of, other than reading it, that is. Then, quite sud-denly, a short distance ahead, I noted a blue-black bundle at the foot of a stunted banyan tree. Strange, that. As I said, nothing goes to waste in India. Detecting a ripple of movement, I made Patsi reverse, which he wasn't very good at.

She was about twelve years old, maybe younger, so emaciated it was impossible to be sure of her age. Her eyes were like opaque saucers in a tiny shrunken face. She appeared to be a lifeless doll, except for the tip of a tongue that endeavored to solace blackened lips as she struggled to speak.

As I picked her up to lay her in the back of the jeep, I thought I heard the word "Ma."

"Gaduliya Lohar," announced Gopi Lal, ostentatiously climbing into the front passenger seat beside Patsi, who gave him a curious unwelcoming stare.

"You're sure she's Lohar, Gopi Lal?"

"*Aaccha*, and flea-crawling and disease-ridden, into the bargain, Uncle. Per se."

"Lohar womens," said Patsi, spitting scarlet juice through broken, betel-stained teeth to land on his dirty-white trousers. That seemed to clinch it.

As I wet her lips and tried to force a little water into her mouth, the incredible thought hit me like a hammer blow that in some sort of preordained, pre-programmed set piece, I now had a representative aboard of each of the three tribes that I postulated made up the rootstock of the Rom. I paused and looked up at the sky. It just wasn't possible. . . .

Despite ourselves, there is an element of superstition in us all and at that moment I felt an overwhelming sense of fate, of karma, come over me. The other thought was, Who the bloody hell is ever going to believe you?

She was sitting up and taking notice of her surroundings by the time we found Gopi Lal's lost city – Bariyada – that evening, which in itself was a major miracle. What with Patsi ignoring Gopi Lal's directions and Gopi Lal being hopeless at map reading, it was about on par with Christopher Columbus coming across a McDonald's in the middle of the Atlantic. It had the effect of giving Gopi Lal and Patsi an entirely exaggerated idea of their direction-finding capabilities, which was to prove in future very expensive in time and petrol – 20 to 30 percent extra mileage on any trip more complex than going up the High Street for a chappati and toddy would not be an unfair assessment. But at least their mutual self-congratulation (just stopping short of back-slapping) at having found the place without the Lord Krishna's divine intervention had brought them closer together.

A camel party out of Jaisalmer had beaten us to the only decent camping site and so we parked Jas Tilak* on an incline in the shadow of the crumbling city walls. Carved *Sati* stones rising from the earth commemorated warriors fallen in battle and the devotion of their widows immolating themselves to join them in Heaven.

A young man with a spaded Rajput beard – a Canadian teacher – came up, eager to impart information about this "lost city."

"It was built by the Paliwal Brahmins about two hundred years ago – descendants of the priests of the Pali tribe who, because they were traders (as well as bankers and landowners), were forced to give up their priestly vocation. They turned this area into a veritable Garden of Eden: the valleys between the stone ridges and the sand hills grew great quantities of wheat and prime vegetables. They dammed the rivers and built a splendid township with exquisitely carved doorways and ornamented walls, meeting places and many superb *chhataris* (memorials). Suddenly, one day, they abandoned everything and moved south to Gujarat."

"Why so?" I asked.

"Controversial. Take your pick. Some historians say they

---

* Literally, "mark of favor," the name of Maharana Fateh Singh of Udaipur's favorite hunting elephant.

left because Salim Singh, the prime minister of Mooj Raj II of Jaisalmer, raised their taxes to unbearable levels. Others contend he lusted after a Brahman *yakshi* (maiden) and desired her as his concubine. Her father, unable to face the shame, fled with the township behind him."

"I'd go for lechery over taxes, any day," I said.

"You could be right. By the way, as one romantic to another, when you get to Jaisalmer, look up the story of Princess Moomal who lived not far from here in the Palace of Meri – *Moomal ki Meri* in Hindi – and her lover, the Prince Mahendra. Pure Goldwyn. Ah, well, back to that camel. Catch you guys later."

An eerie place, this lost city. I walked into it alone, Gopi Lal sheepishly ducking out at the last moment. A bit rich, I thought, considering it was his idea to come here in the first place. In the pearl-gray dusk with the image of the moon tinkling faintly on its mellow stone, I walked along streets running straight as a die, reminiscent of an ancient Roman city in its planning, order, and remnants of a sophisticated drainage system. Most of the houses had lost their golden yellow bricks to the local villagers. A town built for anything up to 20,000 people, the Canadian had said. I wondered about the lives the people had led, the spirit of the place. Serene or stressful? Proud and exultant or melancholy, morose?

Suddenly, and perfectly in keeping with the mood of the place, a black-clad figure appeared to step out of a wall some seventy yards in front of me. Then, turning away, it walked, or rather glided, a few paces before disappearing into a corner wall. And I mean into. It was as if Kali the Destroyer had breathed out from solid rock and taken form and substance before evaporating back into stone, or a temple dancer, a "Devadasi," emerging from dreaming marble had spun a twirl or two before vanishing.

I was still shaken when I got back to the campfire and grate-fully gulped down a measure of Patsi's IMFL (Indian-Made Foreign Liquor). The girl we'd picked up – Seelya was her name – had been crying, and it seemed to me that Gopi Lal had taken advantage of my absence to be rather unkind to her. This sur-prised me a little because I had been given to understand that there was a vague kinship between Banjara and Lohar: the same ancestral root or some such – along the lines of both Jews and Arabs issuing from the loins of Abraham.

Pretending not to notice the girl's red eyes or Gopi Lal's sullen, bad-tempered face, I contented myself with the thought that we'd be in Jaisalmer the next day and with luck would come across the group she'd been traveling with. I'd heard that many Gaduliya Lohar made the trek across the Thar to the frontier desert towns when business was bad in the east.

I had a dreadful night's sleep, disturbed by a couple of camels who'd managed to untether themselves for a bit of splendor in the grass and later by a succession of cries and sobs and once a piercing scream, all coming from Heaven knows where.

"You were crying in your sleep last night, Uncle," remarked Gopi Lal the next morning. "I heard you."

"Nonsense. A touch of hay fever is all."

"Patsi heard you, too."

"Then his hearing's equally defective."

Gopi Lal threw away the rest of the tea in his mug the way he'd seen Gary Cooper do it in *High Noon* and said in a very meaningful tone of voice: "*Aaccha*, kind words butter no parsnips. You will recall I said this, Uncle. Per se," he added significantly and with utter predictability.

I found out afterward that no one ever slept in close prox-imity to the lost city. The place was haunted, the camel drivers said. Indeed, that morning it wore an atmosphere of dank, Elsinore-like tragedy as if habitually waking up to grief.

Seelya, roused by our din, immediately started to cry. One's heart went out to the Lohar waif, lying under the jeep with her head cradled in her arms. She had taken off her blouse and her skeletal back was crisscrossed by welts and was badly bruised. I stared, open-mouthed. Who on earth could have done such a thing? There was absolutely no possibility that it could have been self-inflicted. As if to remove any trace of suspicion from my mind, Gopi Lal came up and stood beside me. I couldn't help myself, and with a furious gesture I motioned him down to the campfire in the little hollow. Seeing it was no use arguing, he walked away and got back into his sleeping bag.

The girl's sobbing went on for a few minutes while I brewed her a mug of sweet tea. When it was ready, she came out shakily from under the jeep to take it from me. En route, her body jarred against the undercarriage – the springs, probably. She just made it clear before the jeep started rolling down the incline, straight to where Gopi Lal lay sulking in his sleeping bag.

Patsi was nowhere to be seen. I remembered he had wandered off with – of all things – a fancy tooled leather toiletries bag that contained a pink toothbrush his father had given him shortly before he died some ten years ago and a flask of Campbell's Royal Stuart Heather twenty-five-year-old, authentic Scotch whisky, distilled and bottled by the Chota Peg. Co. of No. 77a Mysore Lane, off Ranjit Street, Bombay, Scotland. I'd sampled it the previous evening. The only thing remotely aged about it was the cork.

Everything seemed to be happening in slow motion, and when I tried to rise from my crouching position, mug of tea in hand, I found I couldn't move. When I did finally get myself into gear, my feet got tangled up and I fell heavily on my shoulder. On the ground and looking up, dead ahead of me, I could see Gopi Lal's wide-eyed, terrified face. He, too, seemed powerless to move as Jas Tilak, gathering speed, trundled inexorably toward him. What a way for the bloody picnic to end, I thought.

Suddenly, a slight figure flashed past me, stooping to pick up a rock that I swear would have weighed in the vicinity of thirty pounds — not far below her own weight — and racing down the incline, jammed it in the path of the front nearside wheel. A split second later, she'd taken off in a monkey jump into the front seat and I saw a look of fierce, almost snarling triumph as she pulled on the hand brake with both her small brown hands. The jeep stopped in a cloud of dust as a vicious shower of small stones filled the stunned, transfixed air. Suddenly it was all over.

Gopi Lal was safe.

From that moment onward, Gopi Lal Banjara became Seelya Gaduliya Lohar's father, brother, sister and mother, too. Nothing was too good for her. As far as he was concerned, there was no longer any question of her leaving our happy group. He made only the most perfunctory enquiries in Jaisalmer when we got there to trace whichever glittering band she'd been traveling with. And Seelya was no help either. It seemed more than likely she had been intentionally abandoned rather than inadvertently mislaid as she wasn't in the least bit unhappy at not finding her kith and kin. Indeed, quite the reverse. She gave every indication of relishing every minute of being with us, certainly something she had no intention of forgoing in favor of biffing an anvil twelve hours a day, seven days a week. And besides, I had the distinct impression that she thought we three males needed a bit of organizing.

Be that as it may, by the time we left Jaisalmer I was pretty well satisfied we had done our best to find her people and could continue with an easy conscience. Maybe we would run into them on the road. (With Patsi's driving, the expression assumed a positively concrete dimension.) Selfishly, too, if you like, the enormously exciting idea of following those thousand-year-old footsteps across Asia Minor with the three representatives of the original Romani Trinity completely overpowered any desire to continue what had already turned out to be a fruitless search.

We stayed at a delightful pension in Jaisalmer run by an ex-Begum (a queen, but of the Moslem faith as opposed to a Rani, her Hindu counterpart). She served us superb food while presiding over the communal dining table with a mixture of Girls' College decorum and giggles and looked after us like a mother hen — except for Patsi, whom she detested on sight and immediately relegated to an area hard by the chicken coop so he could keep the snakes away.

With great good humor, she accompanied Gopi Lal and Seelya on shopping expeditions to stock up on the provisions we would need to continue our journey over the inhospitable terrain ahead of us on the next leg.

Jaisalmer. Every stone reeked of sieges: the insanely brave acts of *Johaur* (suicide) when the men rode out to certain death while their women immolated themselves to prevent dishonor. Its glowing yellow sandstone ramparts and *havelis* (mansions built by the rich merchants) made it richly deserve the name Golden City.

For the Bhatti Rajputs who built it in the twelfth century with careless disregard for the fact that the whole area was called Region of Death, it was an ideal place to resist the Moslem onslaughts to come and a good place to retreat to after raiding their Rajput neighbors to the east. From every point of the compass the city is surrounded by moonscape desert, barren ridges and glittering sand dunes. A land controlled by the camel. The camel pulls everything, carries everything on its back, is the measure of time, distance and age. Slender-legged females, tree-trunk legged males have intricate designs carved into their neck fur. The pace of the camel and the people are one and the same.

Jaisalmer, where chivalry and military daring were the only virtues. Where then as now, inside massive gates the streets are infinitely narrow and winding, cool and dark. You squeeze, making yourself wafer thin, between two advancing cows. As you turn a corner, atop a recessed waist-high ledge, three feet of goat leer down with black-orange eyes. The coat is shaggy, black and with white tips. "The goat holds its horned head high. The goat disdains. The goat virile is. The goat is of assured power," recites Gopi Lal's cousin, Rajendra, who teaches English at the high school and has a strange, mesmeric way of speaking.

He gave me a brief run-down on the caste system, mainly I think because Gopi Lal had been complaining to him about having to share air space with Patsi but also, charitably, to improve my understanding of things Indian. He prefaced his discourse with subtle references to how different and peculiar he found things when arriving at Cambridge to read Philosophy. "Yes," I assured him, "a lot of English people feel that way about Cambridge." I yielded later to temptation and told him that we in Britain had a caste system every bit as unyielding as the Indian but which was so well-hidden that only the British realized it was there — which probably explained why, when the Brahmins tried their effortless superiority act on the Colonel Blimps — the bit about having a private arrangement with God — they found themselves relegated permanently below the salt by the merest twitch of the old school tie.

"*Aaccha*," which means he has no idea what I'm talking about — he carries on regardless. "There are four main castes, occupational classes you might call them: priests, warriors, tradesmen, agricultural workers. Every Hindu falls into one of these. However, within each caste people have a variety of callings and accordingly each is subdivided into sub-castes. To complicate matters the weeniest bit, sub-castes are in turn divided into *gotras* or family groups. Hindus must marry within their own caste but not within their own *gotra* to avoid interbreeding, in practice not with a relative closer than the seventh degree. All quite straightforward, wouldn't you say?"

Sanitized rather than straightforward, I thought. "What about the problems of marrying outside one's caste, or tribe?" I enquired.

Rajendra seemed to pass into a state of shock. "What problems? There are no problems. It is not a realistic situation you postulate. Now," he continued, hurtling over my next objection, "I did not mention the fifth class. I won't call them a caste. To the Mahatma [Gandhi] they were the Harijans, the Children of God, known popularly as the Untouchables, so called from the belief that the higher castes risk defilement if they touch them."

He coughed delicately and I could sense that the punch line would not be long in coming. "You see," he continued, "from all I have said how difficult it must be, Mister Roger, bearing in mind their respective traditions, for an educated, high-caste Hindu to have to associate with a Harijan on a daily basis and in conditions of the most intimate proximity. Eating together and so forth." He gave me a beautiful, sincere, mild-eyed gaze.

For my part, I couldn't think of any reason to keep Patsi on but, on the other hand, I couldn't think of a sufficiently strong pretext to fire him either. The fact that he really wasn't very good at doing what he'd been hired to do didn't, in Indian terms, count for a row of chappatis. So I prevaricated and joked that I would speak to Patsi and try to convince him to be a lot more forbearing vis à vis other people who hadn't been born with his advantages in life.

Gopi Lal took over the educational process that evening in

a roof-top restaurant overlooking the city. I pointed to the street below us where there seemed to be a continuous stream of men sliding surreptitiously into small doorways.

"Uncle, in every town in Rajasthan, the less privileged classes and castes such as the Jagirdar, the Bhagats, the Nats, the Sonsigs, the Statias, the Berias and, of course, the bloo. . . . the Kanjar, practice prostitution. The street in which they operate is called – as that one is – *Patarieon Ka Mohalla* – the Street of Prostitutes." He leant back as if he had proved a very important point and in his bright black eyes I could almost see fifteen-love being registered.

Later that evening in a more mellow mood after a fine meal, Gopi Lal, tiring of firing snide shots at an absent Patsi, got onto the less tendentious subject of what Jaisalmer meant to him. As with me, it was his first visit, but ever since he could remember it had formed part of his life.

"My grandfather told me about his days as a child when the Banjara were a power in the land. That is," not being able to resist a backhand volley down the line, "before the British Raj came along with their railways and made paupers and criminals of us." Graciously accepting my shoulder shrug as a gesture of apology on behalf of Queen Victoria, he went on. "In those far-off days we Banjara used to load our bullocks with salt – anything up to twelve thousand animals was not uncommon – at Pachapadara, 250 kilometers southeast of here, or at Sambhar Lake in the Jaipur region and sell it from village to village, town to town while trading information with the local princes and chieftains. A spy network stretched across the whole of northern India, believe me, Uncle. They would bring the salt up to Jaisalmer and, following the trade routes, transport it for sale into Pakistan, Afghanistan, Persia even. Or they might travel west to Gujarat and the Rann of Kutch or east to Delhi. Sometimes, if the prospects were good, down south to Bombay and Hyderabad. Always I see in my mind's eye my grandfather as a boy trailing at the back of the caravan, stepping around tons and tons of bullock droppings." And he laughed his high and low dipping laugh.

For a moment I had a vision of a cheeky-faced urchin with a loose turban around his head, carrying a cattle prod taller than he was, marching tiredly but ever determined along a path beaten smooth by four thousand years of his ancestors' journeying.

On the eve of our departure from Jaisalmer, Patsi exited from a drunken argument on the future of the Punjab with a fiery Sikh with severe injuries to his one good arm. Gopi Lal couldn't or wouldn't drive – hinting at certain religious reasons impossible for a non-Hindu to comprehend. Seelya begged to be allowed to share the driving with me. Well, why not? After only one lesson it was obvious she had a natural affinity for it: a strength of wrist to control Jas Tilak under even the worst conditions, and an in-born stamina, which meant she had to be prised away from the wheel even after ten hours of continuous driving in the pouring rain or over rocky terrain.

"Anything that is of a mechanical nature," said Gopi Lal proudly of his protégée, "the Lohar have a talent for." He beamed at our frail slip of a girl (although padding out fast on the strength of two square meals a day) taking her place behind the wheel, bursting with pride and happiness, a great big melon slice of a smile bisecting her face, shining eyes expressing pure delight. Of course, she'd been up well before dawn to check the oil, water, petrol, tire pressures, windscreen wipers, mirror positioning, etc. etc. That little girl was as close to Heaven as a human being could get, short of becoming a mystic.

She was invaluable, too, in other ways. She not only cooked but mended our torn clothes, took over the laundry and acted as nurse to Patsi until his arm got better. Someone had to feed the poor chap and change his dressings and Gopi Lal, for one, wasn't about to turn into a Mother Theresa for a bl ..... Kanjar.

Among her other accomplishments, she learned to speak English with remarkable speed and, curiously, with what I could only categorize as a Dutch/Flemish, ever-so-slightly Afrikaner accent – but charming for all that. Patsi never did learn, except for a few words. When he didn't use sign language (which with only one arm lost a fair amount of quality in descriptive power), he spoke to me in Kanjar, taking my look of blank non-comprehension as agreement with whatever he was proposing.

And so there we were, a happy, united band with only the barrier of caste between us. Naturally, being European and a meat eater, I was the bottom of the heap.

But one thing was for sure. I had witnessed, at the beginning of the journey, the instinctive, inherent antipathy among the three different tribes – Banjara, Kanjar and Lohar – gradually grow into a co-dependence. Admittedly, it was taking a lot more time for Patsi to lose his distrust of the others, but then the Kanjars just were a wilder, more untamed race of people. They'd been outside the pale of society since history began – hunted and persecuted like wolves with every man's hand against them. And that just for being what they were: free, kissing the hem of no man's robe and believing that the present was all a man ever had.

So, therefore, it could happen – at least on a mental/emotional plane – this coming together of the three species. But what about the other aspect? The physical interbreeding? The miscegenation that had to have taken place? Was it possible? Likely even?

"No," said Gopi Lal with a shudder. "It could not ever happen. Would antelope mate with elk? Or eagle with owl? Or camel with bullock? It is unnatural. Per se, against all the laws of God and man. I plead with you, Uncle, not to persist with this most sacrilegious, impracticable and damn bloody profane notion." No doubt about it, Gopi Lal's command of English was improving daily thanks to contact with me.

We left the enchanted city of Jaisalmer and it seemed that for ages its towering fort was saying good-by to us. All went relatively smoothly as we pressed onward toward Afghanistan. But the further we traveled along this, the route that the Ghaznivite invaders would have used to bring back their slaves and plunder, the worse little Seelya slept, even on one occasion again awaking with welts on her back and shoulders. Yet, I was certain that nobody had been near her.

Gopi Lal and I discussed the phenomenon at some length. Patently, it was a form of stigmata. Had she had it before in childhood? Who knows? Seelya, by the time she had drunk her first mug of tea in the morning, had forgotten whatever dream/nightmare it was or, more likely, simply didn't want to talk about it when Jas Tilak needed all her energy and attention. The only plausible explanation – or rather let's say, the one I favored – was that the surroundings through which we were passing had somehow brought to the surface a race memory deeply buried in her subconscious. Of a trek . . . a forced march her ancestors could have taken as long as 1,100 years ago as newly captured slaves; months of excruciating agony carrying large loads of booty, sobbing blindly in the wind at all the pain there was in the world, stumbling on lacerated feet toward mountain-girt incarceration in the heartland of Afghanistan, driven mad by writhing hunger and thirst, not daring to pick up a pebble to suck for fear of unsettling the monstrous load on their back; prime slaves trussed in coarse sacking and slung over the backs of camels to preclude escape. Was it that the plasma of their agony had adhered itself irremovably to the stones of the road for all time?

"I say, Uncle," cried Gopi Lal. "Let's not get carried away. Couldn't we just put it down to a change of diet?"

The day after we left Amritsar, we rose early after falling asleep talking around the campfire. Our days were calm. Groups of blackbuck and *chinkara* (gazelle), cows, sheep, goats, camels wandered around isolated villages, shifting sand dunes, rocky outcrops. The Ker, Aak and Rohira trees were in flower. Do the people wear bright clothes to offset the lack of color in the desert? Bleached cattle bones drove home the message of mortality. Words of wisdom from Gopi Lal were imparted in my ear: "A peacock passing the traveler on the left is considered a good omen. A monkey crossing one's path from right to left is auspicious but bad luck the opposite way. Meeting a Rajput with a sword on his shoulder (we didn't see too many of those) is a good omen." Wild grasses, shrubs, Jungli crows, peacocks, myanas, blue jays, bulbuls and robins. The Imperial Sandgrouse arrives in the third week of October and leaves at the end of February. Too bad — it was now April, and we missed His Highness.

The captured slaves would have followed the River Indus through dry, sandy country, bare of grass but scattered with low-lying desert shrubs until they reached Multan, green and well stocked with game, famous for its camels.

Then the final leg for those still walking: Peshawar followed by the never-ending, back-breaking Khyber Pass, Ghazni and, finally, Dasht i Nawar.

En Route to Jammu

All the way north to Jammu to consult with Johnnie Pathania, a noted Indian Gypsiologist, Gopi Lal and I discussed Dasht i

Nawar, picked the bones of it so clean that they became part of me, embedded in my psyche and in my reactions to the Gypsies. And all the time I had this dream of turning up there with the three of them: Gopi Lal, Seelya and Patsi, each one a segment of the heart, brain and body of the Rom.

There we'd be, perched on a barren rock, overlooking its desolate, God-forsaken barrenness. I'd be thinking what a bloody miracle it was that we had got there in one piece. Then I'd think something deep about how I was gazing down at the crucible of the Rom. My eyes would take in the great dried-up basin where once the lake had been. Maybe we would see, traversing far in the distance, a group of Pashtun nomads who frequented the place – but only in the summer months when light dispelled the shadows, and then for only the briefest of halts en route to the south and Pakistan. It was said that they believed the spirits of the dead haunted the place – or guarded it – I was never sure which. They were the only ones to come near Dasht i Nawar; the locals gave the area a wide berth. Even lost goats, it was said, tried to get lost someplace else.

And gazing down on the erstwhile camp from our flinty foothold on the mountain side, it would not have been difficult to see why. From all accounts, if there was ever a place that cried out "Abandon hope all ye who enter," this was it. The sight and sound of absolutely nothing, the very end of the world, the place where earth meets the void center that lies at the heart of chaos, that which Christians and Hindus call Hell.

Maybe in the hyper-emotional state we were in at having reached our goal we'd feel that layer of spirits pressing down on us. Possibly, too – stretching it a little – our ears would pick up bygone wails of those about to die, mouths praying for abso- lution. Standing there in an icy wind that swept the mountain slopes like a glacial scythe and thinking all these deep, deep thoughts. All except Patsi, that is, who'd be happily gurgling in the middle of a close encounter of the Chivas Rajah kind.

"But why do you place such store on nomadic tribes, Uncle?" Gopi Lal asked, breaking in on my daydreaming with all the subtlety of a juggernaut at festival time. "Per se, Mahmud of Ghazni — to take but one of our many invaders — would have brought back any Hindu capable of putting one foot in front of the other. Is that not so?"

I forced myself to respond one more time. Just one more time, I promised. If he doesn't get it this time, he never will.

"I think by the time Mahmud came along, after three centuries of raiding experience, the sheer common sense of enslaving nomads and nomads only — as far as practicable — would have been recognized by the Afghans. And as you are aware, Gopi Lal, the predominant northern Indian nomadic tribes at the time were the Banjara, Lohar and to a lesser extent the Kanjar."

Gopi Lal continued to look skeptical but was clearly enjoying the discussion as much as he had the ninety-nine preceding ones just like it.

Weary but unbowed, I went on: "Look, Gopi Lal, there are lots of reasons why nomads would have been preferred: physical fitness, better survival characteristics, a skill or craft at their fingertips, to name but three."

Again that nod. I had the beginning of a feeling I might be getting through this time.

"And there are many others. For instance, what do you think would happen to a slave turning up at Dasht i Nawar in those days, without friends or fellow tribesmen to take him in hand, show him the ropes, protect him?"

"I don't know, Uncle. But I know you will inform me."

"He would have stood zilch chance of surviving the first week, that's what."

"I cannot altogether believe that, Uncle."

"Look, the inmates would have been starving. At best the system of food distribution would have been shockingly ad hoc. Every man for himself. Women and children last. But . . . but . . . if the Moslem happens to be targeting just three nomadic tribes, for instance, well, you can recognize the benefits, can't you?"

"Yes, Uncle," Gopi Lal replied very slowly. "Yes, I think I can. It would mean that each slave coming into the camp would be greeted by someone of his own tribe . . . possibly even of his own *gotra*."

"In other words," I broke in, "immediate protection and an instant introduction about how to survive the system without really dying."

It was not until after dinner, lying in our sleeping bags under the cold stars, that the battle started on its next – and I hoped final – phase. But still the feel of the camp eluded me. Was the prevailing atmosphere orderly and efficient or simply chaotic and brutal?

"I am thinking I am not happy with your idea of marriage between tribes, Uncle, even though the utmost conditions of closest proximity may have encouraged same. A few instances perhaps, but never in the irresponsible, completely uncontrolled fashion you are imagining in your mind. Slavery may have destroyed the social structure but never the religious taboos built up over three thousand years."

Not about to retreat an inch, I pressed home my own attack. "The fact of the matter is, Gopi Lal, that when you've eliminated the impossible, you're left only with what could have happened. In this case, a physical blending of the races is not impossible within a context where every day might be the last. I think it had to have been that way. The three tribes – their characteristics, skills, behavior, looks, etc. – when melded together, *make* the modern day Gypsy. There is no doubt in my mind the Rom are a mixture of all three. Surely you can see that after decades, if not centuries of praying to the old Hindu gods for their release from bondage and not having their pleas answered, sooner of later the rule book would have been thrown away."

I paused for breath. "I read once that the Ancient Egyptians produced the temple cat which they worshipped as a deity from a blend of the domestic pussy and the feral, jungle cat."

"But they'd still be wild inside," said Gopi Lal.

"Of course, wild like cats . . . you can't change nature."

Just before we turned in, Gopi Lal remarked inscrutably: "Remember, Uncle, in the leg there are also five fingers."

I'd given up working out his little aphorisms. "I'll do that, Gopi Lal. Just you remember that it is a foolish man who looks for a ripe mango in the middle of a coconut grove."

That stumped him.

The next day, Gopi Lal showed me a piece of rock he had picked up. It had been carved – quite crudely – but was just recognizably part of a bird's wing. A definite attempt had been made to outline feathers. For some reason, Gopi Lal seemed very attached to it and made some feeble excuse when I tried to take it from him to examine the craftsmanship more closely. He even went to sleep with it tucked into his sleeping bag.

All that night Seelya muttered and cried out in her sleep while Gopi Lal tossed and turned restlessly. Small wonder I couldn't sleep either. Patsi joined me by the fire, gesturing for me to share his bottle. Idly I wondered, and not for the first time, how he managed to conjure up this bottomless well of ersatz Scotch. The parable of the loaves and fishes didn't even begin to compete.

"*Yah sone ka samay nahim hai, Sahib,*" he said, which I translated as "this is not the time to sleep." I guessed a nightmare had woken him up. I nodded in sympathy. He put some order in that turban of his, which was always coming undone.

"Many mens, Sahib." He waved the bottle toward the black night. Maybe he meant ghosts. There certainly weren't any people. Not even a bird or a goat. Just to make sure I understood, he threw in a few basic words that any foreigner could understand, like: "*takliph*" (trouble), "*bimari*" (sickness) and "*bhadda*" (ugly). I thought I had the picture.

We made a dent in the bottle before Patsi went back to bed in his customary place at the back of the jeep, but he bore little resemblance to the boisterous, rollicking, "anything for a laugh and a drink" Kanjar we knew and loved (well, some of us). To the extent of which he was capable, he was a deeply troubled man. I had the idea there were things circulating in his churning brain that his limited education and vocabulary simply couldn't cope with.

He was an uncomplicated forty-year old, hawk-faced, tall, slim but with the hardness of a knobbly tree and utterly fearless. One arm or not, Patsi would take on a barroom of opponents with fist, feet and knife and give a good account of himself. Despite forty to sixty *bidis* (Indian cigarettes) a day against a stiff backcloth of semi-raw alcohol, he was capable of trotting for six hours straight behind the jeep in rocky terrain when necessary. He could go without food and water without complaint, and extremes of cold and heat he appeared not to even notice. Until tonight I would never have imagined the slightest suspicion of nerves or of internal tensions of any kind. Patsi was on earth to enjoy himself. He laughed, sang, smoked, drank and danced and thought the world a wonderful place.

Gopi Lal, too, upon wakening appeared deeply troubled, with a drawn, haggard face, great staring eyes and a paleness beneath his skin.

There was little point in proceeding that morning. All I could envisage were a batch of sprained ankles and twisted knees. My motley crew of the living dead would be no match for the arduous trek over the rocky plain and the deep ravine, perceived in the far distance, which we were to negotiate on foot in the hope of coming across stray artifacts similar to the bird's wing.

As we took our ease, sprawled around the fire, soaking up the early morning sun after a freezing cold night and with strong splashes of Patsi's whisky in our tea mugs, Gopi Lal started to describe the dream — more like nightmare — that had so traumatized him during the night. But I soon shut him up. I was in no mood for spooks that morning.

"No, no, Uncle, I must relate it to you. It may well have the utmost bearing on our researches within the context of the historical disciplines we are following. Per se."

"Another time, Gopi Lal," I said firmly, and we left it at that. At any normal time I should have been most interested in hearing about it, but not that morning. With the sun rising deep and sullen and bruised red in the sky, I had a firm feeling that via his dream Gopi Lal had somehow been in communication with the spirits of his ancestors. He had touched something. A form of energy, a resonant morphology that could not be separated from the very molecules of the air we were breathing.

After all, we love, live, laugh, cry, suffer intense pain and chagrin, enjoy moments of ecstatic happiness while the dreams we dream may well touch on and mingle with the dreams of others in an eternal jeweled necklet of sound and movement. But nothing of us, not a dream, not a thought, not a look or the touch of another's gaze, ever escapes the world in which we are contained. They are there. Always there. Waiting to be resurrected, brought to life again in someone else's mind. Well, that is what I believed very strongly that morning.

I had a deep-rooted feeling that Gopi Lal ought to keep his dream to himself, and not let it out to complicate things and unnerve the day any more than it was already.

When we got to Jammu the following day, I found it impossible to settle down to anything. It was raining cats and dogs and a pall of tear gas overhung the city like a sodden shroud. A friend of a friend, and the Indian Gypsiologist whose work I admired the most, Johnnie Pathania, arrived at the hotel – chosen for security reasons rather than comfort – retching and coughing from the fumes but hanging on grimly to the portable typewriter I had asked him to bring.

"We were hoping you would eat with us tonight. My wife and daughter are looking forward greatly to meeting you. It will be quite safe by taxi there and back."

In the face of that warm invitation I could hardly say no. Tonight, if I was right, it was going to be Gypsy dialects with Johnnie, European fashions with Meera and the latest changes to the English tax system with Tipoo, their eighteen-year-old daughter who was studying taxation at university. Tonight I would be in the bosom of a Hindu family I instantly counted as friends. It was going to be love and warmth and banter and all the things I had been missing for such a long time.

We drove through deserted streets while Johnnie explained the background to the latest insurgency, which had mostly to do with the Kashmiri separatist movement and the eternal struggle between India and Pakistan, but not much relation to common sense and settling issues in a grown-up way. Even after his exposé, I wasn't that much more informed, so very wisely I held my peace. I had enough trouble understanding Gopi Lal, let alone Jammu's 200,000 revolutionary spirits.

We drove past shops selling gold jewelry. Whole shop fronts brilliantly lit, were full of the wonder of masses and masses of gold, gold, gold – rings, bracelets, necklets, eggs, rich as dreams. I can see them now. For the first time I understood the attraction – nay, the lust – that mankind has for the metal.

We passed the spot where, earlier in the day, the Indian police had *lathi*-charged (a *lathi* is a long staff) a mob of stone-throwing youths, only to swerve at the last moment as the youths held their ground, to drag three silvery-haired ladies from their rickshaw and beat them senseless – what you might call choosing the path of least resistence, but hardly the way to influence the population on the desirability of continued Indian rule, one would have thought.

Certainly, the separatist movement was gaining ground all the time in Jammu, where Alexander the Great had halted, nervously eyeing the unknown mass of the subcontinent, before his army made him turn back. Adjacent Kashmir, grown rich on tourists, was now forsaken. Only the week before, a houseboat with six apparently foolhardy tourists on board had been attacked by guerrillas who subsequently found out to their cost in the ambulance taking them to hospital that their innocent prey were actually well-armed members of the Israeli Secret Service. All in all, millions of dollars had been lost to the economy. What a mess it all was, I thought. When will the politicians learn that India was people and not a bottomless treasure chest to provide them with wealth and lifetime privileges? In the past thirty years, there had hardly been one riot or instance of sectarian violence that hadn't been instigated for political reasons. And if that failed, the Pakistani threat could always be taken out of the closet and dusted down and the saber-rattling would start all over again while the millions dying of starvation were conveniently swept under the carpet.

India was fragmenting under New Delhi's inefficient and corrupt administration. First Pakistan, to be followed inevitably by the Punjab, Jammu Kashmir, Assam and a whole list of others waiting their turn. Throughout its history, India had been ruled by foreign invaders, starting with the Aryans 4,000 years ago. Maybe the country couldn't do without them? "One thing is certain," an ex-journalist on the *Times of India* said, "unless New Delhi gives the states greater autonomy in the running of their affairs, by the turn of the century they'll just have Calcutta left."

"Why just Calcutta, Ranjit?"

"Because nobody in their right mind wants it, boyo."

When I returned to the hotel later that evening, I wandered into the bar to see what all the drama was about. You could almost touch the thick visceral atmosphere that hit you at the door. The TV was showing Rajiv Gandhi's funeral live from New Delhi. I'd heard about the assassination a couple of days before en route.

There were perhaps two hundred men in the room, but aside from the solemn tones of the commentator, not a sound could be heard as Sonia Gandhi and her children moved slowly around the blazing funeral pyre.

I was about to withdraw – good manners if nothing else suggesting that the presence of a European in the room would be an impertinence – when somehow I found myself pushed gently forward through the crowd to a privileged place at the bar. In close-up, the funeral scene was intensely moving, especially in its melding of a religious faith nearly as old as civilization itself with the barbarity – to my Western eyes – of a corpse being consumed by fire and turned into ashes in full public view.

But the funeral rites weren't the only moving thing. Gradually I realized, when glancing around the crowded room, that something quite extraordinary had happened. There were no segregated groups as was the usual custom. Sikh sat beside Hindu, Hindu beside Moslem. It was unbelievable, but there it was. A common grief had drawn and bonded together three utterly disparate religious sects in what could only be described as a common vale of tears.

All of a sudden, in that Jammu bar, I had a vision of what India, dear India, beloved India, could be like in the twenty-first century.

I pray that I haven't got it wrong.

In the stricken silence that followed the end of the program, I slipped out and went up to my room. I found I was thinking about Dasht i Nawar. The odds were stacked against ever making it there, but there had to be all sorts of aspects of the camp I could explore without moving from my hotel room. It was the funeral pyre that had triggered it off. The connection with the smoking chimneys of Treblinka . . . Dachau. Dasht i Nawar, too, would have to have had day and night furnaces operating in order to dispose of the dead quickly to avoid the spread of disease.

Maybe I'd put a few stray thoughts down on paper. I put out my cigarette and went over to the desk and the typewriter. A small black cockroach was perched on the rim of the water jug, weakly waving a hind leg. I thought I'd pick him up and throw him out the window but before I could get to him, he had jumped and, turning over and over like a circus clown, landed on the floor and promptly disappeared. It gave me an idea.

5. Dasht i Nawar

The Dom slave lay curled in a ball, very small, cracked like a walnut by cruel men and dumped on the mountain side. Immediately below the patch of red-brown earth to which the slave had sunk, the rock-strewn mountain side sloped away as if holding its breath before plunging steeply toward a dirt track leading to the camp below. Some twenty yards to the right, and in line with his splintered body, the precipice fell a full thousand feet to the unforgiving ground below.

It wanted a couple of hours until noon but already the sun had turned the shale-gray mountains white. White, which the Dom called the color of pain. Peaks, blue ice-capped on gold-fire days surrounded the camp like hoary guardians – craggy, wet-daggered, monolithic: emanating a brutal contempt for anything less almighty. The sun shone without favor, too, on the cold flatness of the lake and its environs, picking out individual leaves and making them shine like so many gilded messages to heaven. Overhead, a crescent of white kites wheeled and skimmed in endless patrol for the lake's dwindling stock of fish. Clouds like tight parched marble sat gravely impartial in the blind blue air.

But the slave, twisted into a worm of living torment, was not aware of the birds above the lake. Nor did his eyes take in the embouchure to the west, where the mountains just failed to close the rock ring and which led draggingly to the dreaded Dasht i Margo: the Desert of Death which supported no living thing: not an adder, bush, nor even an insect, it was said. No one had ever crossed its empty tracts without losing his mind or his life. The Shamans of old referred to it as the one place on earth where death, not life, ruled. Rightfully, it was kept apart from the world as being the Devil's domain. . . .

The old Remington was running hot and so for that matter was I. The fan, working at top capacity – that is to say, a lumbering half a dozen revolutions per minute – wasn't doing anything to cool the room, merely contributing an inelegant clatter.

There was a knock on the door and Johnnie came in with his usual bouncing stride. "How is everything?" he asked.

"Well enough, except it's infernally hot in here. You know, Johnnie, ever since seeing Gandhi's funeral on television, I've been struck by the extraordinary coincidence of the Gypsies starting life as a people in one concentration camp run by the Ghazzis* and nearly coming to the end of the line a millennium later in another run by their rhyming cousins, the Nazis."

Johnnie nodded, trying out "Ghazzis" and "Nazis" in rapid succession. "You are right. If it is as you say, then it is truly ironic. God must love them very much to punish them so severely."

I blinked. That was a novel way of looking at things.

"Let me see what you've been typing."

"Sure. Look, it's just my way of generating ideas, you'll appreciate. Throwing balls up in the air to see what comes down. Anyhow, it seems to work for me. Well, sometimes."

Johnnie nodded and devoted his full attention to the typescript.

"Interesting," he remarked after he had finished reading. "But tell me, aren't you making it worse for yourself – you know, reawakening your chagrin at being told you couldn't go there?"

"I'd have thought more like expunging it."

"You could be right," he said thoughtfully. "But I'd forget all about it if I were you – there's far too much for you to do while you're here."

"Like?"

He held up the sheaf of papers he was carrying.

---

* Short for Ghaznivites.

"What's that?" I asked.

"The word roots we spoke of yesterday. A list of a hundred common words in the dialects of five Rajasthani tribes. We will examine them together to see how each compares with modern-day Romanes. A hard day's work but I'm sure most profitable."

I balked. "I could do with some fresh air, actually."

"Good." There was the merest hint of a wicked grin. "I will take you to the house of my great-aunt, who has never before been in close proximity to a white man. She very much wishes to meet you."

As we left the hotel, I remarked on the large number of male staff leaning on their brooms.

"Surely women would do the work better, and they'd need fewer of them into the bargain," I said.

"Yes, but they would suffer the shame of working in a place which we Hindus subconsciously but very powerfully associate with the sleeping habits of men and, by extension, a brothel. No hotel would employ them."

"You mean, it would mean destroying the clubby male atmosphere?"

"No . . . yes . . . maybe. Something like that. But then, here in India, men would not be permitted to carry baskets of bricks on their heads as the women do, working ten hours a day in extreme heat on building sites." A pause. "So you see, it works both ways. . . ."

I could never tell whether he was having me on or not.

We took tea together, Johnnie and I and his great-aunt, who wore her best sari and was obviously very excited to be the only household in the neighborhood to have ever entertained a European. I tried my hardest to live up to her expectations, in spite of the fact that I wasn't at all sure what they were.

One thing that jarred in that oh-so-classic Indian room was

the intrusive resonance of Anglo-Saxon sounds as I spoke to Johnnie's Hindi translation. I wasn't being hypersensitive or any-thing, but it was simply out of place, alien. Johnnie must have had the same thought. I could sense his agile mind working on the problem, determined to make this one of the most perfect experiences of his great-aunt's latter years. Then the quick lift of the eyebrows and I knew he'd come up with the answer. Care-fully, and with delicate emphasis, he took to translating her words to me into . . . Romanes.

Later that afternoon while we were having tea, Johnnie handed me back some fifteen pages. "Are you sure this story of yours is leading somewhere?" Johnnie asked.

"Possibly. I'm hoping that by putting some sort of scenario down on paper we might get more of a feel of the place and maybe, just maybe, stumble across something very obvious but totally ignored up until now. I think it's worth a shot."

"You're just trying to get out of cross-referencing those Rom words with me," said Johnnie, smiling.

"You got it in one, Mister."

Trying for Peshawar

I had arranged for the crew and me to be interviewed by a gov-ernment official with a view – possibly, hopefully – of allowing us to continue our journey to Peshawar from whence I would try to work out a way to get through to the Khyber Pass. But the hope was a forlorn one. We could take the bus to Srinagar only, the end of the line, where the India-Pakistan cease-fire zone started to operate and we didn't.

"That's as far as you and your chaps go, old man," chortled a massively bearded Indian Army officer of the old school. "No question of going on to Peshawar. Of course, we might knock the Pakis for six any tick of the clock if you'd care to hang on a while."

"No thanks, Major," I said, with nothing to lose, "they might reach Delhi this time."

The ultimate bottom line actually was that Mujahedeen guerrillas belonging to the formidable Kauli and Hekmatyar clans controlled all the Dasht i Nawar area, which meant that getting in (if we were silly enough to have a crack at it) was unlikely — read impossible — and getting out rather more so.

I was bitterly disappointed, especially for the crew who sat behind me in the corridor on a hard wooden bench. Smartened up for the occasion, looking cheerful, competent and above all unvocal, they radiated integrity and dependability. Just the sort of people one would have thought welcome in any country. Damn their stupid war, I thought.

I explained the situation to the crew slowly and, I think, fairly unemotionally; Gopi Lal translated for Patsi's benefit. Strange how they'd melded together. They wore identical outfits: loose-fitting Pathan pants, shirt and waistcoat. Seelya's hair, which had grown luxuriantly, was now pigtailed and stuffed under a baseball cap for the occasion.

Curiously they didn't say anything even after, to avoid any possible misunderstanding, I explained to them that the party was over. There was only one thing for it and that was to return to Udaipur.

Back at the hotel — the crew were billeted elsewhere due to lack of space — I placed a call to London. Inevitably, there was trouble on the line. "Yes, caller, I am saying to you your call will take between thirteen and a quarter hours to three days. Your consideration and extreme patience is requested for which it is appreciated in advance."

I pulled the typewriter toward me. Time enough, it seemed, to do some work on my little tale.

The following day when Johnnie had just finished reading the pages I'd typed, I asked him: "Well, what do you think?"

"I'm not sure it tells us much except that consciously or unconsciously you've made the Rom woman come through very strongly, the glue, so to speak, that held the structure together. In that sense, you've put your finger on a very important point. But as for anything else. . . ."

"There's another aspect to that, Johnnie," I said as I turned from finishing my packing.

"Oh?"

"Hitherto, it's always been tacitly assumed that it was the Rom — the man — who had created the most fundamental of Gypsy taboos — the one relating to the essential impurity of the female."

"You mean any woman from twelve to sixty being a source of pollution? That business?"

"Exactly. Now it occurred to me a little while ago that maybe this wasn't necessarily true. Bearing in mind the unquestioned power of the Romni in society, mightn't it have been *she* who created it, and for very obvious reasons?"

Johnnie walked over to the window and looked down on the yard below.

"You mean as a form of protection from male advances within the group?"

"Well, yes, among other reasons."

"It's certainly a novel idea, but still pure supposition."

"I wonder. Couldn't it be a drive not only to recreate the security the woman had back in India but also to guarantee her status as an inviolable being in her own right?"

"I don't quite follow."

"Well, in India, laws of male-female relationships were laid down by the Brahmins, who were always around to check they were being carried out. Now, in conditions where the whole of that social structure was fractured beyond repair, the clever thing would be to invent a series of utterly unbreakable taboos. In effect, the laws of *marimé*.* By making the woman impure, her security within the tribe was more or less guaranteed."

"Put like that, you might have a point," he admitted somewhat less grudgingly. "But I think you'll have to do better than that to convince me."

"Okay, how's this? In Western society it's more or less common practice for men to stare at a pretty woman. Happens all the time: in the street, at the theater, wherever. Over here in India it just doesn't happen. Something stops you Hindus from doing it. Why? Because it's not permitted by the social structure, that's why. The woman always belongs to another male: a father or a husband."

Johnnie picked up a sock that had fallen under the bed. "Uhm. . . ."

"Look, let me give you an example to try to prove my point. A couple of months ago I was gazing down from my hotel window at some chaps working on a boat by the side of Lake Pichola when four of the most beautiful Indian ladies you could

---

* The Gypsy laws of purity. In broad principle, all females, from the onset of menstruation until menopause, are by definition impure.

ever imagine, dressed in gorgeous saris, passed by. They didn't spare them a glance." I paused.

"So?"

"A few minutes later a European woman, a blonde, just short of middle age but well built for all of that, walked past them and they couldn't take their eyes off her. All the nudges and winks in the world followed her retreating back."

"You mean that because she was outside their socially laid-down structure, they felt free to indulge in an exhibition of male lust, etc.?"

"That's precisely what I mean. There were no restrictions or taboos preventing them."

"Uhm. I'll give it some thought the next time I see a blonde walking past the house."

Maybe I was right and maybe I wasn't, but at the time it seemed to make sense. Taboos, superstition, in fact the laws of *marimé*, might well have been imposed by the woman, possibly commencing in Dasht i Nawar in an embryo form, to be codified and reinforced as the race developed, to provide the only sure and certain way the Gypsy woman could feel safe from unwanted male advances and at the same time retain that status of virginal purity that lay deep in her Indian background – even if it did mean she would have to wear long skirts for the rest of her existence on earth!

If I had extracted anything from my little story, I thought, at least it was that: it might well have been the Gypsy woman who had not only kept the race together but was directly responsible for framing its draconian laws.

6. Canada and the Goddess Pathvari

In the Syriac version of the Apocryphal Book of Adam known as the "Cave of Treasures," the following passage occurs:

> AND OF THE SEED OF CANAAN
> WERE, AS I SAID, THE AEGYPTIANS;
> AND, LO, THEY WERE SCATTERED ALL OVER THE EARTH
> AND SERVED AS SLAVES OF SLAVES.

In their Indian past they had been the Banjara, Kanjar and Lohar.

In Dasht i Nawar, the place where the three streams broke their banks to become a river, they became the Dom – the outcast tribe of the Baro Than.

Much later, in Tabriz, they were called Kowlis, Kurs, Luls, Luris or Kavula.

In Constantinople they were referred to as the Roum.

And finally in Europe, they named themselves the Rom.

A few lines of something I had once read came to mind as we sallied forth toward Chandigarh: ". . . and so, with soft insistent calls in the velvet night did the wanton wolf and the moonstruck owl blend their song in love-chant. Reminding the Gypsy maiden languishing by the lake of the land where once her spirit dwelt. . . ."

Ever since I became convinced that Dasht i Nawar had acted as the crucible of the Rom, it had also become the place where three distinct peoples, by merging into one, forfeited their faith and became one of the few races on earth to entirely sever their religious roots. To become that Persian word *Megabyzus* — freed by God or, in their case, might it not have been "freed of God"? It placed an indelible mark on them. To an extent it removed conscience. It splintered their psyche, effectively setting them apart from the rest of us.

This, their original sin, took them out of the mainstream of life, placed them somewhere between the blue-steel frosts of spring and the red-gold of autumn . . . sometimes a brown pebble, sometimes a blue, but never, ever a gray.

In an ordered world of truth and common sense and practicality, they project the not quite true, the half caused, an impression that they, too, deep down, don't feel quite genuine, lawful or legitimate. Not quite right and proper. Fictitious.

The Gypsy removes his mask only to put on another. For essentially he is the epitome of all that is intangible and enigmatically ephemeral in this world. He is the human equivalent par excellence, the flesh-and-blood illustration of the German scientist Werner Heisenberg's famous uncertainty principle, which says that one can never be certain of both the position and velocity of a particle; the more accurately one determines the one, the less sure one can be of the other. That is the Gypsy: this characteristic of quicksilver fluidity.

One interesting comparison between *Gaujo* (non-Gypsy) and Rom arises over their attitude to the Catholic religion. The Rom make it fit into their own magico-religious concepts, adapting its teachings and practices to their own highly complicated spirit world, a world of omens, superstitions, prophecy, witchcraft, legend, taboos and certain rites and ceremonies, the world of *mulesko angelo*, the angel of death, and its connection with the spirit world and dead ancestors.

Animism or spirit worship consititutes the basis of Gypsy belief. It takes illusion and fantasy and transforms them into a simple extension of reality; it puts a thick coating of dreams on everyday reality, makes cats fly and sparrows talk and trees counsel. It is the bridge between the magical and orthodox religions – bearing in mind that over the centuries the Gypsy has been exposed to every conceivable religion. The final result gives rise to one of the most intricate belief systems ever conceived by the mind of man.

As a case in point, let us look at Canada, a country containing up to 20,000 Rom. One of the principal tribes there is the Kalderash, traditional coppersmiths from Eastern Europe whose ancestral stock in India would be the Gaduliya Lohar. I say one of the tribes, because there are also the Romanitchels of British ancestry and therefore Protestant, and the Bayash, who don't seem to follow any recognized faith. Many Gypsies have no particular conviction one way or the other whether God exists but they've known for certain for at least 1,000 years that *Beng* the Devil is alive and well.

To get back to our Kalderash, in most homes there is a wooden box painted blue or green that contains a bottle of holy water and a statue of St. Anne (mother of Mary) of Beaupré. This tiny shrine is called a *Kaplitsa* in Romanes and it stands solitary in a room where no one sleeps since one should not be scantily or improperly dressed in front of her. During times of sickness or trouble, the Kalderash will light candles and pray to her. And if during the year their luck has not been good, in July they will make the pilgrimage – the *Santana* – which brings together the Gypsies of North America all the way to Beaupré, a French-Canadian hamlet some forty-eight kilometers east of Quebec City. There they will toast St. Anne in beer and good whisky to the sound of church bells. No one knows for sure why the Gypsies have this fascination for seeking their luck at the shrines of female saints near rivers or the sea. In France they gather at the shrine of Les Saintes-Maries-de-la-Mer on the Mediterranean to pay their devotions to Saint Sarah. In Mexico it is the shrine of the Virgin of Guadaloupe, and in Bulgaria, the shrine of Saint Sophia. However, it is more or less accepted that these female saints are deputizing for the Hindu Goddess Kali — Kali the Black as she was worshipped on the banks of the Ganges.

The point is that at no time during the *Santana* are any of the Rom worshipping God per se, certainly not in the way their non-Gypsy Catholic cousins are. Their focus is purely on Saint Anne, the bringer of luck.

Fundamentally, the only deity they worship is the one called Freedom. That's what they have lied, fought and cheated for down the centuries: to maintain a nomadic way of life at least four thousand years old. It's the reason that compels them to change their mask so often — to make sure the core heart of the Rom is never exposed to hurt, for that they would find unbearable after having built up their defenses so well and for so long.

In the course of a quest such as this, one dreams a score of dreams that add a thickness, a mood, a spirit flair to airy prose. Certainly the dreams feed the imagination and, hopefully, add something of value to the tale. In one such dream, inspired by a poem I once read, I sit with the Panchayat, a tribunal of five elders enrobed in pale, frozen grandeur. Through the window a blood-red sun hangs wearily in a nightingale's gloss-green air. As melancholy deepens we become fleshless: mere albino marbled skin and bones. It is with our senses, not our eyes, that we perceive the march of the Rom, ceremonious, solemn, emblazoned chest and back with brilliant blood gems, passing out of the valley of death on their way to doomed, despairing freedom.

Who knows but that vestiges of the Goddess Pathvari may

have guided those first shambling steps of the Dom out of Dasht i Nawar, for unique in Hinduism, Pathvari transcends caste, tribe and even religion and can be worshipped by all. She takes no recognizable shape as, for instance, does Ganesh or Krishna or Kali, but is to be usually found in the form of a block of stone at country crossroads, encircled with offerings of ghee, sweets and flowers donated by pious villagers. Pathvari is, above all, the Goddess of Wayfarers, of nomads, of people about to embark on a great journey. She is associated with those making the pilgrimage to Hari Dwera, at the source of the Ganges, to scatter the ashes of their dear departed.

If, unconsciously delving deep into their Indian past, the Dom had summoned a deity to protect them during the first hesitant steps of their flight from Hell, it would surely have been Pathvari, the goddess of those who journey into the great unknown.

En Route to Chandigarh

I had planned on a two-day journey for the three hundred odd miles from Jammu to Chandigarh, but added extra time as the town of Jullundur seemed to merit an interesting diversion. Some fifty miles southeast of Amritsar, the holy capital of the Sikh religion, it had survived a terrifying onslaught by Mahmud of Ghazni one thousand years ago to become one of the most important cities of Mogul Punjab.

I thought it likely that Mahmud had brought Dom slaves with him as water carriers, farriers and the like. Maybe we would be lucky enough to find a reference to their presence in some antique text or other, buried away in the public library. But no, nothing. To make up for the disappointment, we checked out the 150-year-old serai (rest stop) and had a meal by the bus stand which caused us discomfort all the way to Chandigarh.

Chandigarh is a car city designed by Le Corbusier with French logic for a population that doesn't own cars. I took the crew on a visit to its famous Rock Garden, made out of concrete, rubber and pieces of rubbish — very modernistic and the city's inhabitants are inordinately proud of it. It was there, with Seelya and Patsi safely tucked away in the cafeteria, that Gopi Lal ventured to comment on the recent adversity the trip had suffered.

"It is not important that we didn't get to Peshawar, Uncle, or the Pass. Or, indeed, Dasht i Nawar. I think it likely the camp would have been razed to the ground when they left," said Gopi Lal, trying to comfort me.

"Burned down, at the very least," I agreed.

"I wonder how it happened, Uncle," Gopi Lal mused. "Did the slaves wake up one morning and find the guards gone?"

"Might well have been that way, Gopi Lal."

There was a silence between us. I could sense, though, that Gopi Lal was about to ask the big question. Sure enough it came.

"When do you think they left that terrible place on their journey west, Uncle?" I could see from the way he put it that he wasn't expecting me to stick my neck out by giving him a precise answer, so I thought I'd surprise him.

"The year following the Battle of Tarain — twenty-five miles north of Delhi — A.D. 1193 would be my guess. In fact I'd put Patsi's shirt on it."

"The Battle of Tarain, Uncle? I'm sorry, you've lost me there. Who were the protag . . . who was it between?"

"Shihabuddin Muhammud Ghuri representing the Afghan-Turks and Prithviraj III representing the Rajput confederacy."

"But how could a battle in India have anything to do with

the release of the slaves in Afghanistan? And who is this Ghuri fellow anyway? I thought Ghazni, not Ghur, was the dominant power in Afghanistan?"

"Was, Gopi Lal. Was. Would you like me to fill in the background so you can understand just how important Tarain was to the story of the Gypsies?"

"Thank you, Uncle. I was hoping you'd suggest that most meritorious course of action."

So for the next five minutes I talked nonstop as I put to Gopi Lal the background I had assembled and which, in the final analysis, answered that trickiest of questions: the one that Gopi Lal hadn't asked, that is how and why, in what circumstances had they left – or been permitted to leave – Dasht i Nawar.

Sultan Mahmud of Ghazni died in A.D. 1030 and was succeeded by his son, Massud, an alcoholic tyrant who, in the space of a decade, lost most of the empire it had taken his father thirty-three years to weld together by a mixture of diplomacy and the scimitar.

One of Massud's first acts when ascending the throne was to appoint Ahmad Niyaltigin as governor of the Punjab with orders to mount a series of merciless plundering raids aimed at the very heart of India. Six years later Massud himself, at the head of a formidable army, struck south from his base in the Punjab and achieved giant territorial gains. On his way back to Ghazni, though, he was murdered by his Hindu slaves. Too much whip or not enough, no one knows.

During the 150 years that followed until that famous Battle of Tarain, there took place the worst knock-'em-down and drag-'em-out saga of anarchy, palace intrigue, treachery and cruelty ever perpetrated by one bunch of thugs on another, bloody plot succeeding poisonous counter-plot, culminating in Ghazni being invaded by both the Ghuzz and Seljuk Turks. Finally, the neighboring province of Ghur, previously a vassal state of Ghazni, took over as the paramount power in Afghanistan.

Ghazni, reputedly the most beautiful, the most magnificently embellished city on earth, was ground into the dust by Ghur as if it had never existed, its population slaughtered or led into slavery. And so ended the wonder and glory of the age, they said, a court in which four hundred poets daily sang the praises of the Sultan.

In 1174 the ruler of Ghur, Ghiyasuddin, appointed his younger brother, Shihabuddin Muhammud, to extend the eastern borders of the empire. From that moment, one might well say that the fate of India was sealed. It was no longer a question of the Rajput princes resisting once-yearly raiding parties but of trying to hold the line against a foe determined on permanent occupation.

The first Battle of Tarain took place in 1191 and ended with Muhammud Ghuri severely wounded and lucky to crawl back to Afghanistan, "a badly mauled panther with revenge in his heart," as he was described at the time. The following year he was back again in Tarain with a mighty army made up of some of the best and most battle-seasoned troops in central Asia. He was a very determined man, absolutely intent on victory.

Unfortunately for India, the leader of the Rajput confederacy, Prithviraj III of Ajmer, had not retaken the poorly defended Punjab in the intervening time, which he could have easily done, thereby blocking the invasion he must have known was coming as it had done every October for the past three hundred years. In fact, the only time they did not show was the year the opium supply failed in Afghanistan. As to morale, the Rajput confederacy was riven by dissension between the princes and, to cap it all, General Skanda, who was mainly responsible for winning the battle the year before, had been sent on a campaign of no consequence in the northern hills.

Prithviraj was taken prisoner and killed in cold blood. "The sun going down on the plain of Tarain that day witnessed the death of the last Hindu king," mourned the bards throughout the length and breadth of Rajasthan.

Colonel Tod's words best describe the aftermath.* He wrote: "Scenes of devastation, plunder and massacre which lasted through the ages during which nearly all that was sacred in religion or celebrated in art was destroyed by these ruthless and barbarous invaders. The noble Rajput, with a spirit of constancy and enduring courage, seized every opportunity to turn upon his successor. Every road in Rajasthan was moistened with torrents of blood of the spoiled and the spoiler. But all was to no avail; fresh supplies were pouring in, and dynasty succeeded dynasty; heir to the same remorseless feeling which legalised spoliation and sanctified destruction."

After I had explained all this to Gopi Lal, he put on his best mask-like, politely patient expression, which showed just how incredibly under-whelmed he was. "But what has this to do with the reason the Dom slaves left Dasht i Nawar?"

"But don't you see, Gopi Lal? The camp simply wouldn't have been needed any more. What earthly use would Muhammud Ghuri have for the bits of skin and bone at Dasht i Nawar when he'd just enslaved the whole of bloody India?"

"Oh, goodness crikey, Uncle," exclaimed Gopi Lal, in a state of high excitement. "You've biffed the nail on the head, I do believe."

Gopi Lal, like his favorite author, P.G. Wodehouse, imparted an intoxicating exhilaration to the English language that at times arrowed one straight back to the days of top hat and spats and

* James Tod, 1829: Volume I.

Jeeves handing out worldly advice and extra dry martinis to Noël
Coward and Gertie Lawrence.

That evening we were dining in the top-floor restaurant of
Chandigarh's Hotel President looking through the pink-pale
dusk at the Siwalik Hills, the outer rim of the Himalayas. Large
fires were starting in the proximity of the Rose Garden, whether
for wedding ceremonies or funeral pyres was not certain. Wood
smoke drifted up to delight our nostrils.

Gopi Lal talked of fire. Hindus have a love affair with fire.
They offer it flowers and rich presents, including the ultimate
gift, the oblation of their own bodies and those of their beloved.
Idly Gopi Lal murmured the words spoken by a Hindu sage some
1,300 years ago when sentence of death was passed on him by
the Caliph of Baghdad; words of such vital inner meaning that
they grew and grew in your mind the more you thought about
them.

> The earth is dark but the fire is bright,
> And the fire is worshipped since there is fire.

"What was that saying you came out with yesterday, Gopi
Lal?" I asked.

"Are not fire and the sunbeam the straightest roads to God?"
he answered.

"Yes, that's the one. I'll have to remember that."

That night a million billion stars coated the sky as the full white
moon turned the foothills of the Himalayas into a silver ball.

"*Salaam aleikum* – the caravan moves on," I murmured. And
so should we. Now the sad return to Udaipur instead of heading
along the Silk Road toward what were once the very centers of
art and flowering civilization: Persia, Anatolia, Armenia and
Byzantium, their very names the sound of errant roses.

It was galling but there was nothing else for it. I just had to bite the bullet and face the fact that we'd come to the end of the dream.

Finita la commedia.

At some point during the night, unable to sleep, I began to think about how the slaves must have felt when, suddenly, they realized they were free.

Free to go where? Back to India? The turmoil they had no doubt been hearing about guaranteed only starvation and a miserable death by the roadside. Besides, had not their terrible sin made them outcasts in their own land? No, there was only one direction they could take: westward toward Persia and the land of Golden Shadows they carried at the back of their eyes.

I tried to put myself in their place, closed my eyes and imagined them embarking on the grand trek, irresolutely, in dribs and drabs, benumbed or gibbering with fright. After the confines of the camp, they would feel quite lost in the never-ending immensity of the world that stretched before and around them.

Unbelievably, the exodus would lead to some of their descendants being welcomed at the gates of Paris some three centuries later. Simultaneously, others would be leading the lives of hunted wolves in the dark forests of Romania.

They had entered Dasht i Nawar as three separate peoples. Three and a half centuries later they were leaving as a race, the appellations Lohar, Banjara and Kanjar forgotten. Their "Romany roots" had taken hold, miraculously cauterized by the ordeal of the camp.

To those they encountered they were the uncaused, the uncanny. Out of nowhere . . . dark tendrils from a place they never spoke about and tried to forget as quickly as possible. Only Ghazni, Ghazzi, transposed into *Gaujo* would remain in their vocabulary.

It was carried in their eyes, it was in their pain as a shuffling foot courted a viper's bite: a sense of bitter, black destiny. Blood, pain, sorrow, death – the Dom: the outcast tribe of India. What else could they expect?

Little did they know that with exquisite timing, they were heading straight into the eye of a cyclone. An all-conquering, blood-dyed, barbaric force was about to tear Asia apart and follow them into Persia as sword follows strike. And orchestrating this Hell's delight was the most terrifying, inhuman conqueror in history. They called him "The Very Mighty Lord": Genghis Khan.

❋   ❋   ❋

7. Tabriz

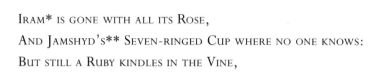

IRAM* IS GONE WITH ALL ITS ROSE,
AND JAMSHYD'S** SEVEN-RINGED CUP WHERE NO ONE KNOWS:
BUT STILL A RUBY KINDLES IN THE VINE,
AND STILL A GARDEN BY THE WATER BLOWS.

EACH MORN A THOUSAND ROSES BRINGS, YOU SAY:
YES, BUT WHERE LEAVES THE ROSE OF YESTERDAY?
AND THIS FIRST SUMMER MONTH THAT BRINGS THE ROSE
SHALL TAKE JAMSHYD AND KAIKOBAD*** AWAY.

— *VERSES V AND VIII FROM THE* RUBAIYAT OF OMAR KHAYYAM:
EDWARD FITZGERALD TRANSLATION

Before leaving Chandigarh that morning, I decided to take the *Lonely Planet* guide book's advice and drive roughly ninety miles northeast to Simla, which before independence had the distinction of being the most popular British hill station of all. It was still, I was assured, steeped in nostalgia for those *Jewel in the Crown* days. Its assembly of whaleboned memsahibs was followed a little later, as the heat on the plains built up, by the sahibs themselves, so that to all intents and purposes it took over from Delhi as the summer capital of British India.

A few miles outside Simla, relishing every minute of the cool

---

* Iram: a sumptuous city now buried somewhere beneath the sands of Arabia.
** Jamshyd: a legendary Persian king. His golden divining cup whose seven rings symbolized the seven heavens, seven planets, and seven seas contained the elixir of life.
*** Kaikobad: a semi-historical Persian warrior-king.

mountain air, we stopped for what Gopi Lal liked to call *tiffin*.

"We must thank our lucky stars it is not winter," he said. "I have heard it becomes rightfully coldish: snow, you know." He shivered dramatically, but I knew he was only showing off. He'd never seen the stuff except maybe in the movies. Saying he was going to offer a prayer to Ganesh, the God of Wisdom and Prosperity, for our safe return to Udaipur and with a meaningful look in Patsi's direction, he wandered off toward a thick copse of trees.

"Well, how did it go?" I asked when he came back. "Is the Elephant God coming to the party?"

Gopi Lal looked crossly at Patsi's dirty, once-white turban, which had come undone again. "Party? What party? The locality is most noisy. Not in the least sacred. How can a person undertake his devotions under a *crore bandar* in a banyan?" Which translated meant: "How can you pray beneath ten million monkeys in a fig-tree?"

Wandering around Simla that afternoon, we paused by a beaded curtain through which came the most evocative aroma of a Persian *horisht*, a stew in full, flowering flavor. Instantly I was transported to Tabriz where I'd been fifteen years ago, with nary a thought of Gypsies on my mind. Then I'd been told that there were Gypsy villages close to the city that had been there since the thirteenth century. Now a great industrial sprawl with hardly a trace of antiquity remaining, I felt certain that progress and the Ayatollah's revolution had swept the Gypsies out of existence — a crying shame. It would have been worth the trip simply to see those Persian Rom. They would have to have represented the purest examples today of the original race as it arrived from Dasht i Nawar.

But aside from the million-to-one chance that Gypsies were still around in the Tabriz area, there was no other reason I should journey to Tabriz except the general one of its having made such an enormous contribution to the development of the Gypsy race. The city was where the Dom, the outcast tribe of India, evolved to become only a short step away from the Rom they were to become in Europe.

Of course, the time to have been in Tabriz was when the Dom were there, very early in the thirteenth century – at the full flowering, the very pinnacle of the city's power and success as one of Asia's wealthiest commercial trading cities, second only to Constantinople at a time when Europe was wallowing in darkness. And the Gypsies had been there to give it that extra panache, that added vitality, to make it sing the purest, most sensuous, highest of notes. Oh, yes, I wish I'd been there then.

That evening I went out onto the terrace for a beer and a smoke and tried to assemble in my mind all I had picked up about Tabriz and the vital part it had played in the history and formation of the Rom. It was a trading center so dominantly important that even the snatch-and-grab Mongols left it in peace in return for tribute. And when, finally, they did move in to take up occupancy, it was almost in the nature of a well-mannered "hope you don't mind" afterthought.

Gopi Lal and I had debated many times the probable year of the arrival of the Dom in Tabriz from Dasht i Nawar – a distance of some 1,500 miles. I had finally settled on circa A.D. 1220, a quarter of a century after I postulated they had streamed out of Afghanistan. The rationale was that even after picking up the Silk Road at Kabul, they would have been obliged to have taken on employment in, say, Herat or Nishapur (or both), the first major stopping places, in order to earn the wherewithal to continue their journey. And, inevitably, too, they would have been forced to split up, one group leapfrogging another so as not to arrive at any single urban concentration in one huge, indigestible blob.

The numbers reaching Tabriz were probably reduced significantly by a break in the ranks sometime after leaving Teheran with still 450 miles to go before Tabriz. Why they split up we shall never know. My feeling is that their numbers had grown to such an extent that it was a case of divide or die. Anyhow, the theory is that one group went northward to Russia, hugging the Caspian coast and entering by way of Baku. Another traveled southward to Iraq, Syria, Jordan and Egypt where they became known as the Nawar (Arabic for Gypsy, as we already know). It is possible that from this group, a splinter party went on to North Africa and there, joining with the Moors, crossed over to Spain and settled in Andalusia.

But the middle prong of the trident, the one that forged westward toward Constantinople and ultimately Greece and the Balkans, is the one this book is concerned with as being by far the most important and the rootstock of those who, entering Europe, thence spread over the globe.

Actually, though, there was a fourth group that people tend to overlook as it stayed "Tabriz local" – and, undoubtedly, it was they I had heard about on my previous visit. They traveled some six hundred miles south to the pleasant land of Shiraz to lead an uneventful existence roving backward and forward on the Teheran-Qom-Shiraz route and in and around the Tabriz area. They were known as Kowlis and in time a separate Kowli language developed, retaining 50 percent Indian content (on par with European Romany dialects), with the balance of the vocabulary being composed of Farsi and Arabic. The Kowlis continued to practice their traditional occupations, all except fortune telling, which came to a stop, but gradually over the course of time, many settled down as peasant farmers.

At the time, Tabriz was the largest city in Persia, famed for its Arg, the citadel from which criminals were hurled to death, and the regularity of its earthquakes. The city had in fact been rebuilt twice following the disasters of A.D. 858 and 1042.

I was certain that the Dom would have spent at least a century in Tabriz being bottled up by the Mongols. There was no other way to account for the extraordinary length of time it took them to reach Europe after leaving Afghanistan.

Why did they stay so long? After all, they were nomads, with the nomadic instinct and all that it implies. Well, the dour answer was that they'd precious little choice. From the moment they got to Tabriz, they were trapped by the Mongol army advancing from the east with incredible speed and ferocity to occupy the area. Wisely, the Mongols didn't take Tabriz but contented themselves by exacting an enormous annual tribute.

I think we can take it for granted that the Gypsies would have been fairly safe inside the city walls and, most probably, as time went by, some of them would have been allowed to roam the surrounding countryside, putting on their entertainments, mending pots and pans, curing livestock – all the usual things. Of course, they were artisans, and as such were looked on favorably by the Mongols. And there again, they were nomads as the Mongols themselves had been – and this would have gone a long way toward creating a certain empathy.

There is no question but that their artisanal skills would have been fully utilized. For instance, they would most certainly have been drafted in the period 1307-1313 to work on the construction of Oljeitu Khan's new capital, Sultaniya, near the town of Qazvin – equidistant between Tabriz and Teheran. A huge army of laborers would have been required to build the citadel, mosques, palaces, residential and trading areas, and the Gypsies as qualified metal workers would have been essential to the project. The great golden domed mausoleum, to cite just one example, would have taken at least a year to build.

Just how did Tabriz affect them? Make and change them? In the first place, it was where they would first make contact with the West: its customs, language, dress and music – above all, its music – where they would learn to co-exist with non-Gypsies in a cosmopolitan, polyglot ambience with powerful Greek and Italian influences woven into a Persian backcloth, sharing a common Aryan ancestry with their hosts but little else.

Dom and Ghazzo (Ghazzi would become Ghazzo and further transmute into the modern-day *Gaujo* or Gadjo) would draw together, for Tabriz was the most benign of cities, but only up to a point, beyond which mutual incomprehension stared them in the face. The Ghazzo/*Gaujo* had a God who stood by him always (or so he believed), but the Dom would pick up any pretty or unusually shaped pebble and it would be his God, his talisman, his luck until its power faded and he found another to take its place.

Music, always in their blood, reincarnated from a distant Indian past, became a dominant part of their culture. They were to master the lute (from the Arabic *al-ud* meaning wood), the sitar, the bagpipes, tambourine and drum. Absorbing the local music, they melded it heart and soul to the glittering Gypsy tunes and made it theirs, producing fluid, cross-rhythmic, light-as-air melodies in which only a trace of harmony lingered, but overlaid with the rich, creamy curves of sound of a Rajasthan heritage they could never lose.

In the dance, and we must remember the extent to which they were dependent on entertainment as a source of income, the women grafted onto the local tradition the movements and gestures of the ritual Indian dances – the graceful arching of fingers, hands and arms; sinuous undulations of the torso; the suggestive rolling of rounded hips. And all the while their bare feet would be pounding, pounding, pounding the earth in an ever-mounting crescendo-tattoo of simulated orgasmic frenzy.

My imagination soared to visualize those Dom, eight centuries ago, freshly arrived, standing open-mouthed in the Grand Bazaar watching richly attired slaves posturing before their master's shop, offering fine wines to a party of Byzantine tourists. The marketplace proposed every enticement known to the ancient world: spices from India, turquoise from Khorasan, lapis lazuli and rubies from Badakhan, incomparable silk carpets from Bokhara, pearls from the Persian Gulf, indigo from Kerman, oils, musk and sparrow hawks from Europe, horses and hunting hounds from Arabia. And, in the slave market, the choicest human flesh imported from the four corners of the earth.

Forty generations earlier, the harmony, point and counterpoint of the Greek language fluently overlapped the elegance of fulsome, flowery Farsi; Zeus was pronounced to rhyme with the Sanskrit *Dyas* (sky); the Hellenistic influence permeating the Persian fabric like fine wine, seeping through its weft and weave. No longer was it a case of what would happen when West met East. They *had* met and mated and produced Tabriz.

For centuries stretching back to Alexander the Great, three centuries before Christ, Greece and Persia had been linked by way of commerce and intermarriage. But Tabriz had improved on that, evolving a way of looking at the world that was neither Occidental nor Oriental, but simply Tabriz style. Unique in its delights, if not its appetites, Tabriz oozed a feline, mesmeric charm barely concealing the commercial energy rippling a fraction below its golden pelt.

I remembered how I'd seen Tabriz as I entered the city on my original visit, cruising the wide streets and boulevards and public gardens laid out with fountains and ornate pools, past the new railway station, the university and the incomparable blue-tiled mosque, the Arg – the citadel – classically simple, with its brickwork still in fine condition.

Tabriz the fair — described in my guide book as the fourth largest metropolis in Iran. Population one million independently minded, often cantankerous people. A city surrounded on three sides by verdant hills. An earthquake zone without parallel and matched only by the temperament of its inhabitants.

I recollected the pension off the Kheyabun Modarres where the landlady cooked like an angel. From morning until night delicate, deliciously fragrant, savory flavors wafted tantalizingly through the house. On the dinner table, steaming bowls of *horisht* — thick stews of lamb and chicken and raisins and various spices — made their appearance. The alchemy she could work on something as mundane as rice defied description.

Getting back to the fourteenth century, I wondered what sort of lives the Gypsies had led in Tabriz, about the initial reception they'd had when turning up at the city gates. Presumably they were welcomed with open arms for their skills and entertainment talents. In those days, Tabriz was an enormous entrepot rivaled only by Constantinople. It was accepted, graven on tablets of stone, that its merchants made 10 percent on all merchandise coming in or going out of the city. It was rich and self-indulgent, could afford the best and actively sought out the unusual. And without a shadow of a doubt, those newcomers would have had an aura about them: a wild, feline quality that would have appealed enormously to its ultra-sophisticated citizenry. In fact, and this is on record, the extraordinary beauty of their women was much commented on, in particular by one of Persia's greatest lyrical poets, Hafiz Shirazi. He referred to them in his poems as Luls or Kavuls, obviously a reference to their Afghanistan provenance.

Objects of curiosity they undoubtedly would have been: ill-kempt, colorfully dressed vagrants, with abrupt, sweeping gestures; wild of eye; dark-complexioned men; exotic, mesmerizing women; children running around brown and naked; speaking an incomprehensible, raucous, highly inflected tongue – but for all their noise and rumpus, appearing to live in harmony with the natural world. The first time a Persian poet (alas anonymous) saw a Gypsy woman dance, he swore she was transformed into solid fire, such was the blaze she emanated.

What type of employment would they have had? In addition to engaging in their traditional occupations, it was likely they would have taken employment as water carriers, domestic servants, guards along the Silk Road or city militia. All were jobs normally reserved for slaves.

But, importantly, for the first time since they left Dasht i Nawar, they would have felt secure – affluent even. They would have begun to lose that sharp edge of desperation, that urge to reach out and grab, grab, grab that would likely have characterized the first period after their arrival.

Certainly the Dom men would have fitted extremely well into this more relaxed life. Most likely as time went by, they would have become more easy-going, indolent even, enjoying gossiping and smoking in all-male company: a leap back into their Indian past. But their music – for it was the men who played – would have gained dramatically from the added dimension lent to it by the wealth of different musical instruments suddenly available. There are some who say that the strange, unique quality of Gypsy music stems from their having taken the Persian chromatic scale and reversed it. Ah, this incredible Gypsy talent for adapting the original and making it his own!

The women, too, would have evolved. Maybe outwardly they would remain subservient to their lords and masters as in the past, but rapidly they could have assumed the breadwinner's role. It was they, the dark-eyed women with the mysterious airs so beloved of the poets, who traipsed from village to village speaking at least three languages as well as the local dialects, selling amulets, pots and pans, sieves and livestock cures made by their stay-at-home menfolk.

It was they who took on the arts and wiles of the dancers they had seen in the tavernas: imitated the rich, theatrical dress of the bourgeoisie, all the garishness, glitz and glitter of a society drunk on wealth and a virile penchant for life in the opulent eastern mode.

Mastering their environment to the extent they did would have done wonders for their self-esteem. Inevitably, the Gypsy character began to be what the women made it. They were the all-important, crucial sales force, the singers, the dancers, the fortune tellers, the glittering, esoteric, dark-eyed essence of the Luri. They were the bricks and mortar of the race, guardians of its traditions, its moulders and shapers, radiating that slow-burning aura of beings placed on earth to fulfill some mysterious purpose.

And then there was the language and the way it was evolving. I think we can take it as read that among themselves they would have spoken their own *chib*, which was then in the course of developing into present-day Romanes. But never a word of Turkish entered into it. Might not that be explained by their inbred hatred of the Afghan-Turkish captors at Dasht i Nawar?

But the Greek, the Armenian, the Farsi they heard all around them, and which they rapidly picked up, dramatically improved their mental processes, speed and subtlety of thought, their ability to comprehend and express manifold shades of meaning, nuances and half-tones. It lent to their *chib* that extra richness of expression to describe all the fresh experiences they were encountering.

One thing the Romani *chib* never acquired, though, was a future tense. Maybe this was a reflection of their attitude to life? Maybe they weren't ever sure there was going to be a future? Whatever the reason, I think their philosophy of life, as I heard a Gypsy once describe it – "Taste the present moment to the full for tomorrow the greedy birds will take your eyes as you dance for the last time under the hangman's noose" – is no mean contribution to the secret of life. Neither is there the verb "to have" or a word for "possession" in Romanes, which I suppose makes sense if you don't happen to own anything.

Now having established, at least to my own satisfaction, the probable arrival date of the Dom in Tabriz from their last stopping place, Nishapur, at around A.D. 1220 (it could have been sooner but certainly not later as they would have been faced with the impossible task of wriggling through the invading Mongols), I set their departure date from Tabriz for Constantinople at A.D. 1335.

To explain the A.D. 1335 departure date: in A.D. 1316 the ruler of Tabriz, Oljeitu Khan, died and was succeeded by his son, Abu Sa'ad, aged twelve. It was then, with Mongol power declining rapidly, that palace intrigues began to multiply and disorder and chaos take over. Looting, revenge murders and robbery became the norm over the next score of years. In the year 1335, the year I postulate as the departure year, Abu Sa'ad died, and law and order in Tabriz and the surrounding areas totally collapsed.

For the Gypsies, the Golden Age of Tabriz would have been well and truly over. In the chaos that succeeded Abu Sa'ad's death, exactly the right conditions would have existed to make escape possible – westward toward Constantinople, naturally, the very center of the world, or so they'd been told.

It came back to my "Feather in the Wind" theory – how the historical circumstances of the time dictated the whys and wherefores of their wanderings across Central Asia, manipulated and motivated, shaped, designed and controlled with absolute inevitability their arrival into Europe. I believed that, indeed, no inner spring but historical circumstances alone were responsible for fashioning the Gypsy race. From the moment they were born, they themselves had hardly taken one positive, unilateral decision in their entire existence that was not forced on them.

Not quite, though. I think they did take that one initiative to leave Tabriz when the opportunity arose, but in any case that, because of the disorder around them and the likely victimization of minority groups carried out by gangs of out-of-control hooligans, probably made leaving the only option they had. But apart from that, from the time they arrived in Persia and during their residency of a century and more, their lives were dominated by one giant of a man and his descendants. He shaped their destiny and their character: Genghis Khan.

Born in A.D. 1155 at Deligun Bulduk in the far northeast of Asia. His mother named him Temujin, meaning the "toughest steel." It is said he held a piece of clotted blood in his fist when he emerged from the womb, and blood it was that bore him all the days of his life. For the next century and a half, he and then his descendants turned China, Samarkand, Afghanistan, Baluchistan, Turkestan and Persia into an abattoir in which, in some areas, hardly a man over bow-length survived.

More than 10 million people died under his sword; untold thousands were boiled alive in giant cauldrons as a warning to others not to resist. The rule was crude but inflexible: each warrior had a target of twenty-four killings every campaigning day. Even the Khan's dogs, it was said in jest, had their target of cats to kill.

He and his descendants shook the old world to its very foundations and changed it forever. From Germany to Korea, his personal standard, the white banner surmounted by nine yaks' tails, led his cavalry in armies of up to 150,000 strong to bear down on their targets with all the inexorable force of a hammer driving home a nail, destroying kingdoms and empires wholesale.

To Islam the results of the Mongol invasion were absolutely terrifying, entraining a huge loss of self-confidence. There is much to be said for the theory that – intellectually, at least – the Empire of the Caliphs never regained its former glory or impetus. The Tartars brought confusion, slaughter, devastation, slavery, destruction and conflagration. The Prophet had indeed foretold more than six hundred years previously the great slayings that must precede the Last Day and this was, indeed, butchery on an incomparable scale. In Ray alone, 700,000 human beings were slain or made captive. The Persian mystic Najm al-Tin Daya, writing of the desert that the Mongols had left behind in that once fair city, penned:

> Hail rained heavy upon my garden;
> of my rose-bush not a leaf remained.

The philanthropist Kamalu'd-Din Ismail, "the Creator of Ideas," meeting with ingratitude from some of the townspeople of Isfahan – recipients of his liberal favors – cursed them in the following verse.

> O Lord of the Seven Planets, send some blood thirsty pagan
> to make Dar-i-dasht like a bare plain, and to cause
> streams of blood to flow from Jupara.*
> May he increase the number of their inhabitants by cutting
> each into a hundred pieces.

---

* A district of Isfahan.

When the mighty Khan died on August 18, 1227, in order to prevent the news becoming known, his escort cold-bloodedly murdered every single person they encountered en route to his burial place at Gods Hill on the Altai Steppes.

Whatever his faults – and no one could deny he had them a-plenty – there he stood, a towering giant of a man who had accomplished the impossible. He had found the Mongols a scattering of savage, disorganized tribes and by sheer force of personality welded them into a nation and implanted in them the vital concept of total obedience to his will. He drilled into them the supreme ambition to conquer the world and, as a result, turned them into the most efficient, ruthless and totally unbeatable fighting force the world had ever seen.

The huge empire Genghis has fashioned with his own blood-stained hands survived him for another hundred years before splitting up into separate kingdoms. It was this loss of power and influence in the western part of the Mongol empire that gave the Rom their window of opportunity to abscond to Constantinople. But, by bottling them up, the Mongols had allowed them to absorb over a long period of time all the gifts Tabriz could bestow. When they left, they were as complete as a race could be. Constantinople added a little panache before they swept into Greece and Europe proper, but only a modicum. They'd bought their clothes in Tabriz. Constantinople just added a better fit – a nip here, a tuck there, so to speak.

We were on our way to Bikaner. By this time it had been clearly established that Seelya was Jas Tilak's number one mahout. Apart from her enthusiasm for the job, she just happened to be the best driver among us and with a sixth sense that seemed to perceive potentially dangerous situations, something I, for one, could never hope to emulate. You were born with it if you happened to be a nomad. From my observation of Seelya, it wasn't so much a sixth sense tacked on, but the heightened capacity to sense danger around the corner by bringing the existing five senses together at the highest possible level of effectiveness at one time.

Patsi was riding shotgun beside Seelya, his role being to spot obstructions in the road ahead (his eyesight was phenomenal) – dead goats, Dunlop tires or Coca-Cola bottles – before we hit them. Being mid-afternoon, he was asleep with his head on Seelya's shoulder.

I was dwelling on this thorny topic of *mochardi* (bad luck) and *marimé*: that mix of taboos and anti-pollution laws, magic and superstitions, as well as fear of the returning dead together with more than a dash of animism that took the place of that knowing awareness. The underlying rationale was that if the Gypsies kept to their self-imposed laws of purity, if their superstitions and taboos were continually being observed and reinforced, then the source of their magic, the thing that watched over them, would be there to protect them. By remaining free from the taint of pollution, they were in a proper state to receive the magic when they needed it. And all that replaced the Gods they had lost.

Tabriz was the key – Tabriz, where by and large I imagined a pretty cushy (that's a Gypsy word from *kushto,* meaning good, fine) life for them, certainly a lot more comfortable than the Dom who ended up in Baghdad, three hundred miles to the south of Tabriz. That was a real horror story and I remember telling it to Gopi Lal one threatening afternoon when we'd barely got out of the way of a flash flood.

"Baghdad? What happened there, Uncle?"

"Well," I replied draggingly, trying to remember the wording in a book I'd read. "It is said that according to Sufi lore, the hidden people, the Marddan-I-Ghai, who are forever flying over the world and who cannot be seen except by those who have the inner eye, were alone able to tell the tale of the sacking of the city of the illustrious Haroun al-Rashid in A.D. 1258 by Hulaga Khan, grandson of Genghis. Every single one, yes, every single one of its 500,000 inhabitants was put to the sword or shot full of arrows or disemboweled in the search for gold and jewels. The echo of that infamy resounded throughout Asia for centuries to come."

"And why didn't that happen to Tabriz? It appears to have been let off scot-free by the Mongols, including your infamous Hulaga Khan?"

"Simply because its position as the nexus of international trade was too important; the revenues which it paid out to the Mongols in the form of Danegeld too vast to be upset. Actually, if anything, Mongol domination of the area only increased the prosperity of the city by making the Silk Road completely safe for merchants and their caravans. And because of this additional security factor, more and more Italians and other foreigners arrived to set up trading houses in what became known as the Venetian Market."

"Did any Gypsies escape? You know, trickle out over the years before the main exodus?" Gopi Lal then asked.

"More than likely. In fact, it seems fairly certain that some reached Constantinople, where they earned a living as entertainers, sieve and comb makers and fortune tellers, profiting all they could from the intensely superstitious nature of the Byzantines. Also it seems certain that some went on to stray into Greece and thence Eastern Europe. We know for a fact that a number crossed over to Crete and Corfu, as their presence was recorded there in the early 1300s, a quarter of a century before the Gypsies fled en masse from Tabriz."

Sometime later on the drive to Bikaner, I got to thinking, idly at first, about how the Gypsies, all of five or six generations of them, might have reacted to their confinement in Tabriz. It had been a long time. The first thought that came to mind was that, little by little, many would have lost their Gypsy identity and merged into the polyglot stew that was Tabriz. There again, the old pecking order based on physical strength or courage or leadership qualities would have vanished to be replaced by an economic structure in which some were poor, some very poor and some comparatively well-off – particularly the skilled artisans. A man's position in society was related to his earning power.

It seemed logical to suppose that a certain fragmentation would have occurred, a reversion to the three original tribes. There'd be a smithying quarter, for instance. Then another for the entertainment fraternity closer to where the popular tavernas were sited. Some would have gravitated to the land and no doubt integrated to a greater or lesser degree with the local peasantry. Then there would have been the "City Rom," those who had gone *Gaujo* and were inevitably enmeshed in the city's language, manners and morals. And last of all, the nomads (a smallish number would have been permitted by the Mongols to service outlying villages), who without doubt considered themselves the only true Gypsies, those of the *kalo rat* – the "dark blood."

The fact of the matter was that, without the freedom to roam, the urban and peasant classes of Rom were no more than bondsmen, with no common religion or culture or written history to bind them together such as the Jews had in similar circumstances. All they had was the *chib*, the language, as a unifying force and, here again, every year would have witnessed more and more of a schism taking place. As time went by, a rural Gypsy might not have understood what his urban brother was talking about. They'd have had to converse in Farsi or Greek to be intelligible to each other, due to the great number of foreign words and expressions Tabriz had introduced into urban Romanes.

I postulate that, after an eternity of kicks and blows and now ensconced in a society that not only tolerated them but even appreciated them for their talents and skills and was even a little in awe of them, inevitably many of them would have begun to look on themselves as a race apart: different, singular, special, better even.

The more I thought about it, the more I believed that was probably the way it happened. Slowly at first but with ever-increasing bravado, they would have begun to look on the Ghazzo/*Gaujo* as a potential source of income, a "mark." Often they would have found him slow compared to their own street-wise cleverness and it would have done something to their character, this strange new feeling of superiority. Inevitably, they would have slipped into the habit of taking all the time and giving back as little of themselves as possible. There was the side of themselves they showed the *Gaujo* – speaking his language, understanding him and his little ways all the way down to the soles of his feet – but, at the same time, they held back, cultivating the mysterious, an aloof, hidden power.

"Like cats," I said aloud. "Just like cats."

My thoughts turned to the Gypsy woman. I could sense how the men were developing but the important thing was, how was she? Just what was happening on that front? Bearing in mind a century of security and relative comfort – but never assimilation – it seemed to me that there was room here for an offbeat theory. Like? Well, like the Gypsy woman, after a few generations had passed, might well have represented the greatest threat to the unity of the Rom. And why was that? Wasn't she supposed to be the glue that held them together? Hers was traditionally the great stabilizing role, but – and this is the big point – in their present sedentary life women's function would have altered radically. In a nomadic existence, it was the close-knit family unit against the world. The survival of the family came first, that of the tribe second. Sedentary life would have thrown up a totally different set of values. Now it was the tribe as a whole that was important. Now a council of elders commanded, the old Indian Panchayat under a different name; later in Europe it was called the Kris. In a word, they had become institutionalized. Decisions were taken by five wise men "for the good of the tribe." Not necessarily, you will note, for the more specific concern of the female, whose role on earth, as always, was her biological destiny as wife and mother. A "man against woman" situation of epidemic proportions might well have been in the cards, with the woman not prepared to surrender an inch. After all, in nearly every family, it was the Gypsy woman who was the breadwinner and the major influence on its customs, deportment and character, with the man more or less dependent on her sales, entertainment or begging skills. The men might look impressive all done up like peacocks but it was their wives and mothers who pulled the strings.

So all things considered, I thought to myself, the Rom might well have been heading straight for a monumental pile-up. And my guess was that before it could happen, they got out of Tabriz. It was probably the only way they could have saved themselves from self-destructing.

※　　※　　※

Bikaner

We'd been in Bikaner for a few days staying in a comfortable Tourist Bungalow on the Pooran Singh Circle in air-cooled rooms and where for an extra five rupees a day we were supplied with three buckets of hot water. I arrived back very late one evening after a full day visiting the mystical Karni Mata Temple and being repulsed and repelled by thousands of sacred rats having the run of the place. Despite the lateness of the hour, Gopi Lal met me at the door, his face ashen.

"Patsi's been taken to the hospital. He is in a most serious condition. The preliminary diagnosis is – here, I have written it down on this piece of paper: heat stroke, epilepsy, cerebro-spinal meningitis, hysteria or alcoholism."

"Singly or all together?"

"Take your pick, Uncle. I know which one my rupees are on," said Gopi Lal, recovering fast.

I drew a long breath. "What exactly happened?"

"He had the fever all day but said the whisky would put it right. Toward dinner time he began to twitch and then the tremors came. The manager took his temperature: 106. Then he went into a muttering delirium before losing consciousness. We telephoned the hospital and took him there in a taxi."

"And it was at the hospital that the doctor gave you this broad-spectrum treasure chest of diagnosis?"

"Yes, Uncle. There is some doubt he will recover."

"Not if he's got all of them, he won't, Gopi Lal. Not even a bloody Kanjar."

Two days later, after tests had been run and *P. falciparum* found in the blood, the diagnosis was confirmed. Cerebral malaria. The treatment: quinine administered intravenously. There was a pos-sibility of recovery but no one at the hospital had ever come across the condition before – in practice, that is.

"According to the textbooks," said the young doctor, "if the legs do not become spastic and there is no incontinence in the urine, he might just pull through. But, I repeat, the prognosis is not good. Death is far more common than recovery."

Three weeks later Patsi was released with a noticeable absence of regret on the part of the staff. I gathered there had been problems. Two of the senior nurses were on temporary leave of absence. Their professional poise, the doctor indicated, would take time to regather strength and continuity. With great tact, he took pains to indicate an alternative hospital in case a relapse should occur. In Jodhpur!

Sure enough, Patsi once ensconced in the best bedroom – mine – was, indeed, a changed man. Gone was the bawdy, devil-may-care Kanjar of old. Despite every care and consideration, he became more listless and apathetic as the days went by. Home-sickenss was the obvious answer, and I got Gopi Lal to discreetly pump him on the subject. No, it wasn't that. He was quite content where he was: liquor and food on tap and the softest bed he'd ever slept in. He had no desire to return to Udaipur. "I have the thought in my head there may be a wife in the background, Uncle."

"So?"

"Uncle, you do not know the Kanjar women. It is they who earn the majority of the income and give only small amounts at a time to their menfolk. And they have the reputation of being the most dreadful chicken peckers, although very beautiful."

Chicken peckers?

That certainly went a long way toward explaining Patsi's aversion to the female sex. I had never seen him so much look at a woman. Well, if it wasn't homesickness, what was it? Malingering was out of the question. Outside of drinking hours, the man was totally committed to the active life. Independent, tough-minded, taking nothing from anyone, entirely his own man. Cynical, yes, but with a sense of honor such as you'd never dream of, the epitome of the world-weary adventurer with the instinctive reflexes of a St. George. Deep down he was a sentimental bloke but one who kowtowed to no man.

My diagnosis – reached most reluctantly – was that he'd simply lost interest in life.

Gopi Lal and I held an emergency meeting. The doctor had told us that Patsi needed at least another week in bed without being moved but it was obvious the poor chap was sinking fast. What to do? The Scotch wasn't working – not even the Bottled in Scotland stuff I was lavishing on him. Then Gopi Lal came up with a surprising suggestion: "I think you should tell him a story, Uncle."

"I don't know any bawdy stories in Kanjar."

"No, a proper story. Something to give him an interest in life. He is not interested in what they say on the radio, cannot read, and has nothing to do all day except think. Which is a thing he is not very good at. Never had much practice at it, don't you know. So he's thinking the same stale old thoughts hour after hour, day in, day out.

"And we don't help at all," he went on, "running around busy with our important affairs. So all he has to look forward to is our company at dinner. He needs something to occupy his mind during the day. A story, Uncle, in my judgment is the answer to the Kanjar's prayer."

I must say there were times when Gopi Lal fair took one's breath away. But I could see the direction his adroit mind was taking. "You mean a sort of Thousand and One Nights saga . . . carrying on from one evening to the next?"

"Precisely, Uncle, that is what I mean. Per se. And I will translate as you speak."

"But what's this story supposed to be about?" Selfishly, I could see a huge slug of my time being taken up with this bedtime story caper and was hardly in raptures about the prospect of playing Scheherazade to Patsi's Haroun al-Rashid.

"It would be about the Rom. About everything you have put together about their life in Tabriz in the days before they fled to the West. An imaginary ancestor of Patsi's living in Tabriz, maybe? I leave these details to you, Uncle. That is presuming he wasn't in jail at the time, which would be the most likely place," he added broodingly. And then with a spurt of excitement: "And Seelya could be in it, and me, of course. Everybody, except you, Uncle. No Europeans need apply. A simple tale that Patsi could identify with, that he could dwell on and embroider in his mind during the day. Also, Uncle," he added winningly, "it will no doubt assist you in putting together a clearer picture of those ancient times."

Time to take a stand. To dismiss Gopi Lal's idea, firmly and irrevocably as quite, quite dippy.

"Look here, Gopi Lal, I must tell you, once and for all . . ." And then, in mid-sentence, I changed my mind. That last phrase of his had really struck home. It was a terrific idea. It would make me really think, really use my little gray cells to imagine how those people actually lived and died. Maybe I could tape it as I went along in case I could use bits of it later. ". . . it's a bloody wonderful idea. We start tonight."

Gopi Lal looked quite dazed, reward enough I thought. Into my head popped this business of the richly attired slaves serving drinks to a group of Byzantine tourists on a shopping spree. Just to set the scene and get me in the mood, I might open up with that.

8. Moonddkata – The Price of Blood

FOR IN AND OUT, ABOVE, ABOUT, BELOW,
'TIS NOTHING BUT A MAGIC SHADOW-SHOW,
PLAY'D IN A BOX WHOSE CANDLE IS THE SUN,
ROUND WHICH WE PHANTOM FIGURES COME AND GO.

— *VERSE XLVI FROM THE* RUBAIYAT OF OMAR KHAYYAM:
EDWARD FITZGERALD TRANSLATION

We were all assembled in the big bedroom early that evening around the bed – mine – in which lay a wasted Patsi. They'd told him the Sahib was going to tell a story. His expression registered a Kanjar skeptical "so what?"

Gopi Lal was to do most of the interpreting but Seelya would chip in as and when she thought a point worth expanding on or embellishing for Patsi's benefit. It was amazing the way she had absorbed English in the short space of time she had been with us. She was now as near fluent as makes no difference and the faint Afrikaans overshading lent her speech an attractive, low-purring quality.

I thought I'd employ a highly florid style, throwing in bits of Romanes and the odd word of Hindi to give color to the fairly flimsy tale I'd be making up as I went along. Let my ego, such as it was, parade rumbustiously around the bed chamber in the manner of the old-time bards at the Court of the Rajputs as Colonel Tod had described them in his *Annals of Rajasthan*. That was the effect I was aiming for so as to jerk Patsi out of his comatose state: booming decibels of sound alternating with low-pitched, gravely-voiced, theatrical whispers. Years ago I'd seen Laurence Olivier do it in *Othello*. Admittedly, we weren't in the same league, but it was a good model.

It was thus, in my opening speech, in best booming bardic style, that the hotel manager, Mr. Mujerjee, came into the room and caught me in mid-boom, so to speak. I can still see his eyes popping out of his head as he sat down abruptly on the only vacant chair. But not even the Lord Krishna himself could have interrupted my flow of oratory now that it had finally taken wing.

"I, the Bard of the Golden Mouth, take leave to address this assembly here foregathered. Be it known that as my voice issues from the red, dreaming mouth of the bard, as it rises and falls, rolls and roars and rivets the tale into your pliant minds, the recital will reach a bittersweet timbre never before heard as I tell the tale of a hero, one uniquely blessed by the gods, known to all as Patsi the Mor. Aye, Patsi the Peacock, on account of the splendid way he dressed, the gold and gems he bestowed on his noble person and, above all, that proud magnificence of bearing he shared with Vishnu's blue and green bird of splendor."

You could have heard a pin drop. They hadn't been expecting an opening twenty-one-gun broadside like this. Patsi's eyes showed white surprise in the way only a Gypsy does as the translation came through to him.

At that moment, Mr. Mujerjee's wife and daughter tiptoed hesitantly into the room and sat down on the floor by his side as there were no more chairs available. Someone must have been responsible for the advance hype, I thought, casting a dubious eye at Seelya and receiving an innocent stare in return.

"In all of Tabriz there never was such a man as Patsi the Mor. None his equal when it came to wenching, fighting or drinking. In antique times in the Baro Than he had been of the people of the Kanjar. But now the Mor, he was of the Jangle Dom, the free Dom, and of them he was their Rai."

There was a chorus of oohs and aahs — none louder than Patsi's. Fire burned in his eyes. His one good hand reached for a *bidi*. I started to relax and, as the tennis players do, prepared to put that extra crunch behind the shots.

"When my tale, a stirring saga of many years gone by, commences, we find our hero, the admired of the Jangle Dom, those of the pure *kalo rat*, with his right hand strapped to the left hand of Gopi Lal, a Ker Ginghar* — a House or City Dom — and rival for the hand of the beauteous Devadasi Vat,** renowned throughout the land for the grace and charm of her beauty, the sharpness of her wit and the magnificent dowry she would bring a husband.

"The two men, both in the pride of their youth and strength, due to the bad blood between them by reason of their sentiments for the beauteous Devadasi Vat — whom henceforth we shall call by her pet name, Ytzka — had been condemned by the Panchayat [the tribunal] to the *Moonddkata*, the Price of Blood. In their free hand each holds a razor-sharp, broad-bladed knife used for the slaughter of bullocks. One of them will die before the hour is out. Maybe both will expire swallowing their own blood.

"Their eyes are grown large as frogs' eyes. Sweat softens the lines on their faces. The crowd presses forward. The circle around the combatants grows tighter. The pungent smell of excitement at the anticipation of death — so closely akin to the

---

* *Ginghar* actually means "cockroach" in Romanes.
** Choosing a name for the woman who was to be Patsi's grand passion in this tale of love and duty was not easy. Eventually I hit upon Devadasi (which simply means temple dancer) and then Vat. One, it sounded vaguely Indian, and two, Vat 69 was the only imported Scotch I could find locally to assist Patsi's convalescence. Needless to say, its price was well above that of rubies.

sweet scent of blood – hangs thickly corded in the air."

There was a gasp from my audience as this was translated. Gopi Lal whispered in my ear: "You will not be killing me off in the opening scene, Uncle?"

"No way, Gopi Lal, every good story needs a heavy."

After an impressive clearing of the throat, I continued: "If either of these brave champions could overcome the other, the assembled Dom were wagering on Patsi with his powerful body and brawny arms that could lift a young bullock. Had he not triumphed in two previous contests against other opponents? A feat unsurpassed in the annals of the Dom. Gopi Lal, by contrast was more slightly built but lithe and well-muscled and very quick with his hands; at weddings and celebrations he was renowned for his ability to catch flies in mid-flight."

"I like that, Uncle. Young Krishna against Goliath, eh?"

I ignored him. "Strapped together they walk to the middle of the circle traced in the earth. They who are about to meet death look up at the incomparable beauty of the Zagros Mountains and each reflects on the loveliness of the countryside he soon would leave behind forever. The way the Elburz, running alongside the Caspian Sea catches the clouds from across the water to bring its blessing of life-giving rain. The majestic snow-covered Damavend rearing its crown of glory up into the clouds; the beautiful verdant valleys that gleam abundant all around them. Would that Heaven were as enchanting."

A cough from Gopi Lal. Tetchy sounding. Impatient even. As he spoke it seemed to me he was limiting his translation of my poetic scene setting to an economic "fairly pleasant sort of view when it wasn't raining."

"At a signal from he who was the first and oldest of the Panchyat, each would turn and strike. There was no skill to this butchery. A man hacked, slashed or plunged his blade toward the other's heart. Bound together, neither could evade the thrust. Death came in a single second. If the first blow did not succeed, others would come until one or other fell to the blood-soaked earth and gasped out his life, staring blindly into his opponent's eyes.

"Casually, as if taking his ease among friends, Patsi the Mor removes a small leather sachet from around his neck and tosses it to the ground. The crowd roars its good humor at a well-appreciated joke. The Dom wore spiders or wood lice in a bag around their neck when suffering from a malady – in Patsi's case, earache. As the insect slowly dies, so does the sickness gradually leave the body.

"The Phuri Dai now approaches and says a prayer over them in her deep man's voice. '*Bachta te Del o Del*.' God bless you. Then, in an expectant hush, with the crowd hardly drawing breath, she asks them one last time if either will bury his pride and his quarrel and bow to the will of the other. Gopi Lal says not a word. The Mor answers in his usual manly fashion: 'Speak to my arse, old hag, my head is tired.'

"'The *Moonddkata* is to be paid. The Price of Blood is Death.'

"The *diklo* [kerchief] is dropped and flutters slowly to the ground. In that split second, both men slew in toward each other in a furious release of pent-up energy. Their knives are flashes of naked light on their way to torture . . . carve . . . split asunder frail flesh."

"Oooooohhh," from my audience. The manager's daughter's dark-eyed attention riveted on Patsi – the rabbit and the snake. Outside, the yellow ocher languid sun of India setting.

"To the astonishment of all, no blood splurted to the thirsty earth. No cruel blade had sunk itself into flank or heart. Instead the knives arced sparklingly to the ground. It was a moment before the two astonished gladiators and an equally amazed crowd realized what had happened. Simply, each had swung round-arm and low, stabbing for the navel. A clever tactic this of directing the blow at an unprotected area. And what had happened? The tips of both knives had met in a million-to-one chance encounter and had been jerked summarily from the owners' hands.

"The fight was over. By Dom law they were to return to their *ker* [houses] and never again attack the other by tongue or deed under pain of expulsion, the harshest penalty a Dom could suffer, cutting him off from everything he knew and held dear. Death followed lingeringly. There was nothing to live for. How could a single branch survive by itself?

"Thus the situation remained as unclear as ever. If only her father had thought to ask Ytzka's wishes in the matter. For, in truth, the fair maiden had her heart set on being the wife of Patsi the Mor."

Ignoring what sounded like a disbelieving giggle from Seelya and a low sound of protest from Gopi Lal, I continued.

"For hark to me, if this tale be of anything, it is the story of a love, an inextinguishable desire of a woman for a man: the passion of a queen among women for her prince. For in truth did the estimable Ytzka yearn for her Patsi with all the power of the love-loaded arrows from her fawn-like eyes. As Meri Bae loved her Rahda, she loved the Mor for himself . . . loved him for the dangers he had passed."

I thought that bit rather good, actually, but all it got by way of a response was an attack of spluttering and a "Steady on, Uncle" from Gopi Lal and from Patsi what sounded suspiciously like an explosion of wind. It was obvious I would have to go easy on the mainstream romance or risk defections from the ranks. I flung myself into oratory as a swimmer into a cool lake on a hot day. No more candy floss . . . no more puff pastry. Well, maybe just a wee bit more.

"But who asks woman for advice? The world deems her

understanding shallow. Yet what is the world without women? Are they not at once thieves and sanctuaries; vessels of virtue and of vice, of knowledge and of ignorance? The man of wisdom, the astrologer, can calculate from books the motion and course of the planets, but in the book of woman he is ignorant. And this is not a saying of today, it has ever been so." Nods of grave assent from Mrs. Mujerjee, Miss Mujerjee and Miss Seelya Lohar.

"To return to our peerless Kanjar. He was not rich by the standards of Ytzka's father, Suleiman, but in his own right owned two hand fingers of sheep and a pair of fine horses. Among the Jangle Dom he was counted a man of substance. Did not the Mor sit among the men of power like a lotus in water, his mind as generous and profound as the ocean?" At that point, with a muttered excuse, Gopi Lal left the room coughing loudly. There was just no pleasing everybody.

I made a sign for Seelya to take over Gopi Lal's interpreting duties and carried on, but at a slower pace.

"And was that not the crux of the problem? Yes, he was a Jangle Dom — a nomad — and as such was looked down on and despised by Suleiman, the father of the beauteous Ytzka. But was it entirely the father's fault? How could he have known that from the moment his comely daughter had set eyes on her gallant Kanjar, she had become as inseparable from him in her mind as flame is to fire?

"And yet again, did not Suleiman and the Ker Dom [city dwellers] daily proclaim their superiority over the Jangle Dom? Did they not criticize their lack of responsibility, condemn their work-shyness, their easy-going morals, their fecklessness?

"But had they ever taken pains to see the world as their nomadic brothers saw it? That a man having no possessions — nothing he could not fit into his tent at night, or that his back could not carry by day — was free of the world and all its snares. Of course, the Jangle Dom had no sense of time. They never promised 'I'll do this or that next week' and meant it. They were practical people. Who among them knew if he would be alive then?

"But, my distinguished audience, to their great credit, it is also true to say that they never set gold a place at the table as the Ker Dom did. Theirs was a different world; a world of charms and portents and good luck things and bad luck things, of spells and curses and incantations, of trees and streams but never of wealth or what it could bring.

"Gopi Lal, on the other hand, was acceptable to Suleiman as a son-in-law. Gopi Lal's father, like himself, was a *bavales* – a rich man – who owned two shops selling pots and copper housewares in the bazaar. The marriage of their only offspring would merge their fortunes. That Gopi Lal's father, Danesh, was of Banjara extraction and Suleiman of Lohar descent did not in the least interfere with a good business deal. And besides, they had much in common: were they not united in their contempt of their Jangle brethren? Those dirty nomads who by polluting the countryside with their lewd ways gave the Dom a bad name.

"'By Allah,' Gopi Lal remembered Suleiman exclaiming when they had met some weeks ago in the bazaar, '*Beshotar lasa* [I pray you muchly], when do you become my *phral* [brother]? Daily the maiden shrivels as a ripe fig in the sun.'

"'*Kon djaneri?*' Gopi Lal had replied in the language of the Dom. 'Who knows?'

"But Suleiman, unctuous as the holy oil of the Balamo [Greek Christian], would not leave it at that. 'Hear me, Gopi Lal, for I am a Person of the Book. Understand my words well. Some women of the Dom cut their hair and become harlots for hire in the tavernas. But others, touched by the Prophet's grace, are the iris of their father's eye. *Unghen* [awake], *diken* [look], Gopi Lal, *ti bakht nakela* – your future passes before you. Take what is yours while it is yours and sweetly ripe and rich into the bargain.'

" 'I hear and take heed of your words,' Gopi Lal had replied politely and gone on his way after adding the customary '*Salamn Agha*,' so prized by the Moslem Dom.

"And now, here he was, riding back to Tabriz, happy to be alive but with the melancholy knowledge that nothing had been settled by the Fight of the Knives. He shouldn't have been drawn into it by the Mor's guile in the first place. To make matters worse, he wasn't at all sure that he wanted the woman as a bride – she whom her father described as the *Nikaleskoro i Luludi* – the Little Flower of Summer. Those Dom like Suleiman and his ilk who had adopted Islam gave themselves all sorts of airs and graces. Gopi Lal's lip curled as he saw Suleiman in his mind's eye: a corpulent man in his mid-fifties, bearded, with dark eyes and a full, sensuous, tongue-darting mouth. The spotless white caftan, the gold-embroidered waistcoat with the black pearl buttons; an amethyst (definitely fake) blazing in the scarlet-red turban. And gold, gold everywhere about his person. If you had it, show it, was his future father-in-law's motto.

"The more Gopi Lal thought about it the more he realized he was only going through with the marriage for his father's sake. He was a Dom and of the *kalo rat* whatever they said. His was a pride of blood, of being different in the world of men. But Devadasi Vat – she who would be called Ytzka – and her family were followers of Allah and *that* was their pride. It was the same old story: ask a Greek what he was and he'd say Greek. A Genoese and he'd say Genoese. A Dom and he'd say Dom or Kauli or Kavul or some such. Ask an Arab, though, or a Turk, an Afghan, an Egyptian and most Persians and they'd look up at you and say: 'I am a Moslem, of course.'

"That's how important it was to them. For to be united under

Allah, you had to abandon your roots, your blood. It didn't take much imagination on his part to visualize that within a year, Suleiman, that pompous hoof print of a blown-up pig's bladder, would have him facing Mecca with his arse in the air five times a day.

"It was a matter of pure chance that, unthinkingly, Gopi Lal took the long way round to his father's house and thereby passed by the slave market at the top end of the bazaar where the Tuesday afternoon sale was being conducted.

"The bazaar. It was a part of him. He had grown up in it and knew its ways like a lover those of his mistress. Proud and independent, always it had been its own Lord with its own laws and self-appointed rulers. Now from a rise in the road he looked down at the very heart of it.

"Richly clad, tall-turbaned merchants seated on piles of carpets, drinking tea: buying, bartering or selling. Calling five times a day on immortal Allah, who had led them from darkness into light; on their knees facing Mecca, praising his name. Brazen clamor and the sound of many tongues greeting the new trading day. The air an odorous stew of cooking smoke, rancid fat, rotting fruit, roasting meats, spices, urine, dung and offal overlaying the sweat and body smells of a people who were born and were destined to die in the bazaar's liquid dark womb. No one went naked in its narrow winding lanes: each carried the full tight armor of his own greed and envy.

"At the far end, by the great wall, he could see a woman being stoned to death. For adultery, no doubt. Her screams seemed to add extra frenzy to the barrage of rocks that smashed into her body. One, thrown in a looping arc, splintered her kneecap. Unable to stand, slowly, as if equating the kiss of paving stone with sure death, reluctantly, the blood straining through her white chador, she sank to her knees. Silence. The silence of the shame-faced. The silence of the triumphant.

The silence of men who lust for women silent or dead."

"Do I come into the story now, *Misterji?*"* asked Seelya a trifle petulantly.

"Yes," I said. "Break a leg, Marilyn Monroe, you're about to make your debut.

"As Gopi Lal drew near, his eyes were taken with a young maiden of outstanding beauty standing a little apart from the others — a sable child of the wind with a mane of glossy black hair and a head proudly set on finely sculptured shoulders, so different from the Moslem women who carried themselves *bango* (curved round): taught from birth to be submissive.

"Her name, as he would later find out, was Seelya.

"In the time it took to blink, Gopi Lal's heart was scorched. He waited until she was offered for sale and found himself bidding against a *kala kakh* — a pig's armpit — of a fat Armenian who wanted her for his taverna."

Gopi Lal came back into the room, drawn by the sound of his name, and took up his interpreting duties anew without, as it were, skipping a beat. He had washed his face and combed his hair, which he always did in moments of stress.

"Oh, no, *Misterji*, don't let the fat Armenian have me," cried Seelya, much distraught. "Gopi Lal must buy me and take me to his fine house and feed me dates and marzipan and honey cakes and bottles of Pepsi-Cola."

I gave her a stern look. "I will accept no interference, young lady. This is *Misterji*'s story."

Mentally blocking out this unexpected intrusion into my creative thought processes, and in particular a highly disapproving look from Frau Mujerjee, I went on.

"But Gopi Lal stuck it out determinedly and at last the

---

* Honorific title that can be added on to anything, thus Nehruji, Gandhiji.

Armenian dropped out of the bidding. On arriving home, Danesh, his father, went red in the face when he learnt how much the girl had cost and straightaway put her to work in the kitchen to earn her keep.

"But the damage had been done. Arrows of love had been fired. Gopi Lal's mouth grew slack, his mocking eye dull, all appetite gone. The maiden Seelya had stormed his heart and he could think only of her in the solitude of his room."

"Eeeeh," cried Seelya, in exaggerated revulsion. The manager's wife placed a protective arm around her shoulders and gave Gopi Lal a fierce look.

I took no notice and continued with my tale, making it up as I went along, chimpanzee-like, leaping from branch to branch and hoping for a happy landing.

"And thus things went on for month after month until Ytzka summoned up courage to confess to her father that Patsi the Mor was the beloved of her heart. '*Dadoro* (little father), I have taken the scent of the young Rai between my breasts forever,' she said, oozing daughterly submission."

"What about me, *Misterji*? I want a young rajah," cried Seelya. "Why do I have to have dull old Gopi Lal? Can't you find another woman for him? Someone who'll make him stop talking all the time? Please, *Misterji*, I don't want to eat his sermons for the rest of my life."

"No, I can't. I don't know any young rajahs. It's Gopi Lal or the fat Armenian for you, young missie." I could sense a mutiny brewing. I pressed forward.

"Gopi Lal's father, Danesh, a solid man, and well accustomed to having his own way because of his worldly success was in black anger with his son for ever finding excuses to put off the wedding with Suleiman's daughter.

"He was about to test him to the limit by ordering him to

either set a date for the ceremony or leave his house forthwith, when news of the introduction of the *chao* — the new paper money — hit the bazaar like a tidal wave.

"The situation had come about because the Mongol ruler of Tabriz, Gaykathu Khan, with the palace coffers empty and heavily in debt, decided to copy the currency system that was working so well for his Mongol cousins in China. On that fateful day, the twelfth of September, A.D. 1293, he introduced the paper *chao*. Everyone had to exchange their gold and silver for this paper or '*chitthi* money' as the Dom called it. Any merchant or individual who didn't, or who refused to accept it from someone else, would forfeit his head.

"The men of business and shopkeepers like Suleiman and Danesh were distraught. They could foretell what was going to happen: the bazaar would close down as its traders lost their sources of supply. No one outside Tabriz and the jurisdiction of the Khan would be foolish enough to accept their paper money in return for good merchandise. Close down the bazaar and you killed the beating heart of Tabriz. No more would the Gypsy stall-holders murmur '*Devlakuino*' — the day is of God — as they stood, palms outstretched, facing the rising sun.

"Of course, the greedy Khan was going to spend their gold settling his debts and holding magnificent receptions and, no doubt, building a grandiose mausoleum for himself. And when all the gold was gone, Tabriz would be bankrupt. No one anywhere would deal with her or supply her with goods. Tabriz dead. Killed by the Khan and his paper *chao*."

"Patsi wants to know when he's coming back into the story. He says he's not interested in the Khan's money problems, he's got his own," Gopi Lal translated.

"Right away," I replied promptly, turning to face our young Lochinvar.

"Nobody had any idea what to do, except Patsi the Mor. He had learnt that the nomadic Jangle Dom were not included in the scheme. They weren't thought to have much gold or silver and, for the little they did possess, it would be too much of a bother scouring the countryside to collect it.

"Full of himself and his plan, he went to see Ytzka's father, who listened carefully to what he had to say before having him thrown onto the street by his servants."

"'*Kala kakh* – pig's armpit,' growled Patsi as he dusted himself down. 'He makes himself comfortable on my neck while I tell him of golden ways to save his wealth. I urinate on the mustaches of your ancestors and make wind on you, Suleiman. May you who have known the pudenda of a woman eat only the penis of a donkey from this moment on and may the black bird of sorrow take your testicles.' His voice was harsh and bitter and rough with rage. Not many dared to treat him so. He was a big, blunt, square-shouldered young man with an ax blade of a face and black, commanding eyes."

Back in the room, a thoughtful look came over Patsi's face as he lit a *bidi* and slowly straightened himself up in bed. It was plain to see a change was coming over him. In Western cine-matographic terms, he was no longer Patsi, the one-armed Kanjar, but suave Rhett Butler sardonically putting match to cigar and not giving a damn.

"But cunning as a fox was Patsi the Mor and resourceful. His whole future was at stake. There would never be another opportunity like this. For three days and nights he dwelt alone in the desert, talking to the sad white moon, lofting his prayers for his undertaking into the pale wind, focusing with all the power under his eyes on bending the inner mind and will of Suleiman. Many rites did he perform with fire and water and kneaded flour. During those days, with his concoctions and incantations and spells and dark magic, he grew into the earth and out of it as the power rose in him. And, at last, the bronze-skinned, black-of-hair-and-eye Gypsy with the heart of a child witnessed with his own eyes the moon turn into white fire and smile at him from inside a basket of spikes of green flowers as naked he jigged with intricate steps to and fro across the blue-black sand.

"And at last, at long last, he *saw* sounds.

"When next day he awoke from the sleep the Gypsies call birth after death, his first sight was of five wild geese flying from right to left. He knew then that he would never again shed hot tears for what he could not have.

His will was to touch with his mind
the wind and sky:
Air which had taken air,
Side by side with the wolf of his desire.

Grieving, un-laureled, past Dom bones
Clap in time with the music
As the Domni maidens swirl in
Rama's dance of the mulé* dead.

He had carried his dreams as the *Gaujo* his cloak . . .
Loosely,
With melancholy;
Wrapped in pale amber.
Accustomed to them
Falling on jagged rocks.

---

* Spirit of the dead.

But no more.

Pray. Pray. Pray.

Dev.* Dev. Dev.

Pray that the stone mind of Suleiman

Turns to pink-tipped bosoms and fragrant thighs,

And away from the skull of the Mor

Whose tongue is raw from pleading;

Whose eyes, eaten by tears, can no longer see

His pale *grai*** grazing

In the lime cave of the yellow dawn.

No one will eat the bones of the Mor,

Is he not become golden ashes of fire's flame?

"The feeling of invincibility was on him. Avatar. For the space of a heartbeat, the Mor had overviewed the world and seen it his. He had found the path of destiny. He cut the vein of his wrist and let the blood soak drop by drop into the sand of the dawn-blue desert. Naked he bayed at the sky like his cousin the wolf; lips drawn back in a snarl. *Balvai i kormi* [thunder's wind], no one will break the bone of the Mor. He is become the burning flame of fire.

"Oh his way through verdant valleys to pay visit to Suleiman, the Mor reflected on the past two years of his life – ever since the title of Rai of the Jangle Dom had been conferred on him. All the turnings in the road that had changed a carefree Gypsy into a hard-eyed Rai who used his powerful body and the crushing power of his will to cower and dominate his people. A man with

* God.
** Horse.

a desire for gold and a lust for the heart and yielding haunches of
a Moslem Ker Dom, the fruitfully favored Devadasi Vat."

I'd got a bit carried away there with the yielding haunches
but luckily there were no cries of shocked horror from my audience. Relieved, I took up my theme again.

"Patsi the Mor cast his mind back. Oh, he'd been a devil-
may-care lad in his time, right enough. The Genoese woman
in Tabriz, he'd saved her life when her carriage horses bolted.
Madly in love with him she was. Couldn't keep her wet mouth
from his Gypsy skin and the body smell of him. A lusty woman
but innocent-hearted, although having tasted many times of
man. After a while, when she thought to own him by her favors
and fortune, she'd asked him to give up his former life: his
family, his nomadic ways, his drinking in the tavernas. 'Such
a small sacrifice, my Prince of Love. Will not Thea be by thy
side throwing gold coins at the moon; bathing with thee in
asses' milk?'

"But he'd grinned back saying he preferred not to be put
into a cage with a pile of gold, that there was much he, Patsi
the Mor, had the power for. He could give a woman love, put
fullness in her belly, crack a man's skull who dared slight her
name. All these things and more. But what he could not and
would not do was to forge a chain for a woman to lead him
around by the neck like a dancing bear."

I could hear Gopi Lal making strangled noises. Time to
soft-pedal the Patsi hype or risk my Banjara assistant throwing an apoplectic fit. Interestingly, the *numero uno* player was
wearing what could only be described as a tortured look. It
came to me that his brain must be undergoing an almost
impossible task, churning over the twists and turns of the story
and trying to project himself into the personality of someone
who bore his name but was, quite evidently, a very different

person from the one he knew himself to be. But, in some respects, quite similar.

Gopi Lal spoke in a hoarse stage whisper. "I cannot endure any more of this sickening, sycophantic, fawning adulation over a worthless *dacoit* [robber]. Uncle, it is making me very unwell."

"It's called psychological remedial therapy, Gopi Lal. It encourages the patient to transfer his identity to that of a much stronger person. A role model. At least I think that's what it's all about. In any event, might I point out that it was your idea in the first place?"

"But, Uncle, after this, *he'll* want to be driven."

"Look on the bright side. Might save an accident or two, Gopi Lal."

"Upon his return to Tabriz," I continued, "Patsi paid a visit to the house of Suleiman. This time he took care to call him 'Hafiz' as a proper mark of respect. This time Suleiman, his head full of wraiths and spirit calls and the fingerprint of the *mulo*, the spirit of the dead, on his heart, had no difficulty in thinking of Patsi the Mor as *hurskanp* [manly]: not a bad chap after all. He listened with interest to the persuasive oil of the Mor's words and such was their puissance that he agreed with only the barest resistance to the proposition put to him.

"Our hero, seizing the power of the moment, went to see Danesh – Gopi Lal's father – and spoke just as earnestly and convincingly to him before obtaining his approval also to his plan.

"And so it came to pass that when an emissary of the Grand Vizier called on Danesh to deliver his gold to the palace in exchange for the *chao*, he was informed that his entire wealth had been lent to Suleiman to make up the dowry for his daughter. This in turn was confirmed by Suleiman. 'Yes, Hafiz, Danesh's gold together with all of mine has gone to Patsi the Mor – my son-in-law to be – as dowry for my daughter.'

"'And where can this Patsi crapule be found?' the hard-faced man from the palace demanded.

"'He's a nomad. A Jangle Dom. Could be anywhere. However, he's due back in time for the wedding next month.' And with that the Grand Vizier's lackey had to be satisfied – for the moment. But he left with a wicked heart, knowing for sure that the Great Khan had been cheated by those worthless, no-account Gypsies."

I took in all of the assembled company in my gaze. "You will be in no doubt that the Peacock had pulled off a masterstroke. Aside from the prospect it opened up of his marrying his beloved Ytzka, it put him in the extraordinary position of being the only man in Tabriz with gold to invest. The opportunities for an astute man were enormous. By the time the Mongols came to their senses and went back to the old system – as everyone knew they eventually would, especially now that the bazaar had closed down and the life of the city was grinding to a halt – he would be the richest man in Tabriz."

Patsi was positively beaming: all betel-stained teeth in an unshaven face, not a sight for a weak stomach.

"As had to happen, the plan went badly awry. Danesh and Suleiman couldn't resist boasting about how clever they'd been in safeguarding their wealth: how the Mor had made it multiply like fleas on a dog. Word got back to the Palace. (There was no shortage of jealous people around, you may be sure). Suleiman, Danesh and Gopi Lal were arrested and thrown into jail to await the Grand Vizier's sentence. It came a week later. They were to be sold into slavery – proceeds to the Palace.

"Seelya, brave and resourceful, wasted no time in going in search of Patsi the Mor deep in the countryside. There was just time to get him back to Tabriz to purchase the freedom of the two fathers and Gopi Lal via an intermediary. Upon his release,

Suleiman promised the Mor that as soon as practicable he should marry his daughter, the iris of his eye, the fulsome, felicitous Devadasi Vat.

"All went well until a month later when Suleiman, entertaining an important customer from Balkh, having drunk too deeply of fine Greek wine, blabbed the whole story of how his clever son-in-law-to-be had bought him out of slavery with gold which, if you look at it in a certain light, actually belonged to the Khan.

"The next morning the buyer from Balkh, eager to ingratiate himself with the Palace, relayed the story to the Grand Vizier's office.

"This time the consequences were drastic. The two families, Suleiman's and Danesh's and their entire households, including Seelya, were judged guilty of treason and sentenced to be flung from the Arg. A great spectacle, including tumbling and juggling and animal acts, was put in train. The Palace hoped it would turn people's minds away from the chaos around them; the disintegration of law and order; the unsettling psychological effect of citizens falling down dead in the street from lack of food.

"On the morning of the execution, a big crowd gathered around the Arg. Monkeys and bears performed tricks, entertainers danced and sang and did clever things on stilts. Cool sherbet was offered freely by street pedlars. There was a happy, holiday atmosphere as the condemned Gypsies appeared at the rim of the Arg to be exhibited to the crowd. Behind them, guards with long, iron-tipped poles stood ready to prod them over the edge at a given signal.

"The crowd hushed. Not a sound could be heard. All eyes were on the terrified faces of the victims. Gopi Lal and Seelya clung fiercely to each other. Do what you like to us, their expressions said, at least we will die in each other's arms.

With Gopi Lal, who looks bashful and pretends I'm in charge. Shanera Royal Castle, Udaipur.

BELOW: Patsi's typical expression when surrounded by "womens."

BOTTOM: Seelya, ruling the roost with that smile.

THE KANJAR

Mother and family, encampment at Balotra, Rajasthan.

Women working on a building site, Balotra.

Outside of Bikaner, Rajasthan.

Temporary encampment, outskirts of Bikaner.

THE GADULIYA LOHAR

Encampment at Ajmer, Rajasthan.

Travelling cart, Ajmer.

Jaipur, Rajasthan.

Smithying, side of the road, Jaipur.

THE BANJARA

Gopi Lal (left) with wedding party at Banjara Tanda (village), Udaipur, Rajasthan.

Cooking the evening meal, Udaipur.

Banjara woman with firstborn child.

Anticipating the evening's entertainment, Jaisalmer, Rajasthan.

TOP: Banjara women returning from the well, Thar Desert.

ABOVE: Topkapi Gate, Constantinople: Point of exit for the Rom, and where their diaspora began.

LEFT: Gypsy nightclub owner, Istanbul.

"No sound. Not a child cried or a dog barked. The silence of the damned. Slowly, remorselessly, the guards moved in."

There was utter silence as I broke off.

"Well, Uncle?" said Gopi Lal.

"Well, *Sahib?*" said Patsi.

"Well, *Misterji?*" said Seelya.

"That's it, folks. The bard's gone dry. Tune into the next install-ment this time tomorrow." And I fled to the verandah for a drink, closely followed by Mr. Mujerjee, who had the same idea.

Midway through the next morning I spoke with Gopi Lal.

"Well, how do you think it went last night?"

"First class-ish, Uncle. Patsi kept me up until after midnight talking and asking questions. He's quite his old self this morning. I must say you laid it on a bit thick at times, by crikey."

I disagreed with him and said so, concluding: "The main thing is that it seems to have worked. All things considered, and if our Patsi's up to it, I'd like to deliver you chaps back to Udaipur quick smart so's I can get things organized to go on to Istanbul by myself just as soon as practicable."

Gopi Lal gave me one of his long sideways looks and walked away without a word. I had the distinct impression I'd said some-thing out of place.

That afternoon I had an appointment with the professor of Sociology at the university – a Brahmin – to enquire more into an off-shoot of Hinduism called Shivism, which, in turn, had given birth to the mysterious cult of the Tantra-Mantra-Yantra, a sect that appeared absolutely tailor made for the Gypsies to have latched onto – like iron filings to a magnet – if they'd come across it, either in India, Dasht i Nawar or during their extended stay in Persia. Could there be just a possibility that they arrived in Constantinople from Tabriz with something other than just pots and pans and baggage? It was intriguing, this exotic, erotic religion suddenly coming into the picture.

But, taking it one stage further, if they had adopted the Tantric cult, why didn't they bring it into Europe with them from Constantinople? But there was no record of their practicing any religion at all when arriving in Greece and the Balkans. Did that mean they had abandoned it in Constantinople? And if so why?

A magnetic force – a lodestone lure – had drawn them irresistibly westard from one staging post to another, like the sun chasing his sister the moon. And, strangely, a cult that may well have been their aid and comfort during their hundred-year confinement in Tabriz was suddenly abandoned. It made no sense.

Of course, who knows, it might still be at the very core of them, hidden from the *Gaujo* world these past six centuries, a secret voodoo – actually, not so far adrift, as from all accounts some of those Shivite rites were extremely pagan and with the accent on sexuality and with spells and potions never spoken about.

To the best of my knowledge no one had ever speculated or in the vaguest way theorized that the Gypsies were ever bothered by any form of organized religion at any stage of their existence. There were vague remnants of a Hinduism long forgotten, yes, notably the worship of Kali under various forms such as Black Sarah and Santana. Strong leanings toward placating the spirits of immediate ancestors by wearing charms and amulets as, indeed, the Banjara practice to this very day, yes. Pollution and defilement taboos, yes. But that's about all if one excludes their skin-deep conversion to the ruling religion of any country they happened to be passing through.

We spent four hours together, the professor and I, and at the end of the interview I was doubly convinced that if, in the whole of Asia, the Gypsies could have had their pick of a religion to carry with them until the end of time, Shivism – the Tantra-Mantra-Yantra cult – would have been it. Also I was sure that, such was its influence at the time of their sojourn in Tabriz, they would undoubtedly have been exposed to its teachings.

I ought to make it clear at this juncture that most Indians believe the Shivism cult to be nothing more than an erotic offshoot of Hinduism, transmuted through a prism of black magic and sex and a live-for-the-day approach to life totally at odds with Hinduism. So, in deference to my Hindu friends I shall not elaborate on it. This will also please a lot of non-Hindus who are bored witless by strange, exotic religions coming out of the mysterious East.

At the outset, the professor grilled me persistently about my reasons for being so interested in this off-the-beaten-track subject. I repeat what I conjectured, namely that because of its inherent affinity with the Gypsy character, the Rom might have adopted Shivism and practiced it in Tabriz for a century or so before taking it to Constantinople. What I could not understand, I told him, was why from there they didn't appear to have taken it into Europe with them – for if they did, they had concealed it remarkably well.

He nodded casually, but his eyes grew profound.

"Of course," he remarked. "It is as you English say: 'horses for courses,' is it not?"

"I beg your pardon, sir?"

He explained. "A people might practice one religion when sedentary – imprisoned is the word I remember you employing. You know, something to fill in the time on a slow evening around the fire in lieu of sacrificing goats or doing unspeakable things to young virgins and so on and so forth. But might they not require a very different religion when reverting to their natural, nomadic form of life? Had you thought of that, my dear gentleman?" And he smiled an infuriatingly benign smile. "Then do, my dear gentleman, then do so by all means." This was accompanied by a condescending look as if he had single-handedly solved the mystery of creation.

Despite a cushionful of ruffled feathers at being treated like a third former, and not a particularly bright one at that, I had to admit that looking at the situation "in the round," the way he had done, certainly put things into a much clearer perspective. Anyhow, one way or another, Istanbul had to throw some light on the business. There had to be *some* traces I could connect to. Actually, a whole number of mysteries remained to be solved. Crack one, and five others seemed to shoot up in its place like the Hydra snake of Greek mythology.

There I was, alternating between despair and high excitement as I confronted the challenge of proving that the Gypsies actually took a form of religion with them into Europe. Such proof prima facie would have tallied spectacularly well with the obscure in their nature: the fortune telling (which at times was unnervingly accurate), the laying on of the curse, mystic glimpses into lives past or future. A naive people's attempt — and possibly the closest the human race has ever got to it — to respond to Paul Gaugin's questions (still unanswered after 10,000 years of civilization) scrawled on his last canvas as he lay dying, uncared for by the world: "What are we? Where do we come from? Where will we go?"

Maybe they *had* found such a religion, discovered the way through the prism, but then fearful of God's retribution had deliberately concealed it. Damn it, I thought, why couldn't they have kept written records as the Jews did throughout their history?

In any case, just what is this thing we call religion? An attempt to find God so as to give a higher purpose to our lives or something primeval buried in our old-new dinosaur brains? Closer to the sacred, inborn drive toward order? Is that what God is about? Simply order? Because we, the human race, fear chaos even more than death?

I remember asking a very dear friend, an ex-Jesuit priest, in his cool smoke-dark flat in Madrid. He was a man who had lived through every torment and storm of soul before emerging into calm water. It was the middle of summer. We were drinking cold beer while from the kitchen came sounds of the afternoon meal being prepared by Inez, smooth-faced and pregnant, his wife of eight months.

"What does religion mean to you now, Paul?" I asked.

"Bit sudden, wouldn't you say?" The deep brown eyes appeared to focus inwards. He put down his cigarette.

"Blame it on Spanish ale. Also, I might never get another chance to ask you."

And I never did. He died the following year from lung cancer.

"Ah well, one's duty as a perfect host and all that." Pausing. Smoothing his thinning hair. "I'm inclined to the view that it's wrapped up with man's search for another dimension. One he instinctively knows exists from the moment he is born and spends the rest of his life trying to find, endlessly putting the wrong key in the lock. The way an ant has only the faintest glimmering that we exist on the same earth but knows just enough to keep on searching. But certain races, those who have lived cheek by jowl with nature for a very long time, may have come close to lifting the skirt of this further dimension. The Australian Aborigines, the Gypsies, the Shamanistic nomads of Central Asia, for instance."

"None of your Catholic mystics, Paul? St. Hildegard of Bingen, for example?"

"You'll have to ask her, old boy."

And there we left it as Inez called us to table.

The next morning as I followed Gopi Lal down the corridor toward the dining room, Istanbul was very much on my mind. I'd got as close to the true history of the Rom as one could get, I thought, *up to this point*. But Istanbul was the golden opportunity to put the Gypsy fairy firmly on top of the Christmas tree. Somehow, I had to find out why the Rom left Constantinople after apparently such a short stay, together with any remaining traces of this mysterious Shivite cult. It was a tall order, but without the crew with me, I'd have that much more opportunity to concentrate on the business in hand.

"I think he is fit to travel, Uncle," remarked Gopi Lal, inhaling a carcinogenic dose of whisky and *bidi* fumes as we passed by Patsi's bedroom.

"Well," I said, "the rent's paid up to the end of the week so there's nothing to stop us pushing off tomorrow. I'm sure we all want to get back as quickly as possible." Gopi Lal gave me the benefit of another of his long under-the-lashes looks but didn't say anything.

"Hey, wait a minute, Gopi Lal, what about my story? I'm just getting into my stride."

"Polish it off tonight, Uncle. We don't want to get boring, do we?"

I put in a good stint that afternoon: last minute good-bys to a host of new-found friends, visiting the museum to check a manuscript, settling up with the hotel for food and drink and having Jas Tilak checked out so she'd be in prime condition for the drive back to Udaipur.

Actually, I was half-expecting some sort of reaction to our departure from the manager's daughter (I never did find out her name). She was in her mid-twenties and stood very little chance of marriage now. Somewhat over-expansive around the hips, not even her large dreamy brown eyes could alleviate the excessive plainness of her face. She moved very slowly in a cocoon of studied deliberation, especially when serving breakfast, which had a tendency to drive Gopi Lal — who was at his hyperactive best between 7 A.M. and 9 A.M — right up the wall. But she was a grand woman who had been staunch and true during Patsi's convalescence. It was clear she'd been doted on by her parents all her life and this may have been her first opportunity to devote herself heart and soul to another person. Unfortunately for her and for her marriage prospects, that someone else was Patsi.

Her tender feelings had been very evident from the way she let him order her around in a manner quite feudal. Of course, it wasn't in the slightest measure reciprocal. Patsi's general attitude toward women was that they just about passed muster when approaching silently with a tray of food and strong drink in his direction.

That evening I delivered the second part of my story to an expectant audience. I was beginning to feel like an actor in a one-man show, an ersatz Richard Burton performing a Dickens evening. Patsi had renounced the bed and sat back on an armchair looking positively rakish in a Kashkai belted sheepskin coat (mine) and a black fur hat pulled down over one eye, relaxed but with a brilliant glitter-glitter in his eyes, which meant that either he was thrilled to the core at the prospect of the (or rather his) forthcoming performance or the Scotch was sloshing about in his bloodstream that much more powerfully that evening.

"You will recall that when we left our story yesterday, the two families and the maiden Seelya were held on top of the Arg. Mongol soldiers were advancing step by step to thrust them over the parapet. Down below, all around the citadel, a vast crowd waited expectantly for their bodies to fall to the ground. One by one they would hurtle down, the remaining victims growing more and more terror-stricken as they waited their turn, some uttering high-pitched screams, shrieking out invocations to Allah, Jesus of Nazareth, the Buddha and Bes, the oldest and most mysterious of the Gods of Asia. That was the part the crowd liked best, apart from the crunching, squelching moment of impact on the unyielding stone: the intangible, obscure second when life passed into death.

"That morning, Patsi the Mor was camped within a few miles of Tabriz. A brazen sun beat down on him and his escort of a score of Jangle Dom lounging in the shade of the great cart that was to carry his wealth to Constantinople. Dev willing, he would soon be lost within the body of a caravan. He had but to give the order to swing west. And yet he hesitated, walking this way and that while his men waited, heads cocked for his word of command. 'What does he do, our Rai, making his road, throwing his salt to the fish?' they muttered.

"Patsi cursed himself for his indecision, cursed Suleiman and all his ancestors and progeny for putting him in this position. Why was he frying his brains for the sake of a woman and her mutton-brained father? He had saved them once. Was that not enough? He was a Jangle Dom not a Balamo saint. So the woman, Ytzka, had *lias mi godi*, taken his mind? So what? In a year's time he would not even spare her a coin or a thought. He was a *bavales*, a rich man now. But the thought refused to leave him that with gold and a brave heart he could save them from the fate that was to be theirs that day. That which he had taken the odor of in the fire-brands the previous night as his face became fiery and brilliant and the red cloud under his eyes told him of death in the morning. The way the hunted dog sees death through his nostrils.

"Overnight he had become as a scorpion shell. Gone was his sense of heroic *vesto* . . . the living out in grand style of the greatest adventure that had ever been in the world, that of his own life. His heart had gone from him, stolen by cowardice.

"Child's foolishness. He spoke in his thoughts, his eyes closed. He was no *kovlo manush* [sweet man]. He was a Rai, a chief. For him and others like him there was no shade on the mountain top. And besides, what was there to like about Ytzka? She was bossy, fiery, too quick to make decisions and incapable of changing her mind. Too, her face was on the thin side. All in all, more of a consort to a Turkish warlord than an accommodating wife of a Gypsy Rai.

"In any case, he preferred well-rounded women with full wide hips, preferably sullen, hostile even. That way a man didn't have to think about them for a moment longer than necessary after he'd sown his seed.

"He was rambling. Avoiding his fate. Great tears formed in his eyes. Dev . . . Dev . . . come close to me that I make you my brother, he screamed inside himself.

"But after a moment the *pad,* the way ahead, came to him. He could die on soft cushions surrounded by fine Greek wines and wheat-skinned courtesans, or this day seek madness and cruel wounds spilling out his life's blood. Either way he knew that henceforth he would never be free from the picture of blood that would come under his eyes.

"He grinned his cruel, careless, wolf's grin. Would that all problems were as simple. He shouted to his men to stop frying their brains and get off their arses. 'Shine my horse like silver,' he commanded. 'Sorrow is past on the twelfth day of mourning. Then shall the living rejoice.' "

"On top of the Arg, Gopi Lal, fighting to contain his fear, turned to his beloved and said in a low voice: 'O, thou Gift of the Universe, thou of ruby lips and breath like wine, thou Tongue of Heaven, be with me this day, I do thee pray.'

" 'This day and tomorrow, my love,' Seelya smiled bravely up at him, the two having eyes but for each other.

" 'Would I were a swallow and sat upon your shoulder . . . or a teardrop on your cheek,' he whispered with a catch in his voice.

" '*Kal*' – bending her head to catch his words – '*Kal* [tomorrow] I will put sweet basil between my breasts as the young brides do, and we shall be married.' "

I was halted by a cacophony of coughs from Gopi Lal, followed a few seconds later by a chorus of unrestrained sobbing from the women.

"I say, Uncle, that's a bit thickish, don't you think? You've got me standing there like a prize gherkin mouthing soppy, totally unrealistic prose to a lower caste, when I . . ."

"When you what?" I growled, annoyed at the interruption.

"When I should be leaping around, sword in hand, fighting for our lives, of course."

"This is not one of your Shashi Kapoor movies, Gopi Lal, where a second before the young lovers are decapitated by a giant saw, they switch to a song-and-dance routine on a mountain top with Vishnu gazing down benignly. This, mate, is thirteenth century Tabriz and my bloody story. If you don't mind."

"Suddenly there was a commotion in the crowd. A lick of flame appeared at the northeast corner base of the Arg. In the doorway, a fire sprang to life. Other blazes broke out. Billows of acrid fumes rolled over the piazza. The sound of explosions coming, it seemed, from all directions rent the air. It was too much for the congregation who stampeded in blind panic, their only thought to get away from this unholy place.

"There were some, though, who took thought to shout up to the guards, their voices carried by a sudden gust of wind. 'Fire . . . fire down below. . . . Save yourselves!' In a frenzied scramble for the small doorway, the guards led the way down. . . ."

It was at that moment that Gopi Lal cut in authoritatively and decisively.

"We will take it as read, Uncle, that our hero rescues us from certain death and me from quoting more of that horrible bilge you have been putting in my mouth. Next chapter, please." Very firmly this. I blinked and gave way with good grace.

"The next and final chapter, by special request from Gopi Lal," I proclaimed.

"They journeyed all day and deep into the night to where Patsi's Jangle Dom were camped. It was there, on the bank of a stream, that Patsi was joined in marriage to his Ytzka, Gopi Lal to the maiden Seelya. They marked one another's foreheads with red lead and hand in hand walked around the great fire to make their vows binding. Then followed the traditional dancing and feasting.

"When Patsi and Ytzka had gone to a quiet place in the woods as was the tradition of the Jangle Dom, and after they had lain together, the Mor spoke of some other customs of his people. 'When my hands no longer shake when thou appearest within the ambit of my gaze, when my ears no longer open like flowers at the sound of thy approach, when no more do thy breasts tremble when our bodies brush, then I am no longer thy husband. No more thy *Bashno*, the giant king of the birds . . . the iris of thine eyes.'

"She looked at him wonderingly. A wry smile touched the fullness of her bruised lips. 'Is it when we no longer go without sleep, counting the stars at night, that our wedding vows become as broken pots? Or when — tomorrow mayhap — a heavy stone enters thy man's heart or thy weak mind takes a fancy to roam, that the tree is split?'

"'A man cannot sit by the west wind for all his life's span,' the Mor replied, in bad humor.

"'Then do not,' said Ytzka in an icy temper. 'As *Beng* the Devil is a giant toad so art thou a little tadpole,' and she cracked the Mor's head with a flat stone the size of a hand's span. Without a backward glance, she walked away with rapid steps.

"The Mor was painfully aware that things had not gone the way the elders had foreseen when they had insisted that, as Rai of the Jangle Dom, he keep order in his own *ker*, set an example to others. It should be spoken of in the very beginning between man and woman, they said. And where had that left him? Lying on his arse in a dark forest nursing a broken head.

"Piercing through the throbbing ache, the sound of her voice reached him. 'I clap my hands four times and we become divorced — as if our vows had never been.'

"'That is only for men . . . Moslem men,' he called back weakly.

"'What is good for the wolf is good for the wolf's dam,' she answered. 'Listen.' He heard the sound of a clap. Three to go. He was about to lose the moon of the world. Painfully he rose to his feet and lurched toward her.

"Clap. Two to go. His future was about to break into shards around him. Forcing his gait forward, clutching at his head with both hands, with a last-gasp effort, he stood before her as the third clap sounded.

"He was finished, his life over. What could he do? There was but one thing left. It had been said about the Mor many times that his tongue could charm a bird off a tree. Well, he would see how it went with an angry Moslem wife. The old Indian love song – 'The Banyan Tree' – sung at weddings and buried deep in the history of the Dom crooned forth from his mouth in the velvet air.

> And, oh my lady, beloved mine.
> Thy fragrance wafts from bole to bole.
> Pray, please descend and enter in
> The garden of my soul.

"The fourth clap never came. The black night closed in as the laughter of their unborn children called to them."

"The Jangle Dom left for Constantinople the following day, traveling by night to avoid detection and the heat. They had no means of knowing that twenty years later the Dom of Tabriz would follow in their footsteps."

You could have heard a pin drop in the room. I paused a fraction before my winding-up speech.

"And thus concludes the sweet outpourings of this, your most vaunted bard. My task will have been accomplished if the souls in this chamber carry with them the rapture of the remembrance of the deeds of the most noble Patsi the Mor and his most excellent companions and these proudly formed tributes immortalized in your minds."

My audience pondered . . . considered . . .weighed it up

and, all things considered, found it to their taste. A well-mannered burst of applause brought the evening to an end.

The next morning Patsi being, if anything, in even ruder health, we started to load Jas Tilak. And so the four of us left Bikaner that morning in the yellow ocher sunshine, Patsi sitting self-importantly in the front passenger seat with the map on his knees. The manager's daughter handed him a bag with a conspiratorial smile. It clinked. Like glass bottles clink.

I had the feeling of an iron fist being subtly concealed. Sooner or later when that Gypsy had been given enough line, she'd start reeling him in. A surprise visit to Udaipur in a month or two's time, I shouldn't wonder. Then she'd begin "making something of him." Of course, she was barking up the wrong tree. Gypsies can't be changed or tamed or made to conform. They go their own way, born with a will of iron to resist turning them into anything but what they have to be. But like *Gaujo* women throughout the ages, she would try. And try and try again.

There he was, our Patsi boy, an adam-appled, scrawny, intense, whip-cord muscled, black-haired, unshaven, wildly good-looking, betel-stained Kanjar who loved boozing and singing and telling bad jokes and scrapping in pubs, about to enter the ring in the fight of his life. Worse, he didn't even realize there was a match going on. Serves him bloody well right, I thought a trifle sourly. May the best Mujerjee win.

In front of us were poor villages, ramshackle hovels and houses, high walls enclosing secrets; drab temples, goats, flies, sheep, chickens and more flies. Savage dogs fighting over piles of rotting garbage. We would take the same road to Udaipur that in the first centuries A.D. had stretched westward, boldly marked, circumventing salt lakes and mountain rages, to eventually join with the Via Egnatia to lead to the then capital of the world: Rome.

Traders, pilgrims, holy men and bold adventurers had taken

this highway for over three millennia, prey to freezing temperatures and excruciating heat, beggars, thieves, highwaymen and disease. But beneficiaries, too, of that warm camaraderie of the caravanserai: massive walled buildings, cloistered, with paved central courtyards holding up to four hundred hobbled camels. Upstairs the lodging rooms; downstairs storage of merchandise and servants' quarters.

I felt a sense of belonging to that happy band. "As God wills," I heard myself murmur, thinking of the drive ahead and then the flight to Delhi and onward to Istanbul. Then popped into my head, for no other reason I suppose than it seemed appropriate, the ancient prayer of the Rom at the commencement of a journey. I turned it over in my mind and then — sheer coincidence or mental telepathy — I heard Gopi Lal utter the opening words. We recited it together, firstly in Romanes and then in English:

"*Gule Devla, da me saschipo. Swuntuna Devla, da me baccht, Aldaschis care me jav, le ferin man, Devla sila ta niappaschiata, chungale manuschendar, ke me jev ande dram ca him man traba. Ferin man Devla. Me mek man Devla, ke manga man tre Dev leskey.*"

"Sweet Goddess, give me health. Holy Goddess, give me luck and grace wherever I go, and save me Goddess, powerful and immaculate, from ugly man, that I may go on the road to the place I propose. Help me, Goddess, forsake me not, Goddess, for I pray for God's sake."

En   route   to   Udaipur

A crowd of villagers surrounding a Kanjar maiden, in a bright yellow dress doing acrobatics: dark-ringleted, tambourine in hand . . .

Wooded valleys, silver passes, deep-red, steep, rocky cliffs acting as walls in dark, doom-laden glens. Dry river beds. A brace of snake trainers nursing their charges with warm milk and honey in a pea-green field . . .

Village children gleefully pelting Jas Tilak with stones as we pass through . . .

Patsi, released from confinement, behaving like a child let off from school, full of sly merriment and husking, oddly haunting songs . . . Seelya grave and close-mouthed as womanhood suddenly comes upon her.

"*Taman Shad*," I murmured in Farsi with a wraith of regret for the parting that was to come when we reached Udaipur. "It is done."

9. Udaipur and Good-by

❋   ❋   ❋

O, LITTLE STONE BRING ME A PALACE: MAY THE MAGIC
STONE BY THE WAYSIDE COME INTO MY MOUTH AND SIT UPON
MY TONGUE AND GIVE ME THE GIFT OF GOLDEN SPEECH.

— "THE WANTON GYPSY BOY"

Throughout the journey, Gopi Lal had been making mumbled references to this forebear of his — a Banjara trader who had been murdered for his gold. I was beginning to get the idea that he had convinced himself that the murderer had fled to Istanbul with his ill-gotten gains. Frankly, I wasn't paying too much attention, being preoccupied with planning a comprehensive research and study schedule for when I arrived. I'd acquired quite a few addresses of people who could help me — Gypsiologists, sociologists, historians, linguistic experts and so forth. There were a couple of theories I wanted to check out, including the Shivite cult concept, of course. So all in all there was a lot of planning to do if I wanted to hit the ground running when I got to Istanbul.

"I am thinking, Uncle, that nothing can surpass on-the-spot, hard-mouthed research. It is you who have been proving this to me."

"Yes," I said, coming out of my reverie, "yes to the first and thank you for the second." I still didn't have the faintest idea what he was driving at. But then, I wasn't making much contact with Seelya or Patsi, either. The closer we got to Udaipur, the more buttoned-up they became. When, one day out of Udaipur, Gopi Lal joined the silent duo, all tight-lipped and prissy, Jas Tilak became a veritable quiver of emotional arrows.

Then it came to me. They'd been away a very long time and were probably aching to get back to their old stamping grounds. Nerves, that's what it was. Well, in the past couple of days I'd been thinking about the moment of parting, too. I knew I'd miss them. Of course I would. For a moment the wildly improbable idea of taking them to Istanbul had flashed across my mind. Just think about it: after seven hundred years, one representative of each of the three tribes in Constantinople. Fantastic. But it was totally out of the question. All those passports and vaccinations, the endless formalities and Indian bureaucracy delaying the journey as much as it could at every stage, just to prove who was boss. No thank you very much. There was no way I could afford the time, the energy, the emotional drain or the expense.

Udaipur

You could have cut the atmosphere with a *lathi* by the time we rolled up outside the hotel on the Lake Palace Road. It had once been a palace – albeit a small one – and was now flanked by the super-luxury Shiv Niwas Palace Hotel on one side and a string of gift and souvenir shops on the other. I planned to stay overnight before selling Jas Tilak back to the previous owner the following day and flying out to Delhi in the late afternoon.

Leaving the crew just inside the portal, I was checked in at reception by a gimlet-eyed lady who, waving my British passport aside, demanded to see my Swiss one. What Swiss one? I was rescued by Mr. Singh, the manager, whom I knew well, who bustled up radiating bonhomie and escorted me to my quarters — a big double bedroom with a small adjoining room to serve as a study. To make life complete, a waiter appeared with four large bottles of ice-cold beer. We chatted for half an hour, me about the trip up north and he about a young Swiss girl his wife — a fiery woman from Dacca — had caught him with one afternoon the month before. So that explained it, I thought. That had been his wife just now at Reception, obviously suffering from a bad dose of Helvetic hysteria.

"Ignoring me when I explained I was conducting an examination for chicken pox, she began beating my naked body with the young lady's sandal all the while calling me a worthless Hindu lust-crazed savage."

"Bad cess, Ragubir. And then?"

"With the girl's undergarments protecting my vital parts, I looked her full in the eye and told her that she was in error. I insisted upon being a *Sikh* lust-crazed savage, if I was now to meet my maker." He smiled bitterly at the recollection. "As you saw we are driving a bicycle made for two. She has placed herself behind the Reception desk and refuses admittance to any female under forty. We now have Rajasthan's finest collection of antiques taking their Last Supper every evening, in this," and he made a sweeping gesture to include all of the hotel and the grounds, "the home of the fairest flowers of Rajasthan." Probably true, I thought. Before becoming a hotel, it had belonged to a minor prince with an insatiable sexual appetite.

I suddenly remembered the crew waiting outside. With a muttered excuse to Ragubir, I hastily searched my travel bag for the envelopes I'd made up containing money to keep them going for a few months. I'd arranged with Gopi Lal that Seelya stay with him until her family turned up again, as I knew they would sooner or later.

As I came down the stairs and into the courtyard, I caught sight of them standing by Jas Tilak and thought of all the times we'd been through together, how, in a very positive sense, the impossible had happened and three streams had become a river under my very eyes. It was a damn shame the trip hadn't gone off as planned. Still, the only way to look at it was that we'd have to part sooner or later and now was probably as good a time as any.

It started to rain. Sheltering under an arch I waited for them, too, to take cover. But they didn't – they just stood there, wet and plastered down and forlorn. Inconsequentially I noticed Patsi had taken off his turban and Seelya's baseball cap was on crooked. Passing across the wide entrance to the Lake Palace Road, I could see a team of bullocks lumbering by, drawing a heavy cart, then a couple of Jaisalmer light-boned camels followed by a herd of goats. In my ears were the hoarse enticements of the souvenir and art shop *spruikers* hawking their wares. And looking up, I saw thousands upon thousands of bats winging to feast on the insects over Lake Pichola, thereafter to hang all night like ripe fruit from the tall trees. There, a few miles up and in front of me, the beautiful Matsya Hill, the dusk beginning to shroud its minor temples. I could see, feel, hear, smell, touch and be part of the blue velvet chant of India all around me, so much, so deeply that it made my head swim. And at the same time there was an unutterable feeling of despair and lonely sadness filling my head like wet cotton wool.

A glass of Ragubir's good Scotch will soon fix that, I thought. Then suddenly it dawned on me. I must have been denser than usual not to have spotted it from their behavior these past few days. They didn't want to leave me. It was as simple or as complicated as that. Hindu thinking: it was a tale unfinished and it was wrong. Why hadn't I thought of it before? Sadly, it was too late now.

Without a word, I handed them their envelopes, not trusting myself to speak and not able to either, the lump in my throat the size of a pomegranate. I put pressure on Gopi Lal's slim shoulder to half-push him away from me and toward the entrance. There were tears in his eyes, and Seelya's too, and Patsi was wiping his grubby shirt cuff across his eyes.

That did it. This was doing nobody any good. I turned away and headed back across the rain-fragrant garden. On the way, I started to get good and angry. Just who were these people to be pulling this emotional blackmail? I was free and over twenty-one and owed no one. I could go my own way, where I liked and when and with whom – or without – as I chose. There was no way in the world I could or would lumber myself with those three in Istanbul. What was I, Father Christmas? One of the thousand guises of Vishnu? Well, I wasn't and that was the end of it.

Don't worry about them, I told myself firmly. Give it a month or two and they'll be happily back in the old groove. Of course they will. No doubt about it.

I got to the Ganesh arch and the stairs leading up to my room. Fragrant smells from the little restaurant extended an invitation to dinner. And wafting from the garden, the rich, creamy scent of roses delighted the senses. Feeling safe now, I turned for one last look at them before they disappeared from my life forever. And at that precise moment, Seelya lifted her arms wide in a half-beseeching gesture and took a step forward as the tears streamed down her little Gypsy face. Stupidly, my arms came up and forward as if to embrace and negate the distance between us and then, oh Lord, no, no, no. In a right funk, I folded those errant arms across my chest, cigar-store Indian fashion, thumbs digging cruelly into my biceps, eyes soaking wet from the rain.

❋　　❋　　❋

10. Istanbul

The ancient Greeks had a legend that Zeus, the father of the Gods, caught in flagrante delicto by his consort Hera with the delectable Io, tried to make up for his infidelity by turning his paramour into a cow. Hera, the sadistic spouse, adding injury to injury, arranged for a particularly nasty horsefly to bite the lovely Io on the rump and drive her across the strait from Greece into Asia Minor.

In the language of the Ancient Greeks, *bous* is cow, and *poros* is crossing place, giving us, reasonably enough, Bosphorus, the place where the cow crossed.

As we touched down at Istanbul, in an aisle seat because of my long legs, I turned to Seelya, beside me, who nudged Gopi Lal in the window seat, and we all turned to look at Patsi sitting across the way scowling at his bottle of duty-free Red Label, which the stewardess had refused to let him open.

"Womens bad news," he said, catching our glances.

The Ottoman Turks: Potentates of the Golden Planet

For nearly five hundred years, the Ottoman Turks held more land by right of conquest than any power on earth. It was an empire that took over from that of Genghis Khan and that finally, softly, sightlessly, in the dawn of the twentieth century, imploded under its own weight to allow a cheerfully obliging Britain and France to slip desirable portions of it neatly into their kit bags.

It had become self-evident that I could never achieve an understanding of thirteenth-century Asia Minor, the all-important context in which its populations existed (including the Roum, for it was thus they were called when arriving in Constantinople), without an understanding of the Turks and their history from its earliest beginnings.

Their original home was in Central Asia in the region between the Tinshan mountains and the Aral Sea. But sometime during the sixth century A.D., possibly driven by a climatic change, they began to stream westward seeking new pastureland for their sheep.

Originally they were Animists – worshippers of earth, sky and water. However, in the course of their wanderings, they absorbed other faiths: Buddhism, Manicheanism, Nestorianism, Zoroastrianism, Judaism and Christianity. Ultimately they settled on Islam as being in greatest empathy with their own fierce hardness, their inborn desire to dominate and conquer.

Exploratory raids into Anatolia (present-day Turkey) during the eleventh century – then part of the Byzantine Empire – culminated in the crucial Battle of Manzikert in 1071 in which their warlord, Alp Arslan, shattered the eastern boundary of Byzantium. Subsequently overrunning the entire region, the Seljuk Turkish Empire stretched hugely from the Sea of Marmara in the west to Mount Ararat in the east, with Iznik (Nicaea) as its capital.

In the thirteenth century, the Seljuk Empire began to break up following ferocious Mongol raids from the east, eventually disintegrating into several independent principalities. One of these was centered on the town of Soghut, close to the Byzantine frontier, its first ruler being one Ertugay Bey. At his death in 1281, his son, Osman Bey, succeeded him and set about gobbling up more of Byzantium. In 1299 he declared unilateral independence from his titular Seljuk overlords, calling his principality "Osmanli Beygligi," which later was to resound throughout Europe and Asia under the title "Osmanli Imparatorlugu" – the Ottoman Empire.

It was the Janissary Infantry regiments – formed in 1328 from enslaved Christians – who were the foundation of those spectacular Turkish conquests in the centuries to come. "In the name of Allah, I command you to emerge victorious from all combats in which you take part," proclaimed the revered Muslim saint, Hadji Bektasch, as he blessed their standard. And hardly skipping a beat they did precisely that.

Considering the immense acquisition of Byzantine territory by the Ottomans in 1327 when the Gypsies were making their way from Tabriz along the Silk Road to Constantinople, the capital of once glorious Byzantium was increasingly resembling a lonely Christian pebble on a Moslem beach. In fact, it had little more than a century to live.

All over Christian Byzantium as the Ottoman scimitar remorselessly chopped it finer and finer, mosques were being built to replace churches. As a temporary expediency – a quick, rush job – a minaret was thrown up cheek by jowl alongside a church to transform it into a mosque and the necessary internal surgery was carried out. Priceless Christian religious statues and paintings were destroyed or thrown out. Allah allowed no icons.

Exodus in Bright Indigo

In the plane to Istanbul, I tried to conjure up how it must have been seven centuries ago when the Gypsies fled Tabriz for Constantinople.

I imagined them reaching Broussa. One hundred and fifty miles of Silk Road ahead: pacific, subdued, Ottoman; thirty days' march at the most to reach their pink, gold goal – Constantinople. Like shoalfish they glide through green valleys. The shallow mid-hour of the day, the sun high on their left dazzling their velvet eyes. Climbing, ever climbing as they ascend the side of the fertile valley that lies beyond the city. Poplars losing their top leaves; propped up like tonsured monks, aging, frail. The rising foothills, wild green and ocher against a backdrop of dense black bruised purple mountains.

Impossible to count their number. The entire broadsward of the foothills a weft of blades of dark blue and light green moving in zigzagging sideways trail. A verve, a vitality. A pelt pulsating with inexorable thrust.

The door to freedom open – but only just – and through it they pour, myriad-hued, glistening, relentless, locust-like and avid.

On the move, chippy as piping birds. Peeling off the Tabriz veneer, paring the soul back to the original Dom. Conditioning themselves again to accept punishment, pain, hunger, misery and freedom. To laugh at anguish, daring it to split asunder the bar of iron that is the heart of the Gypsy.

Olive trees in deep-dyed, intense concentric circles. Time to harvest the plump fruit. During the halts some casual tinkering, gabbling a fortune or two for a hunk of bread and goat's cheese. And all the while, a reinforcing of the hemogeneity that had been theirs a century ago before the Mongol had broken them asunder.

Objects of curiosity. The unwanted. The uncanny. The unforgiven.

The Silk Road

They had known it all the way from Kabul and it was to lead them with many a twist and turn and enameled tale of fate through to Constantinople. An on-off love affair that was to be a major influence on their existence as a race.

Going back in history, when trade first started between China and Rome, a route was opened up to cover some of the most barren, inhospitable terrain on earth. It called to only those hardiest of traders with a rock-like determination to make their fortune. The rule was: if a husband was absent for more than ten years, his spouse could claim their entire property, the presumption being that he had perished en route, felled by disease or robbers.

From China to Rome came the product of the silkworm, which so enraptured the heart of the Roman ladies that "glass" togas appeared all around the forum and the fashionable end of town, and finally had to be banned by the Senate due to their diaphanous quality, leading to "lascivious ways."

For centuries the Chinese had hugged the secret of the silk-making process to themselves. But during the reign of the Roman Emperor Justinian, nearly eight hundred years before Marco Polo's epic journey, a group of monks smuggled some silkworm eggs into Rome, hiding them in a hollow stick. The Chinese monopoly had been broken. Silk belonged to the world.

The Silk Road started from Xi'an, the ancient Imperial capital city and now the capital of Shaanxi province. It was in Xi'an, by the way, that the terracotta warriors – one of the wonders of antiquity – were excavated not long ago, dating back to the Emperor Qinshihuan Gdi who unified China in the third century B.C. It was a wondrous place in those days, with merchants and goods and music and customs from all parts of central

Asia pouring into this great city, which housed one of the most important centers of learning in the ancient world.

The very names associated with the Silk Route ring like music: the Karakoram Highway, Kashgar, Samarkand, Anxi. All along its 12,500 miles were meeting places of different cultures: Indian, Chinese, Greek, Armenian, Genoese, Arab, Venetian. Markets abounded in silversmiths, boot makers, barbers, silk spinners, carpet makers and dyers. Small garrison towns housed Chinese troops, bazaars offered the best of the region: sweet apricots, figs and bunches of "Mare's Nipple" grapes, embroidered caps, herbal medicines, sheepskins, saddlebags, felt rugs, tasseled harnesses, leather boots, brown sugar lumps, bags of wool, agricultural implements, beaten tin trunks and brightly painted babies' cradles. The Silk Road: the produce and the people, the grotesque and the lyric, dust and flies. All the way from Anxi to Duhuang, where merchants exchanged horses for camels and purchased supplies to traverse the barren sand dunes of the waterless Taklamak Desert.

Marco Polo in vivid prose gave us an idea of the hardships and superstitions that stalked this leg: "All the way through the desert you must go for a day and a night before you find water. There are some who, in crossing the desert, have seen a host of men coming towards them and, suspecting they were robbers, have taken flight. So, having left the beaten track and not knowing how to return to it, they have gone hopelessly astray. Even by daylight men hear these spirit voices, and often you fancy you are listening to the strains of many instruments, especially drums and the clash of arms."

Marco Polo, who is associated so intimately with the Silk Route, was born in A.D. 1254 and was six when his father, Nicolo, and his uncle, Maffeo, left on their first epic journey to Constantinople and thence through Persia to the mouth of the river Volga, all the way up to Cambaluc in China (now

Beijing) and the Court of Kublai Khan, the supreme ruler of Mongol China.

After their return to Venice in 1271 they decided they would return to China with two friars sent by the Pope and would take seventeen-year-old Marco with them. The journey took them three years.

Cambaluc they described as a noisy, busy, bustling city bursting with craftsmen, shopkeepers and merchants of all sorts, an international metropolis with specifically allocated areas for foreigners while the Mongols themselves lived in the city, which was really a city within a city. The great Khan kept himself protected with a personal bodyguard of 10,000 hand-picked men.

Marco was nearly twenty-nine when they arrived. Joining the Khan's service, he served in a high position for seventeen years, traveling all over an empire linked by an incredibly efficient messenger service. The messengers wore belts with tinkling bells so they could be heard at a distance.

Many novel things struck Marco Polo: bank notes, for instance – strong thick paper cut to shape and printed with a denomination (the infamous *chao* of Tabriz); coal, too, of which he wrote: "This black stone is dug out of the mountains. When it is lit it keeps the flame much better than wood. It can stay alight throughout the night and still be burning in the morning."

When Marco did eventually leave with his father and uncle, it was to escort the ravishing Princess Cocicin to her wedding to the Khan's grandnephew, the Viceroy of Persia. The Khan loaded them with gifts, including two golden tablets of authority and, charging them with messages for the Christian princes, made them promise to return at the earliest opportunity. Sailing from Zaitun in eastern China in a fleet of thirteen junks, they visited Vietnam and Sumatra, Ceylon and India.

In 1294, two years later and with only eight people surviving from their original retinue, they arrived at Hormuz in Persia, where they received the tidings that Kublai Khan had died. Released thereby from their promise to return after handing over the princess to Ghazan Khan in Tabriz, the group set off for Venice, where they arrived twenty-four years after having left it. Marco was now forty-one. It was then he dictated the famous *Book of Marco Polo*, a description of Asia for a Europe that had forgotten all about it. But the book, intended essentially as a business guide for Venetian merchants (notes on cities, the prices of goods and services, etc.) was not taken seriously by his townsmen, who dubbed him "Marco Millions" and derided him until the time of his death.

He was, and probably remains, the world's greatest adventurer. A hero, a merchant prince, public servant extraordinaire, he knew the Silk Road as few have ever done. Not many merchants, in fact, traveled its entire length; it was more usual for middlemen to take over at various stages. Usually the transfer would take place at one of the larger caravanserais built outside the walls of a town or village. They were great compounds, with thick walls lined on the inside with arcades. The open central courtyard held three to four hundred kneeling camels or tethered mules and was open to the sky. Upstairs, comfortable rooms provided lodgings and downstairs were sleeping quarters for attendants and slaves and the storage of goods. These deserted stone ruins today still exert a great fascination on the human mind.

It was the Silk Road that led Marco Polo all the way through to China, and it was the self-same route that the Gypsies followed a century before him, albeit traveling in the opposite direction. It was this journey which has clung to them and dyed them indelibly all the days of their life.

The Silk Road, the Silk Route: the most evocative name in the world to those blessed with the traveling instinct. Named by the famous German geographer Baron von Richthofen over a century ago, for well over two thousand years it has exerted a magnetic pull on mankind's imagination.

It would be inspiring to think that one day the world would be in such a state of profound peace that it would be possible to travel in safety the entire length of the Silk Road from Beijing through to Istanbul and onto the Via Egnatia and thence to Rome, by camel, horse, or mule, just as people once did when the world was young. If anyone ever organizes such a tour, I would be the first person aboard.

Constantinople –
Capital of the World

So here we all were at last (Meredith had flown in from Delhi): Constantinople, or rather Istanbul, as it was now called, the commercial heart of Turkey but not its capital. That honor had been assumed by Ankara in 1922. Originally a simple fishing village, Constantinople later became a Greek city-state before becoming vassal to Rome. In A.D. 330 the Emperor Constantine inaugurated it as "New Rome," and for 1,123 years Constantinople, also built on seven hills, ruled over the Later Roman or Byzantine Empire.

On May 29, 1453, an enfeebled Byzantine Constantinople, still vainly waiting for the forces of Christendom to come to its aid, regained its former glory in a totally unwanted sense when it became the capital of the Ottoman Empire after having been successfully assaulted by Sultan Mehmet II's all-conquering

Janissary Corps.* The city was renamed Istanbul, and Sancta Sophia, the most magnificent church in Christendom, was converted into a mosque.

We took to this city of 6 million people on sight: the bustle of its crowded thoroughfares, its thick oriental flavor mixed with western manners, the honest directness of its people and not least its rich history. It would be no penance to spend time here in this city. But which one? There were actually two: the new (relatively) one in Asia and the original city in Europe with the Bosphorus bisecting them as a diamond cutter a too opulent gem.

All around us was evidence of the gold-threaded, glittering, blood-adorned tapestry woven by the Roman and Ottoman empires; the great schism that divided the Orthodox Greek and Roman Catholic churches; the awe-inspiring nexus of trade and imperial authority that controlled all of the Middle East and North Africa, as well as half of Eastern Europe; the sophisticated melting pot in which Turkish mingled with Greek, Armenian, Russian, Arabic, Bulgarian, Romanian, Albanian, French, English, German, Spanish and Maltese. Never could there be a civilization like it again, a score or more of ethnic peoples referring to themselves by the name of a faith.

"Ah, the Paris of the East," Gopi Lal rhapsodized. "Tell me, Uncle, I am thinking you are desiring we should take the fabulously renowned Orient Express to Paris."

I demurred: "Only if you can prove to me that's the way the Gypsies got there back in the fifteenth century, Gopi Lal."

"I am very much regretting your answer is no, Uncle."

"Dead right, Gopi Lal, but I do admire a trier."

---

* This is not strictly accurate as in a very practical way, Byzantium had already shifted to Moscow, where it lived and breathed alphabet, religion and traditions until November 1917.

Through the good offices of the British Council, who during our stay were most wonderfully helpful, I rented a wing of a very large house in one of the better districts. The other two-thirds of the building housed a shifting population of various nationalities, including quite a number of English-speaking Turks and (more rarely) Turkish-speaking Anglo-Saxons and Celts.

It gave us the best possible introduction to the local scene. Our fellow residents were a mine of information on everything from the cheapest restaurants to the best shop in the bazaar to buy a sheepskin jacket.

Down to business. Gopi Lal and I had more than enough research work to occupy us in the weeks and months ahead, but the question was, what to do with Seelya and Patsi during the day? It was finally resolved by sending Patsi to the Gypsy quarter to find himself a job in one of their nightclubs. Anything that needed a flair for knife fighting and an inexhaustible thirst, as Gopi Lal put it, would be bang on target. Somehow I doubted the clubs would be falling over themselves to grab the only one-armed bouncer in Asia Minor, but happily I was proven wrong and Patsi, demonstrating yet again that Gypsy talent for adapting to any given situation, settled down to "bouncing" in the manner born. As for Seelya, we enrolled her in a day school.

Surprisingly, Seelya found the idea quite attractive. It was a chance to show off her new clothes to girls of her own age. As a secondary benefit, she thought it might be a good idea to learn to read and write. In return she would teach her new friends how to balance the body and spread the feet when handling the fourteen-pound *ganga* (hammer) and how to hold a dagger at just the right angle and with the sun in the opponent's eyes for a killer thrust against the day when another woman cast hot eyes on the man of your bosom.

I couldn't wait to see her first school report.

Next we hired a cook-cum-housekeeper, whom we christened Fatima and who'd had experience in working for foreigners before, mainly Americans. She established a close, almost maternal rapport with Seelya, who immediately took it upon herself to improve the newcomer's English.

A handsome woman in her early forties, definitely emancipated Turkish middle class, she had a rich, translucent skin, large brown eyes with faint, underlying bags and black hair worn in a bun – a figure just on the right side of comfortable. Always well-dressed in a skirt and blouse and good quality shoes that went click-clack on the tiled floor, Fatima gave out an aura of quiet control and a sense of dignified *comme il faut*. Although in the beginning she left us after clearing away the evening meal, she gradually took to staying later and later and eventually ended up sharing a double room with Seelya. Seelya told us at one time that Fatima had been married but had lost her husband early on and now lived with her mother-in-law. For some reason having to do more with glands than common sense, she went sweet on Patsi from the moment she first saw him kicking her Persian cat out of his way. Once again that couldn't-give-a-damn, Bogart-style charm had caused a sober woman's heart to flutter wildly. Just how did he do it?

Gopi Lal and I now felt free to embark on our program of interviewing historians, sociologists, linguists, and other scholars and visiting libraries and, of course, the Gypsy quarter. The questions we had to find answers for were:

- What was the political and economic situation in Constantinople when the Gypsies arrived from Tabriz circa A.D. 1328?
- How did they fare? Were they liked, persecuted or ignored?

- How long did they stay before moving into Europe proper?
- Did they bring the Tantric cult with them from Tabriz and if so why didn't they retain it when entering Europe?
- And the most important of all: why did they leave a (seemingly) safe haven to take a leap in the dark into a tumultuous and hostile Greece?

It took us two weeks to reach the conclusion that Byzantine historians of the epoch – and they included Emperor Chrysolas, Nicolas Khalcocondylis, John Ducas and Phrantzes – had referred to the Gypsies only in the most fragmentary way. Not even the erudite John Cantacazenus, who on his retirement as Emperor had retreated into a monastery to write three voluminous tomes of his life and times, gave them any space. It was almost as if they had been deliberately deleted, for by their very numbers and the essential roles they played in the artisanal and entertainment fabric of the city, they could not have failed to make some degree of impact on society and its chroniclers. It was like the history of France or England since the end of World War Two ignoring the dramatic impact of, respectively, their North African and West Indian migrant populations.

From the rare comments by historians of the time I did pick out a small number to serve as reference points, although some of the earlier, pre-fourteenth-century writings probably related to Gypsy-type nomads who went under the generic name of *Adsincani* – the origin of the Italian *Zingari*, the French *Gitan* and *Tsigane,* and the German *Zigeuner*.

One excerpt from the *Life of Saint George the Athonite*, written at the Monastery of Iberon on Mount Athos in the middle of the eleventh century, by the saint's faithful disciple George the Small, read as follows: ". . . a Sarmatian people, descendants of Simon the Magician, named Adsincani, who were renowned sorcerers and villains." The tract went on to describe how the Adsincani (officially described as a heretic group) succeeded in greatly impressing the Byzantine Emperor with their witchcraft and magical powers.

The next reference could have related to a number of Dasht i Nawar Dom who, bypassing Tabriz and fleeing fast before the Mongols, carried straight on to Constantinople. It stemmed from the pen of the Canonist Theodore Balsamon (deceased circa 1204), who wrote: ". . . and those who lead around bears are called bear keepers. They place dyed threads on the head and over the entire body of the animal. Then they would cut these threads and offer them with parts of the animal's hair as amulets and as a cure for diseases and the evil eye. Others, who are called Athinganoi, would have snakes wound around them, and they would tell one person that he was born under an evil star, and then the other under a lucky star: and they would prophesy about forthcoming good and ill fortunes."*

But there were other, more disquieting references later on, which seemed to indicate a growing attitude of contempt by the Byzantines toward the Gypsies. In one satirical poem, the wolf in contention with the bear calls him "a reservoir of filth, an amusement of foolish Gypsies." And in another segment of the poem, the hare accuses the fox of being "a liar, a thief and a Gypsy."

Overall, it seemed that early in the fourteenth century, the Roum (as the Dom were now called) had occupied a niche somewhere between the slave class and the artisanal. Doubtless their soothsaying and magical arts brought an extra mystery and exoticism to a population that after nine hundred years had just about exhausted the normal gamut of superstitious and occult

---

* G.A. Rhalles and M. Potles (Athens, 1852) in George Soulis, 1980.

practices imported from every corner of the world and that co-existed quite happily with the most fanatical Christianity.

But this fortune-telling activity was certainly not approved by all. There were deep undercurrents present and when the learned Joseph Bryennius in 1340 blamed the Gypsies for all the misfortunes that had befallen Byzantium, one could sense more than a whiff of pogrom in the air.

And then suddenly – from the m id-fourteenth century onward – there was not a word about the Gypsies, not the barest reference to the fact that they had been or were present in Constantinople, not one allusion to them – past or present. They had become "un-persons."

Stretching the imagination, it was almost as if the memory of something so foul on the soul of Byzantium had to be expunged for the sake of its future sanity and/or self regard.

Was this a deliberate cover-up? With anyone else than the brilliant Cantacazenus – who was Emperor at the time – maybe not. But a mind as supple and subtle as his would be only too capable of totally burying anything that reflected badly on Byzantium, its lack of Christian charity or humanity, for instance.

Constantinople was a city desperately in need of all the friends it could get, not just in the perilous early fourteenth century when the Gypsies arrived but well before that. Several times its Paleologue rulers had been ready if not eager to make up to Rome on Papal terms, to heal the schism, to bow the knee in return for assistance, and it was only the furious reaction of its citizenry that had prevented it.

It was a labyrinth with impenetrable thickets all around. There was no way, if Cantacazenus had a hand in it, that the mystery of the why and the how of the diaspora of the Roum would ever be solved. The one aspect of the situation that held firm though, however hard I tested it, was the theory that the majority of the Roum arrived in Constantinople from Tabriz circa A.D. 1328.

From that point onward, everything we unearthed pointed to their leaving Byzantium in very large numbers circa A.D. 1347 to enter Greece and Eastern Europe, where they were welcomed as smiths, horse handlers and entertainers of quality by the landowners and princes.

We were talking about a stay in Constantinople of a mere nineteen years. What made them move on from this seemingly broad-minded and tolerant city? And, at the same time, leave not an iota of historical record to describe what had to have been a considerable shift of population, an exodus that, without the slightest doubt, would have left a very considerable vacuum behind it?

It was not as if we were talking about a few hundred migrants drifting out of the city. Certainly, one can't put a finger on it but the number is likely to have been upwards of 50,000 to 80,000 people, maybe more. Granted, this represented only a small part of Constantinople's one million population, but still it is roughly 5 percent. Such a movement would definitely be noteworthy, especially as they would have virtually monopolized certain entertainments and crafts such as sieve making and household utensil repairs.

Back to the drawing board I went, to the concept that had guided me all along. Starting from the year of their arrival, Gopi Lal and I would assemble all the historical circumstances encompassed in those nineteen years, everything that had happened to Constantinople on a year-by-year basis. I trusted the answers would pop out of the woodwork by themselves.

Or course they didn't.

At the end of the first month, I had to admit that we hadn't progressed much at all in the effort to come to any valid conclusions. Sure, I had set down on paper the political and economic situation prevailing in Constantinople when the Gypsies arrived from Tabriz but that was all. Even though I felt sure that the answers were in there somewhere, I simply could not put a finger on them.

To take it from the beginning, most of that period was undoubtedly the last golden age for Byzantium before the darkness set in. In fact to arrive when they did was a superb piece of luck. But alas, the best of all times turned out to be the worst in the end.

Let me recapitulate. Approximately a century and a quarter before the Gypsies – the *Tchingéné*, as they are called in Turkey – arrived, the city had been sacked by the Fourth Crusaders. Two-thirds of it was reduced to ashes. On April 13, 1204, the Byzantine Empire ceased as a world power. For the first time in its history, the city had surrendered to a foreign invader, ironically, one that hitherto had been considered an ally and brother in Christ. Had not they been fighting the same Holy War? Was not their cause identical: the redemption of the holy city from the Saracen? With friends like the Crusaders, who needs enemies, the Byzantines must have thought.

The Latin Crusader occupation of Constantinople lasted fifty-seven years until 1261 when Michael Paleologus retook the city and, evicting the Catholic priests, reinstated the Orthodox Patriarchy.

The year 1328 not only witnessed the arrival of the Roum but more importantly for the city, the enthronement of Andronicus III (1328-1341) who together with his Grand Domestic, John Cantacazenus, was to devote his considerable energies to shoring up the weakened Empire. To improve his defensive position vis-à-vis the Turks, he sought a reunion of the two Christian churches under the leadership of Rome, but was turned down flat by the Pope, Benedict XII, with disastrous results for Constantinople a little over a century later, as we know.

During his reign, Andronicus III proved himself a brilliant general, master diplomat and superb administrator. He lowered taxes, abolished abuses in a system generally reckoned rotten to the core, and earned a reputation for humanity, generosity and genuine regard for his people.

While Andronicus was alive, the Roum undoubtedly enjoyed a secure existence, the artisans among them in strong demand following the retaking of the city from the Latins. Parts of it had been entirely destroyed and others left in a deplorable condition: buildings crumbling, streets with their cobblestones ripped up turning into muddy paths and so on and so forth.

As well as the extensive repair work going on in Constantinople proper, the Italian merchants in the new city of Galata across the Bosphorus in Asia were also paying artisans excellent wages, having built up immense fortunes transporting the Crusaders backward and forward over the past three hundred years. It was a complete city, entire of itself, this Genoese Galata, with its own ramparts, fortifications, churches, palace, bazaars, warehouses and entertainment venues and an Italian governor who took a high place at the Byzantine Court.

Even in its declining years, Constantinople – including Galata – was still the largest entrepot in the world, still the major contact point between east and west, with ships from every country jostling in its port and with financial resources estimated at over 3 billion pounds sterling. But it would never recover the pre-eminence it enjoyed prior to its sacking by the Fourth Crusaders. A state of shock had set in. The sharks were circling around the rim of a steadily shriveling empire, while the problems facing Andronicus III were enormous. He had to contend not only with the encroaching Turks, Serbs, Bulgars and Tartars but also with his own hired mercenary, a certain Roger de Flor who, in lieu of payment, was ravaging what was left of the Empire with a company of 8,000 Spanish Catalans.

All in all, Constantinople maintained a very fragile, highly tenuous hold on its existence and this accounted to no mean degree for the volatility – not to say neuroticism – of its people.

So what sort of city smote Roum eyes when they arrived? This fabled center of the world? I tried to put myself in their skin, see it as they did.

In the first place, I imagined their impression would have been of a vastness of scale: of a metropolis much, much larger than Tabriz. Nearly 125 miles of walls, fifty fortified gates, a line of triple defensive walls, watchtowers and a moat protected the city's landward side. Walled harbors and a chain across the Golden Horn prevented it being taken from the sea. If its enormous grain reserves and the largest water cistern in the world were also taken into account, then it was not difficult to see what had made Constantinople so impregnable up to the time of the Fourth Crusaders' Trojan Horse ploy.

The Mesé – the main thoroughfare, which ran from one end of the city to the other – was wider than they could ever have imagined, with good, solid paving stones, arcades on either side and side streets leading off into shopping precincts. The streets were actually lined with colonnades and porticos so that a pedestrian could cross the entire city under shelter to avoid rain or sun. Marble steps led up from the thoroughfare to a second story of shops and houses.

At its peak, Constantinople was quite possibly the finest and most socially conscious metropolis ever to exist. And on top of that, it was the most bizarre, monstrous, licentious, exciting, adventurous urban conglomeration in history. To an outsider, it must have seemed as if it were ruled on alternate days by the

Emperor, the will of the people, and its gangs of thugs called the Blues and Greens. Its population, argumentative and excitable, hated and feared the steadily encroaching Moslems and despised their faith. Equally, they loathed the Latins and their Roman Church. They, the chosen elite, were Greek and belonged to the only true Church. They had been masters of the world for as long as anyone cared to remember and they allowed no one to forget it, not even the Emperor – especially not the Emperor.

The Roum would have had to adapt themselves to a population that lived and breathed not only in the physical world of human desire for power and sex and the everyday framework of war, politics, peace, life and death – the tangible world that rewarded and slapped in equal measure – but also to a supernatural world ruled by Christ, King of Kings, Lord of Hosts, and the spiritual forces of Heaven and Hell, a world studded with divine miracles, guardian angels and Apostles, the thirteenth of whom was the Emperor. It was a world of icons, saints, incense, martyrs, the Kyrie eleison, confessors and confessions, the Son of Man, the Holy Ghost and True Cross. Searching for the word, it could only be described as an intensely luminous world.

And superimposed over and above these two worlds or, looked at another way, acting as a bridge between them, was a positive cross-threading of the brassiest, crudest, most pagan and deceitful superstition.

When they had understood and come to terms with all the contradictions that were Constantinople, the Roum would have blended in well. Doubtless, it would always remain a matter of amusement for them to be able to spot by the color of his clothes what a person did for a living. The ascetics wandered the streets in scarlet robes with their hair bound in a net. The virgins in the service of the Church "glowed" under their somber dark gray and black. Philosophers strolled arm in arm in delicate shades of pale gray. Rhetoricians dressed in crimson and the physician fraternity had a penchant for blue. To that colorful medley had to be added the city's whores, who dressed in every color, style and fashion under the sun, including those of the virginal order of nuns to titillate the sex buds of an ultra-blasé clientele.

Certainly, there was no lack of harlots in Constantinople. As many as 1,500 solicited in the Hippodrome, and five hundred brothels catered to the more well-to-do. Casual sex was not only a daily preoccupation but a major industry giving income to tens of thousands and was as much a part of life as eating and sleeping.

High-born ladies were preceded by a train of mincing eunuchs decked out in gorgeous liveries and golden adornments on their way to the baths of Zeuxippus, there to gossip with other society women and show off their new clothes and jewelry. City prefects in brocaded silks reclined in silver carriages, drawn by four horses abreast. Nobles sat astride white chargers, saddle cloth embroidered in gold. Any person of importance walking around the city was followed by at least one slave bearing a folding seat in case his master felt the need of a rest.

I was trying to conjure up in my mind the overall sensations the Roum must have experienced, the feast of sights, sounds and smells of fourteenth-century Constantinople.

And for amusements and distractions, there were strolling musicians and jugglers, bear and monkey trainers, the public baths, circuses, carnivals, pantomimes, musical performances and the ballet. Apart from the grand bazaar, there were two hundred other smaller ones and more than four hundred caravanserais scattered in and around Constantinople, as well as more than 25,000 shops. Byzantium itself may have been very much on the decline but there was no denying the glory and the opulence that was its capital. One would have had to have been very tired of life to be tired of Constantinople, to mis-quote Dr. Johnson.

On the other hand, it was at the same time a world where a man could never be certain when stepping out of his house in the morning whether in a few hours he would not be lying in his own blood – courtesy of the Blues and Greens. In those circumstances the Gypsy fortune tellers would have done a brisk trade.

But now we come back to the black years. In A.D. 1341 – thirteen years after the Gypsies arrived in Constantinople – Andronicus III died. His son, John V Paleologue, aged nine, and grandiloquently styled Emperor of the Orient, succeeded him under the regency of the Empress, his French-born mother, the strong-willed and fiery Anna of Savoie. It was then, disastrously for the Empire, that John Cantacazenus, the deceased Emperor's chancellor and right-hand man, became the target of a rumor campaign started by the clique surrounding Anna and eventually, when collaboration proved no longer possible, he broke away and proclaimed himself Emperor John VI.

A murderous civil war ensued, in which Cantacazenus received the backing of Serbia and Anna sought the aid of the Ottoman Turks. Five years of horror followed during which Byzantines were beaten, kidnapped, sold as slaves and murdered. No one was safe. Whole provinces were occupied by the Serbs and the Genoese who had joined the Serbo-Cantacazenus alliance to protect their interests.

Brilliant generalship won out, and in A.D. 1345 Canta-cazenus entered Constantinople and forced Anna to have him recognized as Emperor pending her son reaching maturity in ten years' time. Stability and continuity were the order of the day. The only incident that marred the first year of peace was the earthquake that struck the city, tragically destroying the western arch of the Church of the Holy Wisdom, Sancta Sophia.

I say "the only incident," but it had a catastrophic effect on the people. St. Sophia was more than the greatest church in Christendom, it was the protector of Byzantium, the Empire's guardian angel. Psychologically, the destruction to the church would have been on par with the rape of the city by the Fourth Crusaders in the previous century.

And then, as if divine vengeance had still to be satisfied, the plague struck the following year – the unholy, foul-stenched Black Death. Originating in China where it killed 12 million people, it swept across the Mongol world like an Angel of Death. On both sides of the Caspian the results were horrifying. Kwarazim, Turkestan, Syria, Armenia as well as Egypt, Persia, Anatolia and, lastly, Byzantium were utterly devastated. Up to half the population of Constantinople died horribly. Bodies were left to rot where they lay, children roamed the streets and countryside parentless. Civilization retreated abruptly to be replaced by the law of the jungle. Carried from Constantinople, the plague ravaged Europe, ultimately killing over 25 million people.

Well, well, well, I thought to myself. First a fratricidal civil war. Then the city devastated by an earthquake – Sancta Sophia, its greatest icon almost destroyed. Then the plague comes along to top it off. The population would have had a gut-full by then, the 50 percent who remained, that is.

I sensed that I was on to something. I tried to think it through logically. But wouldn't the population have soldiered on? It was an age of violence and uncertainty, after all. Okay, they might have attended religious services more regularly and prayed harder in an attempt to purify themselves in the eyes of the godhead. I suppose, when you came right down to it, they would make every attempt to re-establish good relations with a deity who had not only deserted them, but seemed intent on burying them in ordure.

But no good. I couldn't get past that point. I had the background, but I still didn't know why the Roum took that terrifying leap in the dark into Europe.

Having reached this impasse, I began to explore ways and means of unblocking the logjam. Istanbul obviously hadn't provided the answers, and what's more I didn't think it ever would. However, in conversation with an acquaintance at the British Council, he happened to mention that the Central Library in Athens had an outstanding collection of books on Byzantium, and if I chummed up with the chief librarian I might strike gold. My friend had met him in Athens a couple of times and thought he knew him well enough to write a letter of introduction for me.

He also suggested that I should check out Thessaloniki, one of the main stopping places for the Gypsies as they came into Greece – aside from Adrianople, their first stop. He had heard that a large colony of Gypsies lived there now. Was it possible that among their tribal folklore or race memories, or whatever, there was a recollection of leaving Byzantium for Greece all those centuries ago? The more I thought of my friend's wise counsel, staring at the ceiling in the spare room that I used as my study, the more I made up my mind to leave the crew for a week or two and fly to Greece to tackle the research from another perspective.

Gopi Lal came in and sat down on a camel saddle. After a minute or two of shuffling his feet and looking thoroughly uncomfortable, he suddenly blurted out, "Uncle, would it be to your liking to make me an advance on salary?"

"How much had you in mind, Gopi Lal?"

"The shopkeeper will tell me tomorrow."

"I take it this has something to do with the phone call this morning?

Gopi Lal nodded. He'd been terribly excited about it.

Someone had seen his advertisement in the English language daily seeking to buy a five-charmed necklet. Gopi Lal knew his great-grandfather wore it around his neck: one copper charm for each of his parents and paternal grandparents and the fifth one of gold for the young wife who had died in labor. If he had been murdered for his wealth, then the thief would undoubtedly have stolen the charm-necklet, too, and possibly brought it with him to Istanbul.

"Yes, Uncle. It was a young lady who telephoned, a student with an excellent command of English. It had been in her family for as long as she and her mother could remember, but they were forced to sell it last year. She gave me the name of the shop in the Grand Bazaar that had purchased it and I went there this afternoon but it is closed until tomorrow. She informed me of the price they had received for it so that I would not be cheated."

It seemed the longest of long shots to me, and all in all a bit fairy-talish and I told him so. "That's if it's still there," I said, "and if, indeed, it's the one you're after. It sounds very flukey-dukey to me, Gopi Lal. Don't be too chagrined if the whole thing turns out to be a lemon." Someone had to bring him back to earth.

"Flukey-dukey, as in miracle-prone, Uncle," Gopi Lal in that prim pitch he used to convey the sheer superiority of being a Hindu and directly favored by God (and too damned cocky for his own good into the bargain sometimes). "Flukey-dukey as in bumping into a nondescript ball-basher who confirms in the space of a few minutes a theory which has taken Uncle aeons of time and a positive mountains of good fortune and generous coincidence to assemble."

"Tell me all about it," I said slowly. "The ball-basher chap, that is. Please."

And so with a slanting gleam of triumph in his eyes and a plum-pudding pedantry of speech that together clearly demonstrated that he knew something of highest worth, Gopi Lal recounted his tale.

He'd been out with our interpreter, Roxelana, a twenty-year-old university student, interviewing Gypsies around the base of the fort at Sulukule. They'd ended up in the bar/nightclub in which Patsi worked as a bouncer, one of the few places in Istanbul where he could get free liquor in return for a minimum amount of effort and where, because of the *Tchingéné* content in their speech, he more or less understood what they told him to do.

Gopi Lal showed me the notes he had taken of the Gypsy interviewee Roxelana had found for him. Mustafa, just turned thirty, was a Second Division professional soccer player. His wife of three years, who went by the enchanting name of Birgil (Early Rose), performed in the clubs for bulging Turkish businessmen with heavyweight wallets. Or was it the other way around? But now, expecting their first child, she was going to quit her job. With their savings they were hoping to put a deposit on a two-bedroom apartment closer to the soccer stadium where he trained.

"So very middle classish, don't you think, Uncle?" Gopi Lal, who was middle class himself, detested it in others.

"During his army service some years ago now, Mustafa had come to know non-Gypsies, the *Gagni* (he pronounced it 'gatchni') for the first time. Now, of course, he played with and against them all the time. I asked him straightforwardly, Uncle, man-to-man, whether he felt more Turkish than *Tchingéné* and he replied yes, he wanted most to feel Turkish.

"And listen to this, Uncle. I am making my most greatest and most super attributable point. I asked him why. Simply that. Why did he wish to feel more Turkish than *Tchingéné*?"

"Gopi Lal, the suspense is killing me."

"Uncle, he said that the *Tchingéné* were cursed. And he did not want to be cursed any more. The story was of long ago . . . since the beginning of the world."

"What story?" I asked, beginning to roll my eyeballs at the ceiling.

"How the word *Tchingéné* came into being, of course, Uncle."

"Well, how did it?" I shouted, coming to the end of my fuse.

"That Tchin, the brother, slept with his sister Gén and brought forth a child. That is how the *Tchingéné* came into this world, and that is why they are cursed."

You could have heard a pin drop in the room.

I drew a couple of deep breaths and asked very quietly, very calmly: "I take it Roxelana was interpreting at the time?"

"Yes, Uncle. At that time, yes. Right up to the third drink when I found I could talk Turkish rather well."

"Naturally. You know what this means, Gopi Lal?"

"Yes, Uncle. But then you've always believed in it, no matter what anyone else said, haven't you?"

It was a moment like no other. The tingles up and down my spine just wouldn't stop. After more than a year of talking to Gypsies, reading about them, following their ancient trail, this was the first time I had heard any Gypsy refer to miscegenation as being the origin of the race. And a Turkish Gypsy at that, that much closer to the Dasht i Nawar source than the East or West European Rom.

There it was. A parable. Brother, sister, child as a synonym for Banjara, Lohar and Kanjar. I could have hugged Gopi Lal. I just knew it would all come together sooner or later. And, of course, he was right. It's what you believe in, how strongly, that counts.

Later that evening after another fabulous Fatima meal, sitting around the fire and saying nothing in particular, Gopi Lal perked up and said: "Let me tell you more about this evening, Uncle. It was a wonderful experience. Patsi fits into the club like a camel in the desert. Drinks like one too," he added as an afterthought. "Somebody was telling this joke there and I thought to myself I must tell Uncle this joke, he will like this joke." Was it my imagination or was Gopi Lal still a trifle smashed?

"Well, this woman hangs up a sign outside her door advertising herself as the 'Finest Whore in Istanbul.' Her next-door neighbor and rival for the affections of the local taverna owner also puts up a sign, this time saying 'Finest Whore in the Whole World.' And then the third prostitute, a *Tchingéné*, who has her establishment four doors along puts up a sign saying 'Finest Whore in This Street.' " And Gopi Lal began to laugh and laugh like a drain.

He continued in an excited mood to describe the bar, which we called "Patsi's Joint." Turkish businessmen were lending a casual ear to a trio of *Tchingéné* musicians, two girls were dancing together . . . a slow, sensuous, languid dance. Then Gopi Lal said something very poetic: "It was as if they were dancing, not to the music, Uncle, but to the very saddest of thoughts.

"And my footballer — Mustafa — I can see him now, lounging back, elbows on the bar, his hat sloping down over his forehead, a cigarette between his lips and that half-closed-eyes business the Gypsies put on. Then Early Rose coming in and making a big scene to get him home, but joining us when she found out I was buying the drinks."

"Anything else come out of this evening?" I murmured, nearly dropping off.

"One absolute pippin, Uncle, that maybe you will be able to use. One of the *Tchingéné*, a very small man, was very drunkish in one of the side booths and left the club crying. The story as far as I could put it together — you will appreciate I was flying solo at the time without Roxelana — was that this man, with a name that sounded like Bajiko or Babico or Bali Ko, had lost his wife and daughter to a rich German woman who had rented a luxury villa on the Bosphorus. She has this weakness for Gypsy women, this German woman. She sent her Turkish secretary up the hill to engage two women – real Gypsy women with fire in their bellies – and this man's wife and daughter happened to be the ones.

"He works as a porter at the docks with a saddle on his back, and one day last week he went to the villa and had the dogs set on him. His loved ones were rich now. They drove around in rich clothes in a motor car and had no time for him any more even though they knew it would only last a short time. He was very sad and every drink made him cry more. He had lost everything." Concluded Gopi Lal: "There is nothing sadder in the world than a sad Gypsy."

For some reason, this rather naive story made a great impression on me. I walked slowly to the room I had set aside as my study. It came to me for the hundreth time that I had all the elements at hand to solve the questions that had bedeviled me and every other Gypsiologist. All the pieces of the puzzle were present and correct. They simply had to be fitted together. But for all of that, it wouldn't come, however hard I tried. I left for Athens early the following day.

Athens

From the Greek world, the Rom took a large number of words including many verbal abstractions such as heaven, time, also Sunday and Friday and the numerals 7, 8 and 9. Poetry too: "*Drom te las . . . drom te makas.*" (The road that brings you takes you away.)

I was at the library at 10 A.M.: opening time. From the outside, it was a grandiose, Parthenon-style building, impressive but not a patch on the glowing polished wooden interior, which together with the fixtures and fittings gave out a superb Empire ambience accentuated by elegant nineteenth-century brass lamps and fine paintings. The Reading Room was alive with students from the adjacent university and amidst all the confusion it took me some time to locate my librarian and give him my letter of introduction.

He was an Egyptian who had settled in Athens thirty years ago, charmed by its way of life. He had a delicate ease of manner and aristocratic French, with a discreet hauteur that instantly quelled the rowdiest university student. His large brown eyes looked at you as if you were the only person in the world. He was my friend and has remained so ever since.

Over the next few weeks in an often bizarre but always delightful mixture of French and English, he introduced me to the wonders of the *Paspati Chronicles* in nineteenth-century Turkey. There they were crystallized, bearing that unmistakable Indian mold, frozen in time before they came to Europe and the Gypsy character and appearance took on different shadings to merge in with their new surroundings.

I went through the Paspati writings from A to Z, culled the expressions used by the city Roum in Istanbul as well as those of their country cousins roaming the countryside in age-old fashion. The dichotomy was striking. Ways of thinking, mores, traditions, superstitions were so divergent. One could see how the former had grown away from the original nomadic matrix. Even their language was different as the city Roum absorbed more and more foreign words into their vocabulary.

For the next few weeks I concentrated on taking notes and absorbing everything I could lay my hands on about those all-important first five decades of fourteenth-century Byzantine history. At last, my task completed, I invited my librarian friend to dine with me at my favorite restaurant high in the Plaka district and overlooking in the distance the magical beauty of the floodlit Parthenon.

In answer to his question on how my research was going, I replied that it had not only gone well but was terminated. Over. Finished. I now had a viable theory of the circumstances that had forced the Roum to leave Constantinople in such an indecent hurry, but it needed further consolidating. He asked me whether I had read George Christos Soulis's papers on the Roum — circa 1960s — and their participation in the daily life of fourteenth-century Byzantium. "No," I said, "he sounds exactly the sort of chap I'm dying to meet. Where can I find him?"

"*Il est mort en* 1966 at the tragically early age of thirty-nine. *Bien que d'ici*, born and bred, *il a fait* much of his best work in the U.S.A."

"Where can I get hold of a collection of his writings?"

He hesitated before replying that they did have a copy at the library but it had disappeared. "*Mais j'ai un ami* who might help you. He has made it his lifetime's work to study the Gypsies of Greece and I'm sure he would have a copy. Don't worry," noticing my expression, "*il parle assez bien l'anglais.*" He scribbled on his napkin. "*Tenez, son numéro de téléphone.*" He paused, took a sip of his drink, staring at the Parthenon, lit up like a log cake and seeming to float in the dark. "Do not delay," he added with emphasis. "Every day is critical. Ah," he said, clapping his hands, "*voici notre* alcoholic waiter, Bouzo. Shall we order now while he can still write?"

The next evening I returned to my hotel in the Plaka to await Miklos, the librarian's friend. In my telephone call I had said 1800 hours in the lobby. I paced up and down for an hour waiting for him. I tried phoning his apartment but no answer. Surely he wouldn't be coming now? It was becoming gloomy and quite depressing in the lobby and I decided to go round the corner and eat at one of the local tavernas. It was well past 9 P.M. when I returned and there was Miklos (it had to be him) holding a fawn-colored, rather dog-eared book and waving it tiredly backward and forward across his face in little fanning movements. He stood up at my approach, and I thought how ill he looked and made him sit down immediately.

While we sipped a cognac from the bar, Miklos told me that for the past twenty years, aside from his job with the government, he had devoted himself to the study of the Gypsy population of Greece, had lived with them, spoke their language and knew their customs intimately.

"And for all that, after those twenty years, what have I got to show for it? Where has it led me? Has it given me any sort of a future? A career? A position in life? No. No. No. A good marriage and a happy family? Again no. I was too caught up in my passion to write down my discoveries. With notes I could have done something. It is all in my head, and now it is too late. My head dies with me."

"But surely," I said "these people, the Gypsies, would have given you many moments of joy. In my own experience one lives life with them at a far greater intensity. Isn't that the crucial test? Whether you would do it again or not? The way you did it? Become, as you have, half Gypsy, what the Travellers in England call a *posh rat?*"

"No," he said, and his eyes were very big in his drawn face, the skin stretched tightly over the cheekbones. "No," he repeated, "I would not do it again. These people have a flame. Their fire has burned me. I approached too close." He stood up and I walked him to the lobby door and down the stairs to the entrance, where we shook hands. He took a few paces away, with his shoulders bent and head averted from the sleeting rain. I wanted very much to call him a taxi but he would have none of it. Turning, facing me, he said, "I was wrong. That was not right what I said. I *would* do it all again." And then he disappeared around the corner and out of my life.

My library friend had promised during my final days in Athens to check on some books buried in the inner recesses of the archives that dealt with the scores of esoteric religions that had permeated Greece from Byzantium: cults such as those of the Athinganoi, the Manicheans and the Whirling Dervishes. Some of the tomes dated back many centuries and were difficult to understand even for him. However when I called at the library on that last day, he seemed pleased with himself and said if I liked I could come back at 1:30 and we would have lunch together. "*Cela me dit quelque chose, votre culte Tantra,*" he called out to me as I left. *My* cult?

It was surprising how the most sophisticated and mature of men can become quite adolescent in the face of a new exotic religion that seems to dig down and trigger off a score of primitive fantasies. Was it a reversion to the days when mankind was young and free to wander, felt a part of the totality of water, earth and sky? I wasn't sure that it hadn't happened to me too, actually. But then my flirtation with the Tantric cult had been quite superseded by a far, far stronger drive. I thought I now had the key to the diaspora of the Roum: the circumstances of their departure. And there could be no high for me higher that that.

"*Oui,*" he began over our pre-lunch aperitif. "I agree with you. This bizarre religion: this salad of Hinduism, Buddhism and black magic would have powerfully attracted the Gypsies. *Indiscutablement, j'estime qu'il y a un* strong case to be made that they would have been exposed to it during *les années de séjour à Tabriz. Aussi, je trouve tout à fait raisonnable que les citoyens de Constantinople à l'époque* would have fallen for any mumbo jumbo the Gypsies proposed. *Après tout*, did they not make it *à la mode* to adopt any passing heresy and pop it into their Christian *pochettes?*"

He was right, of course. It had always seemed a little strange to me that the Romans, who at best paid lip service to Christianity by merely dressing up their erstwhile gods and statues with the new faith's veneer, should have been esteemed as being more true to Christ than the Byzantines who possessed a hundred times their mystical fervor for the real, distilled essence of Catholicism but could not help flavoring it with the exotic, the Eastern. All the crosscurrent inflections they put into it and had taken from the Phrygians; the Paulicians, who sacrificed rams in the fourteenth century to attain a vision of uncreated light; the Hesychats, Palamites, Balaamites, the Athinganoi, vilely despised but who alone had the sense not to worship images, the Cross and all so-called Holy Relics. Then there were the Manicheans, who refused to worship a personal redeemer; and all the Gnostics. All were part of the Holy Mother Church and all were pulling the Royal Orthodox Jelly in a hundred different ways and shapes.

While the papacy was happily murdering 1 million French Cathar Catholics to purify the dogma at the beginning of the thirteenth century, half of its eastern brethren were anxiously awaiting the arrival of the Paraclete, the Consoler, the Spirit of Truth whom Jesus promised would one day come to take His place.

"*Voilà*," the librarian added. "*Mes notes. Lisez, je vous en prie.*" And so I read his typed notes, while he fussed, Greek fashion, over ordering the meal.

The gist of what he had set down was that during the period

in question, particularly after the civil war between Cantacazenus and Anna and then most certainly when peace was
restored, a violent resistance to anything that was not con-
ventional Orthodox Church teaching took hold. Only the
purity of the faith could save Byzantium. It was that unstained
creed that had made it a power on earth since Constantine's
day. It was that rededication to its holy, unblemished origins
that would ensure its position in the thousand years to come.

Accordingly, Cantacazenus and Andronicus III before him
laid down edicts banning the practice and promulgation of all
esoteric cults under pain of death. And the rule was enforced
with a rod of iron, allowing no exceptions. Anyone contraven-
ing its strictures was branded a traitor to Byzantium by per-
mitting Satan to stain its resurgent lamb-like innocence.
Overnight anything that was not unalloyed orthodoxy became
anathema. Religious rites grew in number, and it was not
unusual for Cantacazenus himself to preside over two ritual processions a day in full regalia attesting to and re-affirming the
immortality of Byzantium. Despite his brilliance and charm of
manner, he was never a popular ruler, but this devotion to the
faith during hazardous times by the thirteenth apostle of Christ,
as he was called, did draw him closer to his people.

The Whirling Dervishes, the followers of Mani, the Athinganoi, all were proscribed, dispersed, executed, tortured or tied
in sacks and thrown into the Bosphorus. Almost overnight Byzantium became sterilized, pasteurized, deodorized, immaculate.

"So, I take it," I said, finishing the page, "that the Roum
practicing their Tantra-Mantra-Yantra would not have lasted five
minutes, let alone nineteen years."

"*Oui, c'est certain qu'au passage de ces dix-neuf ans — une généra-
tion entière* — it would have been totally eradicated from their
system. *A bas la Tantra.* Only fragments would have remained

to be incorporated into the vague shadowy Hinduism they took over with them into Europe."

So that was the answer, I thought to myself. They may have swallowed the Tantric cult in Tabriz but Constantinople forced them to regurgitate it. A pity. As cults go, it had a lot going for it.

T h e s s a l o n i k i

I visited the Kapardis family on the outskirts of the city. They operated a wholesale electrical goods business and dealt with their fellow Gypsies all over Greece. There was an incredible absence of paperwork associated with the enterprise, mostly just a telephone conversation during which deals were struck. No invoices or end of the month statements; the buyer simply turned up maybe a week, a month or a year later with cash in hand. All they needed to operate was a telephone, a stock of goods and a good memory. They had all three. The network spread over Greece wherever there were Gypsies. The family worked at it with noisy energy, but religiously stopped at noon for a long lunch break and a chance to talk together.

We sat in the office drinking ouzo and eating salted sardines with our fingers. From time to time, a customer wandered in, picked up a radio or TV set, nodded and walked out again. I suppose someone must have recorded it in his head.

The family history was jumbled, not to say confusing. The families of Maria, the wife, and her husband had come to Greece from Turkey in the swap-over in the 1920s when Atatürk and the Greek government exchanged ethnic minorities, both having been originally Greek. Kapardis's father, who was with us, could remember arriving in Thessaloniki and his father opening a small shop. Maria's family went to Bulgaria in search of greener pastures. In some preordained fashion, Kapardis met and courted Maria in Stuttgart where she was doing domestic duties back in the sixties.

Maria was all the Gypsy women you had ever met, whether Indian, Turkish, Spanish or other. In an indefinable way, it was she who adjudicated, but always those large brooding eyes seemed to seek her husband's approval.

Kapardis, a big, burly, handsome, real Romany Rai, could remember all the tales of being driven out of Istanbul in the twenties and yet the way he told them somehow implied that the story itself was of an earlier event – like dreaming a dream you had dreamt before. It took me back to Limerick, Ireland. In a comfortable pub with the fine odor of Guinness all around, I was listening to the tales of the "troubles" and realized, finally, that the man was not referring to the present day north-south situation – nor even to the infamous Black and Tan sadism in the first quarter of this century – but was going back, right back to the stories his grandfather had told him about the atrocities of Cromwell's Roundheads. And the three experiences were all mixed up in the folklore contained in his head. But the "core" story was the Cromwellian one. It is a strange thing this, that the original story can move backward or forward, the facts of it seemingly forgotten, but all the while the pain and flavor and pungency of it keep it alive in the hearts of men and make it the spinal column of all the accounts to come.

I can't explain it any better that that, but as Kapardis talked fluently in Greek and Maria translated it into German, that was precisely what was going through my head. That he was not talking specifically about the 1920 exodus but melding it with a race memory of one that had happened far earlier in time, one that had entered into their psyche, their genes, their folklore, their very being as Rom. The first one from Constantinople in the time of Cantacazenus; a century later, Mehmet's *surgun*, a complex pattern of racial dislocation, enforced as a means of breaking resistance to his authority, and which forced many of them back again. Then the swap-over in 1922 when his grandfather, Turkish for centuries, was expelled because of his Greek name.

Kapardis's two sons and two of their friends drove me back to the city and we got very merry in a vine-roofed taverna. Most of the popular singers in Greece today, and all of the good ones, are Gypsy, they said. But it is only now they dare come forward and say so. Closet Gypsies, one supposed. What else do I remember? Well, exchanging shirts. The contempt of the taverna keeper as he overcharged us and watched us leave without comment. The fact that they felt themselves entitled to a Greek citizen's rights and privileges but somehow didn't receive them. They were Rom, the children of Ham, Noah's banished son. Their nomadic brethren were Gypsies. "Business, love, music," said one of them, "what else is there?

I s t a n b u l

When I got back to Istanbul, they were all waiting for me with the evening meal prepared, and it was not long before Gopi Lal was bursting out with his story of having bought the talisman and how after wearing it around his neck for a day and night, he noticed an advertisement by the Commercial Section of the Indian Embassy for a clerk grade III, had applied for the position, been interviewed and accepted. He was now, he told me proudly, a "functionary" and I could see that ambition had been fulfilled. There was no telling where he would end up. The Civil Service and Gopi Lal were as made for each other as ham and eggs.

Of course, there was nothing I or anyone dare suggest concerning the authenticity of the talisman. Any doubt I might have had as to whether it had belonged to his great-grandfather or that it wasn't entirely instrumental in getting him his job simply had to be suppressed. You can't say anything of the sort to a man with his shirt open down to his navel.

Seelya was doing well at school and took over center stage, telling stories about her teachers and girlfriends, completely at home in Turkish or English and switching from one to the other at will between talking to me and Fatima.

Patsi was absent, as he started work at the nightclub at 6 P.M. and worked until dawn. Gopi Lal had seen him a few evenings ago when he popped into the nightclub.

Later I went into the kitchen to fix myself a hot toddy. Fatima was washing up, and I took the opportunity to have words with her about the future. I explained to her that I was expecting a telephone call from London at any time. My mother was in hospital with cancer of the throat. Obviously, Gopi Lal was going to stay on, and most likely Seelya and Patsi would prefer to stay in the house with her for the next six weeks until the rental period expired, I said. I would pay her wages up to that time.

She nodded in agreement. I had full confidence in her. She was one of the most trustworthy people I'd ever met. And so I said, "If I give you the money for Seelya's and Patsi's return tickets to Udaipur, plus an amount to carry them through the first few months, will you make sure they get it when they leave and buy their tickets?" I repeated it just to make sure and left it at that as soundlessly she started to cry like a wine skin gently seeping.

Later that evening Gopi Lal said he'd seen the porter Bajiko, again at Patsi's joint when he'd popped in. He was still wifeless and daughterless and terribly sad and now he had great boils on his face. For a moment I could visualize the little man quite vividly.

I stood up, under what compulsion I don't know, and as I walked toward my study, the idea hit home. Bang! The pestilence – the Divine Punishment. That was it. Quickly I looked up the Black Death in my dictionary.

"Da, da, da, da . . . principally of a bubonic nature . . . incubation period between three to seven days bringing on nausea, loss of appetite, tremors followed by dilated pupils, congested eyes and terrifying hallucinations. Sickness, diarrhoea, the coughing up of much blood. In the final, fatal phases gangrenous tumours appear followed by suppurating bubons. Nasal and pulmonary haemorrhages foreshadow death between the third and fifth day."

Lord, I thought, there could hardly have been a worse way to die. Just imagine mothers having to watch their infants spit up bloody saliva, parched by the burning heat, jaws inflamed and black sores all over their body. They would have gone mad, ready to strike at anyone or anything.

"Idiot," I shouted at the wall mirror. Wasn't it just as patently self-evident as the nose I was looking at? It was that hell-sent, obscene plague following hard on the heels of the traumas of the civil war and the partial destruction of Sancta Sophia that finally compelled the neurotically superstitious citizens of Constantinople to lance the tumor in their midst. It was a malignant offense in the eyes of God, to be cauterized without delay. The culprits couldn't have been more obvious: those fortune-telling, Satan-inspired, sin-possessed Roum.

Now I was sure I had the answer to why the Roum had left. They had been rounded up and booted out. Next stop Greece. It was the only possible explanation. It just made perfect sense. *They* hadn't taken the decision to leave, once again it had been forced on them.

But if that were the case, why the cover-up? Not a word had been written to describe their leaving. It was eerie. And precious little before that, and what there was was defamatory at best. It was more of an orchestrated anti-Roum campaign and put one in mind of the anti-Jewish propaganda put out by Dr. Goebbels that, in turn, led with absolute inevitability to the extermination camps of the Third Reich.

What reason could Cantacazenus have for figuratively sweeping the Roum under the carpet – their presence in Constantinople as well as the manner of their departure? Surely, on the face of it, it was a straightforward enough affair: "We don't want them, you have them." So why bury the incident so deep that not a soupçon of it had come to light in nearly seven centuries?

I thought and thought and the answer just wouldn't come. Yet there had to be one buried in that mass of information I had amassed. I Just knew it. What to do? I had precious little time left in Istanbul and after that, back in London, circumstances being what they were, I would almost certainly lose the slender thread I was presently hanging on to.

The answer was obvious, even if I had to sacrifice my last night with the crew. I had pressure-cooked my imagination to tell a tale about the Gypsies in Tabriz, and I believed in retrospect that it had brought me much closer to the events of the period, how it felt and smelt – maybe, who knows, how it was.

I would do the same now, bull-terrier fashion, with the specific intention of going after the one element that still eluded me. I would sit down and knock out a story set at the time of the Gypsy exodus from Constantinople.

The idea took hold. Where to make a start, though? For a number of reasons, I thought it would have to start with someone high up at the Palace. That was where all the decisions were taken. But who?

Then it came to me. Quite recently, I had come across a tract describing the Emperor's personal body corps – the Varangian Guard composed of Normans, Germans and in earlier days, Vikings. It was the Byzantine equivalent of the Roman Emperor's

Germanic Guard: incorruptible, steadfast, unmatched – barbarians, devoted heart, mind and body to their Emperor.

Maybe it was the mental image of those fair-haired, blue-eyed giants standing out like totem poles amidst the short, swarthy Greek court that caught my imagination, but I remember mentally filing them away for future reference. Well, why not now? Will the Commander of the Varangian Guard please step forward? Here's your big chance to make a mark on history.

I would toss him in with a few other elements that had stimulated my imagination these past months; like eggs into the mixing bowl they would go and, I hoped, out would come a Yorkshire pudding or an omelette. Well, it sounded great in theory.

I could hear Seelya's excited voice offering to teach Gopi Lal a dance step she'd picked up at school. The music came on. Hesitating to launch myself "cold" into this story, I thought about the tale I'd read about the novelist Pierre Loti (1850-1923), one of the most beautiful and romantic stories ever told. In Istanbul he had fallen under the spell of the Ottomon way of life and had conducted a desperate love affair with a married Turkish woman he called Aziyadé. Summarily transferred back to Paris by the Department of the Navy, he begged her to come with him. She couldn't. Instead the liaison was discovered and she was never heard of again. All his love for her and his nostalgia for the city of his dreams he poured into the most heartrending and popular novel of the day, *Aziyadé*.

From the next room the music started up again. For a moment I hesitated. Then, pulling the typewriter toward me, I started to type. After the first paragraph or two, the story started to write itself. It was more like taking dictation, really. I was just the instrument. I eased back and let the words flow. I was going to enjoy this.

11. Disoibe – Day Dawns

IRON TEARS HAVE SCOURED THE EYES OF THE ROUM.

HIS BONES EATEN BLOWS OF IRON.

THE RIVER IS BROAD WITH HIS BLACK BLOOD.

IN ALL THE WORLD NO HEART'S LOVE,

TO WARM HIS HEART OF STONE.

BLACK GEESE IN THE BLACK NIGHT MAKE THEIR LOST CRY,

CALLING THE MAN OF STEPPES AND STREAMS,

AS BLACK BLIND IN THE EYES OF HIM,

THE GYPSY FEELS FOR HIS HEARTBEAT.

SHONUTO – THE NEW MOON – HAS MADE WHIPS

AND KNIVES FOR THE ROUM.

ONLY THE PAIN IS TO HIM.

HE PRESSES IT TO HIS HEART LIKE A LOVER.

DISOIBE! ANOTHER DAY DAWNS.

For over a century now, the Byzantine Court had been located
in the palace of Constantine Porphyrogenitus. The Imperial
Palace complex was a great sprawling affair housing seven royal
residences and an endless variety of private mansions. It was an
artist's feast of blue and green marbles of Marmara and the
pink of Cyzique – gardens with shaded walks, peacocks, ibis
and pheasants; mosaics that leapt at the onlooker with blazing
color: its pavilions, fountains and fish lakes lending it an air of
Olympus-like tranquility.

It was an important center of business activity too. Twenty
thousand people earned a living within its walls as artisans in

its workshops making fine weapons, dyes and silks or as civil servants, entertainers, court attendants, courtesans, priests and entertainers.

In past centuries it was the most beautiful and supreme example of mankind's search for perfection in architectural form and decoration. And the more the Empire sank into decline, the more magnificent and extravagant grew the richness of rites and ceremonies designed to underscore the Emperor's divinity in these most exquisite of surroundings.

The Palace was also a place of carnivals, theatrical performances, ballet, musical revues and above all of courtly intrigue by powerful cliques of priests and eunuchs: poisonings, fratricide and treachery were commonplace. An evil, decadent beauty walked hand in hand with an Empire that had endured close to a thousand years and was convinced of its special relationship with God. It was an up-and-down, exciting, and highly precarious life being at the top of the mount: a third of all the Emperors had been assassinated, poisoned or tortured to death.

The captain of the Varangian Guard — an elite core of Normans (many from Duke Roger's territories of the Two Sicilies) together with Germans and Norsemen who guarded the sacred person of the Emperor — was by no means a tall man. But what he lacked in height he made up in the startling breadth of upper body. In full armor, he resembled an iron-studded door crossing the courtyard. His massive chest and shoulders ended in exceptionally long and powerful arms that could hurl a war ax with devastating accuracy or snap a man's spine like a dry twig. There was hardly a bone in his face that had not been broken at one time or another. Even his head, it was said, had adapted early in life to the shape of the high-coned Frankish helmet. He was unmistakably Norman: bright

blue eyes; a breezy, direct manner; uncomplicated in thought
and expression; thick fair hair falling nearly to his waist; a
golden-red, beginning-to-gray, square-cut beard; surprisingly
neat, even white teeth. He called himself Harsa, but few
people knew it and those who did were wary of using it and
the familiarity it implied.

The captain had been surprised that afternoon when the
slaver brought along two Athinganoi* wenches and all the
excuses in the world: "Should have gone on Friday like I
usually do . . . best of a bad bunch . . . you should have seen
the others . . . walking disasters. . . . Still, the younger one's a
virgin, I'd swear to it, so I'll have to ask the going rate, you
understand, Excellency, or else sell her up at the Palace. After
all, it's common knowledge that the menstrual blood of a
virgin witch mixed with the pestled gonads of a male bat,
sprayed with the spittle of a hunchback and then sprinkled
with Holy Water at the high altar of the Church of Divine
Wisdom, is a sure cure for any malady afflicting a devout
Christian, and . . ."

The captain had shut him up with a frown and told him
to have the "Companions of the Immortals" – as they termed
the Guards' concubines – locked up in the Records Chamber
until he had time to see if they were worth the price the slaver
was asking.

He had better get down to it soon, he thought: the men
would be coming back shortly from exercises. But before he
could do anything about it, Rollo, a fellow Norman in the
secretarial service of the Emperor, called by.

---

* Athinganoi or Adsincanoi: A heretic Byzantine sect with which the Gypsies
were often confused, hence the various derivative names Zigeuner, Cigan,
Zingarro etc.

"Did you know the Emperor plans to have all the Athinganoi rounded up and held in the Hippodrome awaiting his pleasure?"

"What's he going to do with them?" asked Harsa, puzzled. "And, more important, what's going to happen to the races on Saturday? I don't want to have to deal with a riot."

"They'll have gone before that, I understand. They're being driven out. Permanently. It's a huge exercise the Emperor's planning. Byzantine organization at its best. Pity we're not as efficient fighting the Ottoman."

"But why? asked Harsa, even more confused. "What have the Egyptians done?"

"They're a curse . . . a pestilence on the Empire. It's got to be cauterized and shown to be so in the eyes of God. Or so they do say."

"You mean the people are blaming everything on those poor devils: the Civil War, Sancta Sophia and the Black Death? Ridiculous. Why not accuse God Himself?"

Rollo shrugged. "They don't think with their heads, only with their livers or genitalia. But don't take it to heart. Who concerns himself with the Athinganoi, anyway? We'll both sit down to a good dinner tonight, eh?" And with that he took his leave.

Harsa bade him a hearty adieu but at the back of his mind he was wondering why the Guard hadn't been informed of this turn of events. The fate of the Athinganoi did not bother him — like most Byzantines he considered them an unholy nuisance, what with their begging and petty thievery and preying on gullible people. Still, nuisance or not, driving them out with winter about to set in. . . .

How many of them were there, he wondered? Who knew? They lived like rats and like rats they bred and hid in every nook and cranny. Fifty thousand, 100,000? Any figure was possible.

On the morning of the following day, it was bruited that the Emperor was planning a major religious ceremony for that afternoon. "Not another one," the courtiers groaned. Often more than thirty such ceremonies were held in a month — mostly to reinforce the concept of the Emperor's semi-divinity . . . his equal footing with the Apostles. Gorgeously dressed processions of prelates and courtiers moved slowly in clouds of incense to sit down to a banquet imitating the Last Supper. And woe betide a servitor who dropped a plate. His head left his shoulders a fraction after the last course was served.

Harsa, as ever on such occasions, seeking to go to ground, had been taking the sun all afternoon down by the marble stairway leading from the Palace to the Emperor's Harbor — from where the royal barges set off — when a messenger from the Emperor caught up with him.

"His Imperial Highness wishes to see me?" he asked, surprised. This was most unusual: his orders usually came from the chamberlain or one of the high officials. There was a chain of command at the Imperial Court that generally speaking was quite rigidly enforced.

"Yes, Excellency. I am commanded to conduct your noble self to the radiance of his Imperial Highness's presence."

The captain nodded. It had to be about this affair of the Athinganoi, but still his heart beat loudly. These days nothing was certain. What if a jealous courtier had denounced him for treason? Nervously, he fingered the talisman around his neck, feeling the Chinese characters picked out in emeralds on a gold and jade background. He had taken it from a dying potentate in Samarkand. Superstitiously, he was convinced the talisman had saved his life many times over in battle. Although, in his honest moments, he had to admit it hadn't done the previous owner much good.

Harsa rarely attended Court. This one would be identical to its predecessors. They would still follow all the rites, traditions and procedures laid down by Constantine the Great over eight hundred years ago. Neither would the vice, the corruption, the treachery, the neopotism, alter or deviate one iota either. Fathers — even emperors — still had their sons castrated to fit them for high office.

He followed the messenger across the courtyard past the ex-Empress Anna's apartments. She was degenerating fast. Rollo had told him the gossip was she drank a goblet of wine every time she lay with a man. "No human liver could support that amount of abuse, my friend."

Although outwardly calm and composed, inside he was a worried man. What if he had unwittingly offended Cantacazenus? The Imperial lust for revenge knew no bounds. Who could ever forget the inhumane treatment handed out to the old Emperor Andronicus I by his own family? They'd had him incarcerated in their private dungeon connected to the Imperial bedchamber. There, over a period of time, they'd beaten him black and blue, broken his teeth with hammers, poured boiling water over him, plucked out an eye, then cut off one of his hands. Finally, they'd paraded him through the streets on a sick camel to have additional torture inflicted on him at the Hippodrome in full view of the populace. Ultimately, they'd taken pity on his whimpering body and stuck a blunt sword through his kidneys.

The captain swallowed painfully. Please Bes it never happened to him. Damn it all, what had he to be afraid of? As a Norman knight and a descendant of old Tancred d'Hauteville, the only thing he had to be afraid of was losing his honor.

He had been waiting an hour in an ante room of the Emperor's private apartments before a sapling of a boy, beardless, tall, slim, olive-skinned, with a peerless, perfectly heart-shaped face, presented himself in the antechamber. His appearance simply stunned the gaze. He wore a knee-length, raw silk, wine-colored, tight-fitting coat of a style Harsa had never encountered before. In his right ear a large emerald, clasped in gold, hung down to his shoulder. Gold chains interspersed with ropes of pearls trailed around his neck. A silk-trimmed, stiff cotton round hat such as worn by the Venetians and holding a blood red ruby completed this magnificent youth's attire. Harsa, following him along the corridor to the Emperor's private quarters, marveled greatly at this elegant apparition. Even the youth's soft slippers were adorned with silver and pearls.

At the door to the audience chamber stood two massively built, half-naked Nubians with great scimitars held across their chest. No lightweight himself, Harsa felt positively dainty compared to those two mastodons. All this to guard a man with whom he had shared the rudest of lives, often not sure of a meal, for a whole five years. Life was full of small ironies.

The painted door opened slowly, with enormous dignity. The ceiling caught the eye instantly. It was lofty, with beautiful arches, painted in gorgeous blues and greens and filigreed with gold and pink-white marble representations of swans and long-necked herons.

In the center stood a magnificent table made up of a multitude of rare soft-planed, multi-hued woods that glistened like warm silk in the sun's rays as they entered the chamber through the translucent stained windows. The walls, tiled with exquisitely painted mosaics, depicted peacocks and leopards, palm trees and mountains. Friezes and cornices bore gold-worked flower arrangements. It was a cool, aloof, imperial room, with a cachet of that supreme style and luxury that

could not be matched anywhere in the world, a room that
implied — not too discreetly — that within its precincts the fate
and shape of the world had been decided many times in
between sips of scented wine.

John VI Cantacazenus reclined on a pile of silk cushions.
The floor around him was richly carpeted with the finest
Persian silk rugs. Fragrant wisps of smoke emerged from
pierced brass burners in each corner of the room. He wore a
long silken robe of the same russet wine color as his groom;
his only decoration was a necklet of blazing emeralds. Beside
him, paws outstretched, a gleaming black panther lay, a similar
emerald choke-collar around its throat.

It was glittering, barbaric, richly sumptuous to a point
approaching the unbelievable. It was the essence, the very core
of the world's concept of that mystic, ornate eastern fable represented by the word "Byzantium."

Harsa made a stiff, awkward obeisance but no more. His
initial deference to the sumptuous gold had paled. No longer
impressed by the panoply of gorgeous pomp, his braw nature
saw only the popinjay.

It was a scene such as a painter dreams of. The tall, slim,
charismatic Emperor, all of sixty years, still had a handsome,
unlined face, jet black silky hair and beard. Beside him,
a black silk-pelted feline stretched itself sensuously in a
symphony of rippling muscles. An elegant blade of a courtier
stood within easy reach to refill his master's goblet or catch
his softest words.

And Harsa standing there, massive framed, became
knobbly and bulky as a bull in such delicately refined surroundings. He was deeply tanned by wind and sun in sharp
contrast to the other's pale olive complexion, his blue eyes
were now fading a little, losing their acuity. His long fair

hair was especially combed for the occasion, but he still had
had a broken nose, a chewed-up ear. He was a badly scarred,
half-blind old boar confronting an insinuating, slithery, beautifully marked but quite deadly serpent.

Cantacazenus wasted no time on preliminaries. "Captain,
during the night, the day after tomorrow, that is to say, the
Feast of St. Andronicus, the Varangian Guard will escort the
Egyptians from the Hippodrome out of our city to within sight
of Adrianople. You are to say nothing of this now or in the
future to anyone under pain of our Imperial displeasure."
Harsa knew exactly what that meant.

"You have my life on it, Highness." A long moment of
silence. "Will that be all, Highness?" He couldn't believe that the
Emperor had summoned him just to tell him that. After all, it
could have been relayed to him through any one of a dozen
flunkeys. There must be something else, he thought to himself,
knowing a little of the other's mind. During the Civil War, fighting side by side, they had been close. Each had saved the other's
life more than once but in the five months since his accession to
the throne, Harsa had seen the Emperor only from afar.

He waited uncertainly in the ensuing silence, now beginning to anticipate dismissal but the sign did not come. Instead,
Cantacazenus spoke almost to himself. "They give me no
choice. Even an Emperor must occasionally bow to the will
of his people."

Harsa followed his train of thought easily enough. From
what he had heard during the day, there had been increasing
pressure on Cantacazenus to take action against the
Athinganoi. The people had been demonstrating in the
streets howling for blood while the all-powerful Blues and
Greens had gone on the rampage, breaking into shops, pillag-
ing and setting fire to houses. No maiden above puberty was

safe in the streets. Trade in the bazaars stopped. Food was in short supply. Worse, the 1,500 prostitutes evicted from the Hippodrome to make way for the Athinganoi had gone on strike. The Empire faced chaos.

One thing was unclear in Harsa's mind. "Highness, I understand that within a few hours the last of the Athinganoi will have been rounded up. With your grace, could not they all be bundled out tomorrow morning, thereby clearing the Hippodrome for the races?"

The Emperor's eyes went cold. "Captain, not tomorrow but the day after. Not early morning, but dead of night." He spoke in a soft, almost purring voice, a prelude Harsa recognized to an explosion of sudden, tigerish rage.

Harsa, shaken, recognized he had never been closer to death in his life. His desire to offer commonsensical advice, it seemed, had bordered dangerously on lèse majesty. And that was not a clever thing to do with an Emperor who had been on the throne for only five months and was still reacting very sensitively to his new, semi-divine status.

Cantacazenus relented. "It is our desire that they rest before their journey. Also for their own safety it is not wise that they leave during daylight hours."

"Of course, Highness. I had not thought of that."

"But an Emperor has to think of these matters. We have no wish to go down in history as the butcher of the Egyptians, whatever their crimes. We must hope they will be happier with the Latins."

Harsa was now totally swayed to this view. "It shall be as you order, Highness." Taking a chance now that he'd had the extra minute to think things through, he added, "One point, Highness. The moment we let this riffraff loose into the Latin countries, will not the Pope and the whole of Christendom accuse Byzantium of unloading a horde of hungry locusts upon them, full of satanic arts and black magic . . . anti-Christs?"

Strangely, Cantacazenus seemed only too agreeable to offer an explanation. With a charming smile, he said, "Captain, no one will ever know where they came from. We can always say that these Egyptians were simply passing through our lands on their way west as many have done in the past. We suggest you advise their leaders they'll receive better treatment if they say they come from the Land of Egypt."

"I understand, Highness, like the fabled Treasure of Attila, buried with him and hidden for all eternity."

"Yes, most apt, Captain." Cantacazenus hadn't the faintest idea what Harsa was talking about. "Now, not a ripple all the way to Adrianople, you understand. March at night at every opportunity. Keep them under cover as long as possible. We wish it to appear to the Latins as if they dropped in their midst like raindrops from the sky. We do not, under any circumstances, wish it known they originated from here or that Byzantium had driven them out. I repeat, under no circumstances."

"Certainly, Highness. You may rest assured, the honor of Byzantium is in safe hands."

"Then they too shall be forfeit should you fail." Cantacazenus spoke sharply.

He stretched out a be-ringed foot to be kissed. Dismissal. Harsa ignored it, contenting himself with a deep bow. He could see displeasure written all over John's face. In that he was correct. The Emperor was thinking he should have this insolent dog whipped and thrown in the Bosphorus. On the credit side, he knew that Harsa had the interests of Byzantium at heart and his personal loyalty was unquestioned. How many could he put into that category? But he was thorny to deal with like all the others of his race. He well remembered the story of that other stiff-necked Norman — more than likely an ancestor of this one — Rollo, the first Viking Duke of Normandy who, refusing to bow low to kiss the French king's foot, took hold of it and lifted it to his mouth.

The Emperor stayed without speaking for a long moment as Harsa straightened up and then, with a negligent flick of the wrist, gave him permission to withdraw.

When Harsa had left, bowing low all the way to the door so as not to show his back, the Emperor accepted a goblet of wine from his groom with a tight smile on his lips.

"Balthazar," he spoke softly. "There is to be no record of our audience with the captain. And, we are much afraid, no witnesses either. A great pity. So young and we knew your brave father as a friend for many years. . . ." His voice trailed off.

But then, as Balthazar had always known, a eunuch had to aim high, and to be in the personal service of the Emperor was the very highest of all. Unfortunately, the position never seemed to last very long.

I was reasonably pleased with the fragment of speculative history I'd written so far. It was definitely pointing me in the right direction and I only had to follow it along. But one thing kept nagging at me and that was this business of the exodus taking place at dead of night, as it most likely happened so as not to have been witnessed or indeed, recorded by the population at large. Prima facie, one could understand a civilized, humane ruler not wanting the Gypsies stoned, molested, jeered at and generally harassed as they trudged up the Mesé to the main gate. But, frankly, I had to doubt whether Cantacazenus would have been that concerned about a people he must have thoroughly despised. I had just put it in as a reason he could give to Harsa, without think-ing too deeply about it. Okay, couldn't there have been another reason for the moonlit flight? Well, yes, in the sense that he would not necessarily have wanted the Latin world to know he was dumping a horde of locusts on their doorstep. But then, as he had himself conveyed to Harsa, so what? Vagrants of unspec-ified origin had been turning up at Constantinople on their way to Europe for centuries. All in all, there was nothing of sub-stance in either point to justify the magnitude of the cover-up I was postulating had taken place.

Looked at the other way, just think of the kudos, the popular acclaim an unloved Emperor would have received if he had turned the event into the Byzantine equivalent of a Roman Holiday. Surely that would have negated the modicum of bad public relations potentially emanating from the Latin Quarter?

All right, so there had to be another reason for not making a public spectacle of it – in fact, making a deliberate and most capable and efficient attempt to expunge it from the record books entirely. What was it?

It was early in the morning. The house was quiet. I got up and went into the kitchen and made myself a cup of coffee and sat in the courtyard smoking a cigarette.

I knew I was as close as dammit to finding the answer, mere inches away. My mind returned to the nighttime exodus. That was the key. I repeated it slowly. "Nighttime means that it was virtually unseen . . . un-noticed . . . unrecorded."

Why, why, why?

Maybe if I saw the action unfolding from another point of view? Maybe that would do it. Like an overview of the Exodus. I hastened back to the typewriter.

October 9, 1347 (the eve of the Feast of St. Andronicus, the
Patron Saint of Silversmiths and ironically, a particular favorite
of the Gypsies).

The court painter had been unable to sleep, wondering
how he could put the talent he never used (and knew he had)
to better use than portraying emperors and empresses with
blank oval eyes and oval faces that tradition demanded. He
yearned for something more fulfilling . . . life, real and vivid.
A scene that embodied action, energy, vitality. He had been
putting the finishing touches to yet another portrait of the
Emperor in the anteroom next door when he heard Harsa
enter the audience chamber. He could not resist going to
the door to eavesdrop. So there were to be no records of the
expulsion, eh? No writings? Nothing to record the event?
Well, he'd see about that. His time had come. It might well
be his last if he was discovered but he intended enjoying every
rare moment of it.

And so here he was, perched on a primitive platform
on top of the Obelisk of Theodosius, overlooking the
Hippodrome, his painting materials spread out before him.
The obelisk brought in from Egypt during the reign of the
Emperor Theodosius in A.D. 390 had had its bronze plates
ripped off by those short-sighted fellows of the Fourth
Crusade under the impression they were gold. He was looking
down on the place that had been the center of Byzantine life,
the nexus of the empire for over a thousand years, crammed
full to bursting point with a dark, throbbing, rank-smelling
humanity.

Across the way, Sancta Sophia, the Church of Divine
Wisdom, from earth soaring upwards to the blue, reached
even to the choir of stars. What did they say? If Sancta Sophia
belonged to God and the palace to the Emperor, then the

Hippodrome belonged to the people. How true this night.
There had never been so many here.

Normally, priceless statues from antiquity adorned the
Hippodrome. When building his city – which went up at the
fastest rate of any metropolis in history – Constantine had pillaged the Empire for works of art, preferably statues of pagan
Gods that could then be "Christianized." But that night the
statues had been removed – the magicians, jugglers and fortune
tellers, prostitutes too. No clients were strolling up and down
in couples, jugs of wine in hand, passing knowledgeable comments on the merchandise on display; no Blues and Greens
screaming *"Nika! Nika!* Win! Win!" at their favorite charioteer;
no Emperor entering his box, raising his mantle and making the
sign of the cross; no choirs singing praises to Christ and the
Virgin with passionate supplications for the victory of their
chosen hero. Not a blade of the grass lawn of the arena could be
seen, only in the blue-black darkness twenty, fifty thousand
(who knows?) pairs of gleaming eyes, packed close like stars,
and the pale crescent moon flickering on the dull-gleaming
spears of the men of the Ring of Steel. It was a scene out of
Hades. And he was privileged to be its Recording Angel.

The painter had the concept clear in his head. He was
ready to paint now and threw himself into his work like a man
possessed. In the wildest burst of creativity to ever come over
him, he set down everything: the dark, brooding, self-indulgent face of the ex-Empress Anna in the far left-hand corner;
the Emperor's vital, energetic presence in the middle; his
queen Irene's podgy features, creased neck and appraising,
tawny eyes at the right-hand top. Then, with the Church of
Divine Wisdom faintly in the background, the main body of
the mounted Varangian Guard streaming up the Mesé, flags
and pennants alive in the flare of the torches. And in the

foreground, the Ring of Steel opening up like a steel flower.
The first Athinganoi moving forward uncertainly.

And over and above everything, permeating the tone and
texture of the paint, infusing his artist's work, the voice of
God made flesh as an accusing finger, stretched taut, pointed
down from the sky at the Athinganoi poised between
Purgatory and Hell.

Harsa felt a sense of relief at having got the column under way.
Although he could hardly say he liked them, he could not help
feeling sorry for the Athinganoi in their present state. For
days, without anything to eat or drink, they been crammed
into the Hippodrome with scarcely room to breathe. Why in
the sacred name of Jesus hadn't he been allowed to lead them
out before? In their present condition, they would hardly be
capable of ten to fifteen miles a day. At that rate it would take
an eternity to reach Adrianople.

He couldn't help noticing that many of them were
showing signs of the plague – the traditional boils and so on.
Up to now it had seemed to everybody that the Athinganoi had
resisted it remarkably well. Harsa, himself, being a commonsensical man, had put it down to their inbred hardiness, but he
was aware that most of the population took it as confirmation
of their pact with the devil to introduce it into the city.

He'd be lucky to arrive in Adrianople with half of them
still alive. No wonder after what they'd gone through, all
penned together like that. . . .

"Stop the train!" I shouted in the silence of my little room.
"Hold it right there!" Standing up, I barked my shin on the desk.

There it was, before my very eyes, the first instance of germ warfare ever recorded (or rather *not* recorded) if I had got it right. Never mind the soft soap about resting them before their long trek. Cantacazenus was just making sure they would be as thoroughly infected by the plague as it was possible to be. The man had sent a time bomb into Europe as revenge for the sacking of Constantinople by the Fourth Crusaders and the repeated failure of the Christian princes to come to Byzantium's aid.

If my hypothesis was right, he had perpetrated one of the most diabolical crimes in history, one that was to halve the population of Europe, killing upwards of 25 million people, simultaneously imbedding the Gypsies in the European psyche as harbingers of death and destruction, carriers of dire misfortune wherever they went, so that Europe could with an easy conscience embark on six hundred years of slavery and systematic persecution leading to their near extinction in the gas chambers of the Third Reich.

To be fair, sending plague-infected Gypsies into Europe would not have been the only means by which the Black Death reached it. The ships of the Venetians and the Genoese regularly plied between Constantinople and the Mediterranean. But by sending them in the way he did (and without a ripple ruffling the surface), that brilliant forerunner of Machiavellian cunning, Cantacazenus, was making absolutely sure and certain that Europe would undergo the same horror as Byzantium, thereby satisfying his lust for revenge and, as a bonus, ridding what his clergy and people termed vermin and an abomination in the eyes of the Lord.

Not a bad day's work, he must have thought. All I have to do is to bury the evidence. Erase any records that they'd ever been in Constantinople – but not all, that would have been suspicious — then conceal their eviction so well that no one would ever think to look for it in the first place.

Well, I thought, he didn't do too badly at that. One of the most vile acts of retribution ever perpetrated had lain dormant and undiscovered for nearly seven hundred years. That takes talent and organization. But then all good things have to come to an end sooner or later.

I was just glad that I happened to be the one to have stumbled across it, in the sense that it gave a positive and very final ending to my quest. It's true, the Harsa segment was pure fairy floss but it had served its purpose by answering — to my satisfaction — the one question that had never been asked in the first place. Not when they went. Or how they went. But *why* they went.

I started to massage my neck. It was 6 A.M. It had been a long night. I could smell the aroma of coffee. Fatima was up early this morning. Still rubbing my neck, I wandered out, seeking a refreshing cup. The telephone rang. Gopi Lal must have picked it up because I heard the sound of his muffled voice from the other room. After a moment of silence, he came through the door, hair sticking up, eyes big as saucers — a dramatic entrance, one of Gopi Lal's best.

"It's for you, Uncle. England. The hospital. They say you should come at once. . . ."

I'd checked the day before: there were two planes that morning leaving for London — both only half-full. I was already 90 percent packed. All I had to do was to say good-by. I wanted to do it in the house and leave for the airport by myself. But no way — Fatima commandeered a car for Patsi to drive me to the airport.

There we were, speeding along the open road, the four of us just like old times, except that it wasn't the beginning any more, or the middle, it was simply the end.

Going through Security, this time I didn't look back. I couldn't take the chance. I thought of all the things I could have said to them, should have said, and an awful sadness came over me. The journey of a lifetime together was over and now we'd be off on our separate ways, and however much we'd try to adjust to everyday life it would never be the same again. And neither would we.

"*Taman shad*. It is over, . . ." I murmured half-aloud and got a curious look from the Customs man.

BOOK TWO

✳ ✳ ✳

You know, Uncle, I've lost whole parts of myself since we are traveling together. Layers and layers of "me" gone. Peeled away, discarded, surplus to requirements. Is that what traveling does? Brings us back to what we truly are?

— *GOPI LAL*

12. Reflections

I gave my story a good deal of objective thought on the flight to London. Figment of my imagination, yes. But at the same time, might it not have been a fair approximation of the core truth of the matter? The fact remained that a coincidence of natural disasters – five years of desperate civil war, the partial destruction of a hugely sensitive icon, the Church of the Divine Wisdom, followed by the Black Death, which killed off half their city's population – would have given a strong, if not compelling reason for the superstitious Byzantines to expel the Gypsy scapegoat (already in increasingly bad odor), cauterize the tumor within and render themselves pure in the sight of a God who had seemingly deserted them. At this distance removed, obviously it was impossible to prove. Looked at the other way, it was impossible to disprove, either.

Actually, when I thought about it, the timing of the Rom diaspora was fortuitous in the extreme. Yet again in their history a short-lived window of opportunity had opened for them. Not long after, Ottoman advances into Europe closed the circle around Constantinople, rendering escape impossible. Probably they would have been among the last of the refugees to leave the beleaguered city ahead of thousands of Greeks seeking security for their wealth.

In 1357, bypassing Constantinople, the Ottomans crossed the Dardanelles to establish their first permanent base in Greece. Adrianople, renamed Edirne, was established as the launch pad for the conquest of Europe. Now whether as my imagination and/or *Fingerspitzengefühl* (that lovely word for "intuition") suggested they were booted out not only for chastity's sake but also to assume the role of harbingers of history's most horrifying, infamous act of vengeance, I can only postulate. What I can say with confidence is that for John Cantacazenus and his Byzantine mentality, the temptation to pull off a magnificent double – a truly inspired two-in-one – must well have proved quite irresistible.

And there has to be – must be, by all that's holy – a reason for the complete absence of reference to the Rom after 1347 in a city that was swarming with them and in which they had made such a vital impact on its day-to-day life. As it was, they were wiped off the pages of the history books as if they had never existed.

I rest my case.

Ironically, when Mehmet II finally took Constantinople in 1453, he found the only way to repopulate his new capital was to issue a *firman*, an edict applicable throughout the Empire (which at that time included most of Eastern Europe), offering tax concessions to settlers, particularly artisans, if they would migrate to the re-christened Istanbul. Failing to attract the desired numbers, he gave orders to the army that whole populations were to be brought in by force.

Thus it was that a good many Eastern European Gypsies found themselves dragged back to the city a century after they'd been kicked out. Almost akin, you might say, to the Tribes of Israel being recaptured to solve latter-day Cairo's labor problems. How many Gypsies would have been brought back? There is simply no way of knowing. The only bearing we have (and a pretty intangible one at that) is a rough estimate of anything up to 100,000 in and around present-day Istanbul.

The plane was beginning its descent. I felt a desperate sense of let-down. I'd come to the end of my quest. It was all over.

My object, somewhat conceited I could now see in retrospect, had been to fill in the whys and wherefores associated with the missing annals of the Rom between their departure from northern India in Lord knows when and their arrival in Europe early in the fourteenth century. I could only leave it to those better versed in the subject than I to judge whether I had succeeded. By and large, I thought I had. Or, at the very least, maybe come closer than anybody else to filling in that enigma; one of the few remaining mysteries of our time.

By rights, *The Rom* should have ended here, its mission accomplished. And yet . . . the more I thought about it, the more I felt I should be guilty of an impoliteness by leaving the reader up in the air. You know: "Well, you got them into Europe, then what happened?" A chagrined sense of anticlimax was setting in.

Although the saga of the Rom in Europe has been thoroughly, indeed, superbly well covered by Gypsiologists, a brief chronological record of some of the salient periods of their European existence might not come amiss. I shan't call them high spots, because they certainly were not that. What follows is a potted history of their life and times in Europe over the centuries, a collage of their experiences in some of the countries they dwelt in. Mostly, it does not make for pleasant reading. All one can say is that man's cruelty to man became more and more refined as the centuries proceeded.

While I was writing it, and particularly the Holocaust chapter, it struck me just how much the saga of the Rom had this curious, ill-starred quality about it. In an inexplicable but absolutely inevitable way, it seemed foreordained that, by starting their existence as a race in one concentration camp, they should all but end it in another a thousand years later. It seemed more than ironic that the sign of the swastika, which in their north Indian cradle signified bounteous good fortune and protection against the forces of evil, should be the symbol of their near total annihilation.

13. Gentle Thrace

IT WAS THOUGHT BY THE ROM THAT IN THE BEGINNING THE
WORLD WAS A VOID AND WITHIN THIS VOID THERE WAS ANOTHER
VOID. THE INNER VOID WAS THE SLEEPING GOD. IT HAD NO
BODY, MERELY A BRAIN, AND IN ITS BRAIN GREW A DREAM. AND
THE DREAM WAS MADE UP OF A HOST OF SPARKS THAT,
CONGREGATING TOWARD THE MIDDLE, MADE UP A HUGE BALL OF
FIRE. BUT IT BECAME SO HOT THAT THE MIDDLE EXPLODED AND
FLEW OUT IN EVERY DIRECTION AT GREAT SPEED. WHILE IT
SLOWLY COOLED, TWO GODS WERE BORN: THE GOD OF LIFE,
MOSHTO; AND THE GOD OF DEATH, ARIVELL.

AND THUS IT WAS THAT THE BRAIN OF THE SLEEPING GOD
GREW AND GREW AND ITS DREAM BECAME THE STORY OF ALL
OUR DAYS.

— *OLD ROM LEGEND*

Thrace 1347

It had drawn them from the rich red earth of Rajasthan to the
mountain fastnesses of Afghanistan: threading them through
Persia, Anatolia and thence Byzantium. Now the lodestar of the
Rom was commanding them into Europe.

In a tumultuous band the Rom descended on the golden
plains and gentle folds of Thrace, happily ignorant of the
upheavals, the turbulent political ebbs and flows, the never-
ending assaults of mounted iron from each point of the compass
that swept through fair Thrace and neighboring Macedonia, tall

Norman disputing territory with swarthy Catalan, blond Serb with sloe-eyed Bulgar, chiaroscuro Genoese with golden Greek. And, in the wings, a hooded falcon, talons barely concealed, the Terrible Turk biding his time, waiting to rend and conquer.

Winds of violence and ambition swept over the land of Greece. And in the midst of this carnival of chaos were the Rom, fated to be blown hither and thither like so many fine, floating feathers.

Initially greeted with awe as creatures from another world, sometimes welcomed for their skills and accorded rare respect for qualities they did not possess, they were later to be vilified as vermin, persecuted, enslaved, hunted down and slaughtered in their tens of thousands.

They would not have been the first wanderers Adrianople had seen. Small bands of nomads with artisanal or entertainment skills had been passing through from Asia for centuries. But it was at this city or thereabouts that the Rom separated and struck out in three separate directions. What was the motivation behind this self-inflicted schism, one that destroyed once and for all their chances of establishing their own nation state? We can only conjecture why a country called Romanestan never came into being.

Let us explore a couple of possibilities. One: If the exodus from Constantinople occurred in October, as seems most probable, it would be coming into winter and food would be very scarce on the ground by the time the Gypsies reached Adrianople. Their embarrassingly large numbers would have threatened to strip the land naked. The greater their number, the more certain the likelihood of punitive retaliation from the peasantry whose lands they were scavenging.

Two: Without doubt, a number of them were carrying the plague and were spreading it on contact. A low profile – fewer numbers – would have been mandatory.

Now, although I feel that the above may have been major causes for the split-up, I believe the main reason was that now the first real opportunity since Dasht i Nawar had come their way, they simply divided up according to their ancient origins, reverting to the tribes they had been in India prior to enslavement in Afghanistan, obeying an unconscious imperative to expiate the dark stain of their Original Sin, that unholy captivity-enforced miscegenation.

The instinct to start a fresh life on a new continent, pure and unblemished, would have been incredibly powerful. A subconscious compulsion toward a state of blood purity and undefiled innocence would allow them at last to escape the cruel karma that had been their lot for their entire history.

Hence the final cleavage and the river separating into three streams – northeast toward Russia, due north to Moldachia, and west toward Western Europe. Smiths one way, farriers another, entertainers yet another. Centuries of interbreeding allowed each of the three branches to possess in its genes the skills of the other two, resulting in a rare ability to turn a hand to anything that assisted survival.

Banjara, Kanjar and Lohar reverting to type, rejecting the protection of the whole. Now they would become known by other names – Lovari, Kalderash, Manush/Sinti, and so forth – each tribe considering itself the only authentic Rom, the true people of the *kalo rat*. Intermarriage between them would be prohibited on pain of permanent ostracism from the *Kumpania* – the assembly of *vardos* (wagons) traveling together under one chief.

One of the first problems they would have contended with in Europe was that the people around them had white skins. It was no longer possible for them to merge into the crowd as they had done to date. It increased their vulnerability, their feeling of being exposed. "Their whiteness makes our darkness," said the Rom, with utter truthfulness.

Subsequently, they went the opposite way, over-emphasizing a Levantine singularity, telling fantasy tales of an "Egyptian" past, of a close association with the events surrounding the crucifixion. Finally, and most dramatically, they told of having been sentenced by His Holiness the Pope to journey on a pilgrimage to the principal shrines in Europe for having forged the nails of the Cross. They adopted an air of barbaric nobility, an esoteric flavor of mystery, of enchantment, of dark, magical powers, of a visionary insight into Heaven and Hell. For additional weight, they procured letters of patent signed by the Pope himself, commanding all Christian princes to accord them safe passage and every consideration while in their kingdom.

The Rom invented themselves. And having done so they let the *Gaujo* accentuate and embellish those elements of their persona which appealed most to *his* imagination with what he wanted them to be.

But this tickling of the *Gaujo*'s fancy unfortunately did not stop their destiny taking the form of abject slavery in Eastern Europe and vile persecution in the West over the next five hundred years. Although instances of Gypsy enslavement in Eastern Europe were recorded as early as 1355 – only a decade after they arrived – in the main they were allowed to move around and follow their occupations freely for the first hundred years.

Improvisation, adapting a thing and making it uniquely "Gypsy," was their stock in trade. It was said, many centuries later, that it took the Gypsies to play the czardas better than the Hungarians and dance the flamenco with more panache and passion then the Spanish.

Day comes. And so a black-haired people who took short steps, seeming to glide rather than walk, who danced with head held high, who never traveled at noon for fear of the *mulo*, spread through Europe like a swarm of aberrant djinns.

We skip a century now and come to their arrival in La Belle France. The year is 1427 and England has a bulldog grip on France's throat. But soon the Maid of Orleans will lead French arms in a holy war of liberation culminating in her being burnt at the stake four years later and on her way to becoming Saint Joan of Arc.

❋　❋　❋

14. La Belle France

CES PAUVRES GUEUX PLEINS DE BONNES AVENTURES
NE PORTENT RIEN QUE DES CHOSES FUTURES.

THESE RAGGED TRAMPS FULL OF FORTUNES (TO SELL)
OWN LITTLE BUT THE WORDS OF THE TALES THEY TELL.

VOUS QUI PRENEZ PLAISIR EN LEURS PAROLES
GARDEZ VOS BLANCS, VOS TESTONS ET PISTOLLES.

YOU WHO ENJOY HEARING FUTURES FORETOLD
LOOK OUT FOR YOUR PENNIES, SILVER AND GOLD.

France 1427

They arrived at the gates of Paris one hot August day in 1427.
One hundred and twenty persons in all, according to a con-
temporary report – blue-black hair, hypnotic eyes set in high-
cheekboned faces, dark complexions; the women ringing bells,
whirring wooden clappers, speaking a strange tongue, dressed
in vivid colors, flashing barbaric jewels; frightening the guards
at the Porte d'Orléans and scaring the horses half to death. When
permitted audience with His Most Christian Majesty to be, the
Dauphin Charles VII, they presented him with Letters of Cre-
dence from His Holiness Pope Martin V.

The story they told the future king was one they were to
relate many times over during the next fifty years at virtually
every court in Europe. It was simple, dramatic and with just
the right biblical flavor to make the audience want to believe

it. They became very adept at this type of salesmanship.

The bizarre story ran that when the Holy Family fled to Egypt from King Herod's butchery, the Gypsies refused to help them for fear of offending the Pharaoh. As a punishment, God condemned them to roam the earth for ever more and be shunned by all. The Saracens (they said) had recently driven them out of Little Egypt (wherever that was!) and after wandering through Bohemia and Germany they had thrown themselves on the mercy of the Pope, who had given them absolution and set them the penance of visiting all the major shrines in Europe within seven years.

Impressed, Charles gave them the royal "*Laissez passer*" and the city of Paris threw open its gates, its hearts and its purses. The honeymoon period lasted just one month before the Archbishop of Paris excommunicated "the whole band of sorcerers and fortune tellers" and had them driven out of the city. In addition, any French subjects having contact with them were also automatically excommunicated. Paris had its fill of the Rom. Its citizens could not adjust to their penchant for picking purses while small-holders complained that no chicken was safe within five miles of them.

Within a short space of time, they were ordered to leave the country or be sent to the galleys: "Secured by convict chains – there to serve in perpetuity. The women to be flogged and banished from our kingdom . . ." ran the royal edict.

So much for their debut in France. Actually, when you come right down to it, the French administration's treatment of them has not improved much in the past four and a half centuries. They don't use convict chains any more, and flogging has been discontinued, but in most other respects the victimization is as bad as ever.

And so now we travel on another century, across the

Channel to Merrie England. The year is 1527. The weavers of Kent are rioting against restrictive government policy while severe outbreaks of plague are making tragic inroads on the nation. In London, Henry VIII is explaining to his nobles and the population at large his motives for seeking a divorce from Catherine of Aragon to marry Anne Boleyn.

Even by today's standards, his hold on the marriage sacrament was tenuous: one marriage annulled, one wife divorced, one dead in childbirth, two beheaded. Only his last queen, the sweet and gentle Catherine Parr, survived him.

※　　※　　※

15. Not So Merrie England

OLD MAN (MERRY): "I'M THE ROMANY RAI,
I'M A TRUE DIDDIKOI,*
I BUILD MY CASTLES 'NEATH THE SKY,
AND THAT'S WHY THEY CALL ME THE
ROMANY RAI."

OLD MAN (BITTER): "WE'RE KIN TO THE WHITE CROWS AND
OFF-COLORED FOXES,
THE OTHERS TRY THEIR BEST TO KILL US."

England 1528

They didn't fare that much better in Britain.

An account that year stated there were 10,000 Gypsies in the British Isles – obviously due to steady infiltration over the past century. Two years later, in 1530, Gypsies were henceforth banned from entering the country.

In 1547, Edward VI (1537-1553), instituted a law requiring all Gypsies to be branded with a V on their breast and enslaved for two years. If they ran away and were caught, they were branded with an S and made slaves for life.**

By the 1600s, in Cromwell's time, an active campaign of persecution had been put into place. To be a Gypsy, or to associate with one, meant automatic death by hanging. In George Henry Borrow's famous words: "The gibbets of England groaned

---

* Traveller.
** Kinney, 1973: 45.

and creaked with the weight of Gypsy carcasses and the miserable survivors were obliged to creep into the earth to preserve their lives."

Wherever they went, town or country, an aura of sorcery and superstition was associated with them. To the people, the sight of a Gypsy outlined against a moon-bathed tarn brought them closer to the mysteries of life and the universe than all the sermons by the Archbishop of Canterbury in his grand palace at Lambeth.

And now we flick through the pages of history and stop one hundred years later, in 1627, at Moldachia, present-day Hungary/Romania.

Frans Hals was painting *The Merry Drinker*, Rembrandt *The Money Changer*, and Rubens his *Mystic Marriage of St. Catherine*; the first German production of *Hamlet* was taking place in Dresden and René Descartes was publishing his famous *Rules for the Direction of the Spirit*; Shah Jehan had just laid the cornerstone of that love-poem in stone, the Taj Mahal; and while all this flowering of art and civilization was taking place, Gypsies were being hunted like wolves in the forests of Moldachia, eating rats and each other to survive. And still they were more fortunate than their enslaved brethren on the big estates.

Of all the times, of all the worlds, this was the worst.

16. Moldachia — The Slave

O CHONUT ASAL AMEN	THE MOON SMILES
TE O CHONUT KORHAVOLA	DOWN ON US
TE AMEN DIKHASA	AROUND THE FIRE
KON VAKARELA	WE WEEP

Moldachia 1627

In 1627 the Gypsies had already been slaves for nearly 250 years in Moldachia. It would be another 250 years before they gained freedom — 1864 to be precise, one year after Lincoln issued his Emancipation Proclamation freeing the American slaves.

In 1627 between 600,000 and 900,000 Rom slaves in Moldachia lived a subhuman existence. Even more brutish were the lives of the *Netostsi*, runaway Gypsy slaves living in the forest: savage, half-naked, existing on the flesh of cats, dogs and mice; sleeping on bare ground in all weathers; and, it was rumored, resorting to cannibalism in order to survive.

House and field slaves on the estates were treated with a systematic cruelty and sadism that defies description. For the slightest infraction, they were hung upside down and the soles of their feet shredded with whips made of bull sinews. While the Rom women were regularly used and abused by their masters, the men were seen as a potent sexual threat to Moldachian woman-hood. Gypsy males who had contact with their mistresses during the performance of their household duties were castrated as a matter of course. If, despite all the obstacles placed in his way, a slave did, miraculously, rape a white woman, the punishment was to be burnt alive.

It is difficult to believe that somewhere in so-called civilized Europe only 150 years ago the penal codes of certain countries could include the following articles:

- Gypsies are born slaves.
- Anyone born of a mother who is a slave is also a slave.
- Any owner has the right to sell or give away his slaves.
- Any Gypsy without an owner is the property of the prince.
- Legal unions cannot take place between free persons and slaves.
- Marriage between slaves cannot take place without their owner's consent.

Between the years 1627 and final emancipation in 1864, the treatment of the Gypsies at the hands of their owners had sunk to unimaginable depths of depravity. And in the vanguard of this unholy, Godless conduct as a major slave owner in its own right was Holy Mother Church.

It was as if man were trying to test out for all time the outer limits of pain and degradation he could inflict on another human being. The following is a French journalist's — the respected Félix Colson's — eyewitness report of a mere 150 years ago:

"A typical day in the life of a Gypsy field slave begins at dawn when the '*vatava*' [overseer] warmly wrapped in furs and bull whip in hand, assembles them to assign their day's tasks. A distressing sight, this foul-smelling, haggard, half naked, shivering group, everywhere appearing from stables, kitchens and sheds. The '*vatava*,' always hard and inflexible, flays them as much from fancy as from a desire to assert his authority."

What he saw on his on-the-spot journalistic investigation made Colson sick. He never forgot the experiences and neither did those who read about them.

Slaves belonging to a private landowner were subject to no laws but his, and God protect them if he happened to have a sadistic turn of mind. The churches and monasteries, although theoretically governed by the law of the land, treated their Gypsy slaves with even more inhumane savagery, an indelible stain of blood that the Church will have forever on its conscience. It defends itself by ignoring it ever happened.

The prince, the church, the boyars: the three spikes of the iron cangue buried deep in the Gypsy neck.

Over the centuries, the punishment code was refined and consolidated. By law, the boyars (landowners) had no right to kill their slaves but there was nothing on the statute book to prevent them slowly torturing them to death. Equally, no law forbade the master systematically raping his female slaves or breaking up family units as the whim took him.

If the laws of Moldachia and Moldavia granted no automatic right to the slave owner to kill his slaves, as Félix Colson wrote in 1829, not one boyar had ever been prosecuted for the murder of Gypsy. One of Colson's despatches from the Balkans read: "A Gypsy postilion or courier is often shot through the head or flogged to death upon any cause or no cause, without the murder being noticed, for 'he is only a zigeuner.'"*

Colson's writings go on to describe his visit to a boyar homestead. "In the evening, the master makes his choice among the beautiful girls – maybe he will offer some of them

---

* Chambers's *Journal,* 1836.

to his guest – whence the light-skinned, blond-haired Gypsies.

"The next morning at dawn, I am awakened by a piercing shriek: it is punishment time. The current penalty is one hundred lashes for a broken plate or a badly curled lock of hair."*

Another account from a much earlier period – some hundred years after the Gypsies had arrived from Byzantium – describes the recreational amusements of Vlad Tepov V, known to the cognoscenti of horror as Vlad the Impaler, who became ruler of Wallachia in 1476.

"He invited them [the Gypsies] to a festival, made them all drunk, and threw them into the fire. Another amusement of his was the construction of an enormous cauldron, into which he thrust his victims. Then, filling it with water, he made it boil, and took pleasure in the anguish of the sufferers. When the people whom he impaled writhed in agony, he had their hands and feet nailed to the posts. Some . . . were compelled to eat [a] man roasted."**

The infamous 1834 public sale of three thousand Romany slaves in Bucharest finally stirred public conscience. Western Europe started to take more than a cursory interest in what was being revealed little by little as a satanic abomination carried out by church, state and landowners. Here is Roleine's description of a day that indicted Romania in the eyes of Europe.

"Bucharest 1834. A square. There's no crowd, just a group of people in front of a wagon pulled there by buffaloes. The passers-by quicken their steps and lower their eyes so that they don't have to look at the men and women tearing at their rags in anguish. Dishevelled, dark skinned, these are Gypsies. You can't escape the entreaties of the mothers whose children are being

---

* Robert Roleine, 1979: – article based on Colson's diary notes.
** J.W. Ozanne, 1878: 1189-1190.

torn from them, nor their sobs and screams of fear, nor their curses; you can't escape the cracking of the whips breaking down their stubborn resistance to the separations inevitably to come."*

Ironically, twenty years later, all over Europe, philanthropic societies were springing up with the object of abolishing slavery in the southern states of America. Under their very noses, at the same time, nearly a million Gypsies were undergoing the sort of treatment J.A. Vaillant described in his history of the Romani people, written in 1857.

"What are these animals I can make out over there, through the haze of evening? They're coming and going, sometimes on all fours like rats, and sometimes on two feet, like monkeys. . . . certainly they're not men; they're animals. My God – they ARE men! Gypsies! There are six of them, and an overseer too, keeping an eye on them. Can you see? They're as naked as Adam, and their bodies are smeared all over with a thick coating of tar. There are shackles on their feet and yokes on their necks, and they are removing sand from the river bed. They are wearing 'cangues,' those vile triangular yokes they put on pigs to stop them from breaking through the hedges but whose three long spikes prevent the Gypsies from being able to rest their heads.

"Since morning they have been sweating blood, with nothing to drink but river water, and nothing to eat but bits of bread baked there in the ashes with some boiled leeks and a little salt. At the risk of its being taken away from them by the guard, I gave them each a coin and went on my way."**

Despite stubborn opposition from the landowners, legal freedom, the *Slobuzenja,* came about in 1864. One of the vilest passages in human history was about to draw to a close. Their

---

* Roleine, 1979: 108.
** 1857: 409-412.

former owners received compensation from the state, the Rom merely earned the right to exist.

They fled: northwest to Scandinavia; through Yugoslavia into southern and western Europe. Large numbers embarked for North and South America. Some stayed behind. With no money, broken in mind and body, they sold themselves back to their former masters.

And now we flick on through the pages of history to pay a return visit to England, this time settling on the Victorian and Edwardian eras, and what was indisputably the best of times: the mellowest and gentlest of all the lives of the Rom, anywhere, at any time. It was a lullaby time when they could do no wrong and the people accepted them for what they were. It had never happened before. It wouldn't . . . couldn't happen again. From that point onward, it was all downhill.

But then, as I said, it was the golden time.

17. The Golden Years

Great Britain 1850-1913

It was the age when the Gypsy, a few drinks in his pocket, the moon tucked away in a coat sleeve, rollicked the length and breadth of the British Isles. The era when this dark, feral people left the security of the forest: the owl and the barking fox and the murmur of mossy streams under the quiet, white moon, and emerged onto the new roads linking the expanding cities of Industrial Revolution Britain.

After Wellington's victory at Waterloo, England was incontestably the premier nation in Europe, if not the world. Factories and mills were springing up, using the newly invented steam engine. An amalgam of ingenuity, imagination, dynamism and commercial pugnacity transformed the British Isles into the British Empire within a few short decades. As John Bull rose high, so did the Gypsies, riding the crest of prosperity as to the manner born. Or rather riding the Gypsy wagon – the horse-drawn caravan that for the first time would let them unfurl the full measure of their restless, itinerant spirit.

The caravan became the symbol of their way of life. Midway between farm cart and stage coach, it reached superb heights of decorative splendor, with outside scroll carvings of red and gold and a treasure trove of ornaments and cut-glass decorations inside to bedazzle the Lees, Coopers or Boswells or any other Traveller clan. They would travel from one end of the country to the other to attend horse fairs like the famous

Appleby or drop in on Kent for the hop-picking season. Fifty miles a day was a fair clip on a good road in fine weather.

Mostly they'd be earning money making shopping baskets and clothes pegs from willow and hazel tree branches. A good pegmaker made up to twelve pegs an hour. The whole family worked together. The women collected reeds and branches to make into baskets. The men would "chin the cost" (cut the stick), i.e., whittle butchers' skewers and clothes pegs. The children foraged for firewood, fetched water, cleaned and polished the horse's harness. The rest of the day they were in the woods catching birds, rabbits, hedgehogs and the like for the evening stew-pot.

The wagons rarely rolled on a Friday. It was taboo — bad luck too if a bird flew into the caravan. Then everything stopped until the next morning. You couldn't see the New Moon through glass, cut your hair or nails on Sunday and a thousand and one other prohibitions that made a Traveller think twice before he even blew his nose.

Between themselves they spoke their own highly inflected tongue and gave colorful Romani names to Britain's lakes and ancient mountains as they sat high in their wagons, bemused by the beauty of the purple twilights in the Lake District or in the deep-green heart of the Vale of Evesham.

Summers' golden moons. Autumns bleak after the fall of the flaming leaf. Winters, cloudy: slanting sleet on raw faces. Spring mornings full of dreaming: nights full of ghosts. Blood of my blood in her death-cot under the briared hedgerow. Elfin faeries lighting reverential fires around the holy willow tree. The snowdrop patch by the fox's den. Morning, noon and gloaming. *Kalo chiriclo* was my blackbird. *Kalo cori* the blackthorn on which she perched to sing.

"Gauzo" . . . "Gaujo" . . . turning into "Gorgio" as the vowels broadened. Sorrow tempered by the brief, bright eyes of the children, glistening like glow worms in the shadow dark: teeth a-glitter in the yellow cast of moonbeams. Romani *chal* and *chavi* (boy and girl) braided together (but in mind only) at the pinnacle of their glorious youth. For it was the primrose month and the *kalo rat*, the dark blood, was running bold, unbearably throbbing in young bodies. There would be weddings arranged come Appleby. The boys would wink and nudge, the girls blush prettily while their elders sat down and quietly did the business.

For lo! The new moon has cut the sky. May it bring good fortune, health, wealth and happiness! Jingling coins in their pockets: turning them thrice times over. 'May Shuri the *Chovahani* (witch) spit three times on the face of the new moon on water to bring us luck." And they'd greet each other with "*Sarishan*" (good day) or "*Koshti sarla*" (good evening). "*Kushto bokht*" (good luck) would come the reply as the crescent moon danced on the silver stream.

Dark heads dim-gleaming in the brazen autumn evening, they'd walk into a village trudging over the open leas. Front gardens growing hollyhocks, sweet williams and evening primroses. "The name they gives her is '*Bokht drey Cuesni,*' Luck in a Basket, 'cos when she comes home at night her basket's full of things she's nicked." No fowl, it was said, was safe from her bottomless basket unless plucked, baked and eaten.

The village people thought them odd like cats and treated them with reserve. There they'd be, all nice and quiet, winsome and insinuating on the outside. But give 'em a scratch and the feral core spat through. Untamed. Unpredictable. No sense of time or duty. No feeling of obligation to pay back concern or spontaneous kindness. They went their own way – took what they wanted with never a thank you. A body would never know which way they'd jump. Sometimes a-purring and a-rubbing at your feet and other times you'd swear to see a tail swish as they'd walk away with that stiff, proud back and smooth peculiar glide of theirs.

Like cats, they held their heads high, focusing on the middle distance with that foreign velvety look, for all the world like old-time kings and queens.

Oh lordy, what a fine time those old Romanies had. They had more than their *showhawry's* (sixpence) worth of things *gorgiko-naes* (in the manner of the Gorgio): gin and beer and baccy and tea – especially tea. Up to twenty cups a day some of 'em and more. Of course, they poached the Gorgio's woods for trout and pheasant. What else were a man and his lurcher on God's earth for? Up in Leek Country (Wales), some of the *Tachey*, real dark blood Gypsies, caught rabbits by talking them over when they came out of their burrows at dusk. Just talking nice and easy. A tasty rabbit stew and a mug or two of ale on a Saturday night was top of a Traveller's delight. Nothing choicer unless it be hedgehog baked in clay with a sup of dandelion wine. The women favored hedgehog. *Hatchi-witchu* (prickly thing of the wood) or *pal of the bor* (brother of the hedge) they called him.

They'd sell what they made, the likes of baskets, clothes pegs and fancy wooden spoons. Made a bit of brass repairing pots and pans, knife grinding, telling fortunes (more of that later), selling flowers, and, because it was in the blood, stronger than anything, buying and selling horses. Earnings went on things for the *vardo* (caravan): china mugs and figurines of Queen Victoria and her son, Edward VII; mirrors – lots of them – glittering ornaments, fancy clocks and bright, multi-patterned bed spreads. With the groats (shillings) left over from the tavern – and actually there weren't that many inns that allowed them in ("No Hawkers, Dogs or Gypsies," sign-making being a real growth industry in Victorian England) they'd buy gold. Just for the feel of it; the luster of it shining back at them in the Gorgio's green eyes.

They'd wear the whole lot at once: rings, necklets, bangles, pendants, lockets, bracelets, anklets, chains and crucifixes. Gold, gold, gold.

Like cats they could walk away from the comforts and amenities of civilization into another, totally different and enveloping world where a child was given at least three names, the second of which was secret to fool evil spirits . . . the bad genii, servitors of *Beng* the Devil. Did they but know it, the Banjara, a hemisphere away in northern India, had been doing just that for the past couple of millennia.

The sky was their tent, the earth their carpet, the mild woods their couch and bower. Their glossy-haired children led enraptured lives full of country lore, birds' nests, trout streams, blackbirds whistling, the linnet and the bullfinch answering. The first *koring chiriclo* (cuckoo) of spring. Bare brown legs standing out in the bright, desiring green of newly sprung leaves. It was their "high" time. The enchanted, unique, never-to-be-repeated child-age, captured by the thrilling, trembling ecstasy of the sky-lark reaching up to divine heights of sweet swelling sound.

And in those molten evenings poised between night and day, the children would see queencups and hear rare, mirthful music: love-elfins trilling their Pipes of Pan a-top a green hornbeam. They learned to beware of magic girdles which when placed round a body gave rise to dreams of unobtainable sapphire thrones set in honey-scented emerald palaces. Hesitantly they spoke of these matters to parents who showed – disappointingly – only matter-of-fact acceptance. They, too, when young, had familiarized with the little people. The tragedy of growing up was that the charmed ones no longer sought your company or allowed themselves to be seen at play.

Youth was a brief affair. A short pause between childhood and early maturity. A time of love-darting eyes, of trysts never quite transpiring in caves guarded by the fine spray of the waterfall. Glances that spoke of an eternity of love from sapling to trunk. All remaining firmly in the world of dream-fantasy. Their parents saw to that.

The stripling, Tornapo, could not help himself falling instantly in love with every Romani Chi (girl) his eyes dwelt upon. There was Reyna, dark and sheened as a September plum. Kisaiya, who spared him not a glance as her mother was a Stanley and her father well-off in horses. Mizella and Narrila, who were sisters and never let each other out of sight. And, the queen of his life, Syeira, who whispered to him in his dreams, but scorned him in real life even though he put pellets of bread under his pillow from one new moon to another to make her change the way of it.

It was a society in which personal possessions were accorded scant respect – with the exception of gold jewelry (the more massive the better). A new suit of clothes would be worn until frayed and ragged. Slept in even. Only tools were accorded dignity, passed lovingly from father to son. On the other hand, there would always be a tree along the way that was hallowed to a Traveller. And always the intimate, lurking fox carrying within him something of him. Instances known and related in low voices of the animal surviving the man by barely a day. The amber-eyed, red-gold "dog of the wood," *Beano abri,* born out of doors like the Gypsy and sharing the same wild, untameable heart.

And the joke was, the easier life got, the more draconian their self-imposed taboos, laws and restrictions became. Each year they put another bar on the window, another bolt on the door, until they'd well and truly locked themselves in with their compulsion, their mania for purity.

The laws governing defilement, especially as applied to women, increased in number and rigidity. Women may not touch men with their skirt. Women's shadows polluted. Women's washline linen must not come into contact with men's. Women must not handle red meat or partake of it during menstruation or immediately after childbirth. Cups and plates used by women may not be washed in the same bowl as the men's. Women defiled water by merely stepping over a water pipe. When you got right down to it, unless they were under ten or over sixty, women defiled just by being women.

The Brahmins themselves could hardly have tied a more finicky set of knots. But to the Gypsies the taboos were a vital part of their lives. Lief as curse a Sunday babe as offend against the laws and taboos of *Mokkado*. That is if *Kushto bokht*, good luck, was your desire.

Step by intuitive step the Gypsies returned to India. To the rites, traditions, mores and way of life of a thousand years ago. Back to the very pith and core of their being. Marriages between young couples were negotiated between parents. As in India, the bride lived with her husband's parents. Her own family became dead to her and she to them. As in India, she obeyed her mother-in-law in all things. The money she earned by begging, selling flowers, fortune telling or whatever, went straight into the family exchequer. Elopement marriages — always a facet of Gypsy life — became more frequent as the bride-price went up. After running away together, the young couple would return a few days later, ostensibly shame-faced, ready to face a verbal drubbing (to the sake of keeping up appearances). They they'd settle down, taking their place without further ado in the body of the tribe. Run-away marriages throughout the world are not that common as they rub against a well-ordered society structure. One of its principal exponents, however, were and are today the Kanjar tribe of Rajasthan.

Marriages were entered into for life. Infertility or infidelity were virtually the only accepted reasons for divorce. But every now and again a woman was brought before the council, the Kris (replacing the old Hindu Panchayat) to answer charges of having killed her husband by casting a spell on him. The penalty was permanent banishment from the tribe. The ultimate sanction, spelling out a lingering, lonely death.

The punishment for prostitution or adultery by a woman was to slit her nose and expel her from the tribe. A divorced woman was not allowed to have intercourse on pain of expulsion. An empty-headed flirt who sought the company of the chalk-faced Gorgios was called a *Pauno-mui* (white or pale face) and much looked down upon if not expelled altogether.

For a people who were always having a good laugh at the Gorgio for believing in fortune telling and all that superstitious mummery, they were remarkably prone to it themselves. In a way it was understandable, probably inevitable, as they had no idea of what was going on around them, politically or economically. Everything that happened to them, whether for good or ill, they ascribed to *bokht*, luck. Luck was everything. Omens were everywhere: in the number and direction of a flight of birds, the shape of a cloud, the way a branch shook in the wind. The whole living, blessed day was made up of lucky and unlucky portents and auspices too numerous to mention.

And they were intensely superstitious about death too.

Reyna was about a hundred years old with the face of a wrinkled walnut but a long time ago a man had called her *miri kumli Rumni*, my dear wife. That she remembered as she gazed deep into the glowing embers. The fire brought back other memories too: death and the fear of the dead. Nights on windswept heaths when the wagon of the *mulo*, the dead one, had gone up to the sky in a fire-burst blaze and him in it. And all his worldly goods and clothes and jewelry. His favorite *grai* (horse), lying close by with its throat cut. There was no other way the dead could be placated. That and not mentioning them by name for one whole year and a day. Otherwise, they'd come back to haunt you. Come back even sharper if they knew you were having words about the odds and ends they'd left behind. So the whole lot was burned to avoid *chingaro* (strife). That way when the *mulo* returned it would be as a friend, an ally, someone you could call on when times were bitter.

Country folk in the main were sure the Gypsies had the "power," the gift of vengeance. A Romani oath, a full moon, a silver knife, a piece of fruit and presto! the job was done. How many people envied the judge his fine position, his great house and furs when after passing sentence for some petty misde-meanor, the convicted Gypsy leaving the dock roundly cursed him in strange tongue? How many envied him then? How many of those bewigged *poknies* went home that evening and, con-suming more than their fill of contraband French brandy, woke up the following morning with the stench of fear on the bed-sheets and a clammy wetness gripping their heart?

Dukkering – as fortune telling was called in Romanes – relied for results on a shrewd assessment of the client's facial features and body language as well as a few innocent questions to bring out what he or she most wanted to hear.

Triffeni Scamp and Cineralla Purrun were two famous *Yokki Juva* – past mistresses of the quick filch, ringing the changes and telling fortunes so true they'd as oft be seated in a great lord's castle as in a yeoman's cottage. The man married to either one of them dined well and kept a turnip watch in his waistcoat to pull out on occasion, frown, shake his head and walk away importantly, like the Romani Rai he was. *"Dukker drey my vast,*

Rai," ("read my palm, sir") they'd sauce after him. But he'd
pretend not to hear and direct his gold-mounted sword stick
toward his usual pew in the tavern.

It was the best of lives in the best of times. Never before
and never again would it be so good. Footloose and fancy-free,
the constabulary not bothering them more than a modicum provided they tidied up the camp site before leaving.

Their horses pulled them to Kent, which they called *Levi-
nengriskey tem* (hop country). Up to Lancashire, which they called
Chohawniskey tem (witches' country). To *Coro-mengreskey tem*
(potters' country, i.e., Staffordshire) and the biggest city in the
world: *Mi-krauliskey gav* – Royal Town, London.

Thus they roamed in those never-to-be-forgotten, incomparable Edwardian summers. There they were, these strange
tawny folk, like bright cherries in a rice pudding, with all that
nervous crackle in their smooth-skinned bodies. All that rollicking *joie de vivre*:

> Can you *rokra Romani?*
> Can you play the *bosh?*
> Can you *jal ardrey the staripen?*
> Can you *chin the cost?*
>
> Can you speak Romani?
> Can you play the fiddle?
> Can you eat the prison loaf?
> Can you cut and whittle?

Moving to the big gray cities in winter, they congregated
on open common ground. In London from the 1860s onward,
Wandsworth, Battersea and Clapham commons were the most
frequented.

Those were the days when many Romani words made their way into English, mostly via the criminal underworld who used them as a secret language to deceive the police: pal, duffer, jockey, bloke, chivy, tiny, mug, nick (to steal), birk (breast), bar (one pound sterling), mush (man), put the mokkers on (curse, damn). Those were the days when the "Purrum" clan (onion in Romanes) became the Lees; the "Rossar-mescro" (duck fellows) became the Herons; the "Grai" (horse people) became the Grays. And a host of other transformations.

To the unsuspecting Gorgio, the Gypsies were one homogeneous race, whereas in reality they were nothing of the sort. If the outside was lyric smooth, the inside was serpentine. The fact of the matter was that they were composed of a number of extremely diverse subgroups, each operating a caste-class system every bit as severe as in their land of origin. In effect the Gypsy, ensconced in his own hermetic group, recognized only it as being truly Gypsy. This superiority bowed its head only to the *Tachey Romani*, those of the old sacred race, who had never slept under a roof in their entire lives, or spoken any word save Romanes. But, by that time, most of them had disappeared, all except a few in the remote fastnesses of the Welsh hills and valleys, as ephemeral now as a half-remembered tale on a grandfather's knee.

18. The Holocaust – Horror Play in One Act

Last - Chance Lament from Limbo

Once again they were the victims. The all-purpose, disposable martyrs. The sacrificial lambs. They and the Jews: the eternal scapegoats for the human race.

Some who had been born into slavery in Moldachia now found themselves in the twilight of their lives become again the shadow dead. This time death would not come slowly: from toiling until they dropped, or the lash, or the violence of their master's passions, but quickly, expeditiously, with a modicum of fuss. But still painfully. Always painfully.

They were to be rendered as atoms of dust. No frills or furbelows. Straight to the heart of the matter. Ground and plowed into the face of the earth.

The clock was to be set back. If every harlot was once a virgin, by the same token there was a time when Europe was Gypsy-free. There was nothing medically, chemically or surgically that could be done regarding the former, but a great deal the Third Reich could do about the latter.

The scene is set in limbo. Four men are grouped around a table. Three of them have the faded look of the very aged. The veiled desperation of men with one last chance to put their case. The other one is a Gypsy. They will call witnesses as and when required.

Dr. Josef Mengele: "You must remember that long before the Nazis came to power the Gypsies had been treated like vermin not only in Germany but all over Europe. The Führer alone cannot be blamed. A 'Central Office for Combatting the Gypsy Nuisance' was created in Munich as long ago as 1899. As a point of interest, gentlemen, you might care to note this agency was not closed down officially until 1970.

"It is a matter of record that when the Nazi Party assumed control over the destiny of the German people in 1933 it inherited anti-Gypsy laws that had been in force since the Middle Ages. You might truthfully say that we National Socialists merely accelerated a process which had been going on for over five hundred years without anybody complaining, least of all Britain, America, France and a great number of other countries who were all carrying out identical policies of discrimination and persecution against the Gypsies.

"The German race, I like to think, simply approached the problem with the orderly efficiency and energetic despatch for which it is renowned."

Anton Weissmann: "With the same painstaking attention to detail and sophisticated finesse you brought to the final solution of the Jewish race, Mengele?"

Mengele: "The end result was the same but the background was different. If we go back in history, the period when the Gypsies first appeared in Germany was surrounded by fearful and inauspicious events: the coming of the Black Death, which killed half the population of Europe, the conflict between the three Popes, the battle of Agincourt, and I could go on. The whole of Europe was in turmoil. It was only natural for the German people to associate the arrival of these nomads and their foreign, barbaric appearance, strange customs and lower earth language with the unnatural events that were occurring."

Weissmann: "What I have never been able to understand is why you dumped the *Zigeuner* in the same non-Aryan basket as us Jews. Surely it was German scholarship that proved conclusively that the Gypsies originated in northern India and were, in effect, as Aryan as Siegfried and Brunhilde?"

Mengele: "I agree this presented considerable difficulties in the beginning. We did toy with the idea that the extermination of the Gypsies should be based on the biological factor: that the Gypsies' originally 'Aryan blood' had become impure due to mixing with other races during their migration from India. However, this seemed like hair splitting to Himmler, who was always a straight-down-the-line sort of fellow, and we eventually settled on 'social factors' as the determining reason. Evidence of 'inferior race' attributes: inbred characteristics such as immorality, criminality, work shyness, ineducatability and the burden they placed on the social services were cited. 'Elimination without delay' was the only possible verdict he could reach."

Raklo: "Is that all you could think of? Exterminating us? Couldn't there have been other — more humane — options open?"

Mengele: "Well, I do remember our Austrian cousins put forward a scheme to the League of Nations to transport you people to form a colony on one of the Polynesian Islands. Or was it Madagascar?"

Raklo: "That would have been about the time, during the first months of Nazi Party rule, that an SS study group recommended that all Gypsies in Germany be taken out to sea and the ships sunk. What did you monsters use for brains? Dynamite?"

Colonel R.D. "Zak" Stillwell (ex-Nuremberg War Crimes Prosecutor): "What beats me, Mengele, is why you Nazis couldn't have put forward the same proposals for the Gypsies as you did for the Jews back in the thirties. You know, inviting foreign governments to take them off your hands before you put them through the mincer?"

Mengele: "And what was the reaction from the 'foreign governments,' Colonel? 'No thank you very much, not right now, Herr Ribbentrop, keep your Jews.' The response would have been identical in the case of the *Zigeuner*, I have not the slightest doubt."

Raklo: "But why treat us Roma twice as badly as you did the Jews?"

Mengele: "What do you mean, 'treat you twice as badly'? We put you both through the same hoop. No favorites."

Raklo: "Let me put some facts before you. On September 15, 1935, the Roma became subject to the restrictions of the Nuremberg Law for the so-called 'protection of blood and honor' which forbade intermarriage or sexual intercourse between Aryan and non-Aryan peoples. In fact, the criteria for classification as a Gypsy were twice as strict as for the Jews. If two of a person's total of eight great-grandparents were even part Gypsy, that person was Gypsy and had to pay the penalty. On the other hand, the Nuremberg decree, if you remember, defined a Jew as being, minimally, a person having one Jewish grandparent, i.e., someone who was one-quarter

Jewish. Were our Romani genes that much more powerful?

"And you were sterilizing Gypsies as early as 1933 — but not the Jews. And, in that same year you established camps to hold us — four of them, I believe — although it had not crossed your mind to incarcerate the Jews at that time. I sometimes get this weird feeling the Jews came along as an afterthought to you: a tactical diversion to get at the real target: us."

Mengele: "Look here, Raklo, I cannot remember all the fine nuances and subtleties of our policy. My recollection of the prewar period was simply of a party committed to finding an intelligent way out of a dilemma."

Raklo: "An intelligent way? Like, for instance, in 1939, Johannes Behrendt, a spokesman for the Nazi Party, declaring that 'the elimination of the entire Gypsy population must be instigated immediately.' Thoughtfully adding that a number of families would be kept in a compound for anthropologists to study. A sort of Roma cage next to the gorillas and the chimpanzees. A curiosity for the Sunday crowds. 'Look, Papa, it says not to feed the Gypsies. It only makes them used to it.' Was that the idea, Mengele?"

Bishop Bland: "It has always seemed curious to me that among the victims in Hitler's Germany, the Jews and the Gypsies alone were considered so genetically degenerated as to pose a threat to German racial purity."

Mengele: "In our view there was no difference between them. Later on, of course, we added homosexuals, drug addicts, deviant writers, intellectuals and most Slavs."

Weissmann: "The *Endlösung*, the Final Solution."

Mengele: "Yes, it does have a certain Wagnerian ring to it in German."

Weissmann: "Of course, we will never know from the Gypsy point of view what you went through, Raklo. None of your writers survived the war."

Raklo: "That is certain. If it hadn't been for your Jewish chroniclers, our part in the Holocaust would have been overlooked entirely."

Raklo (addressing himself to the Bishop): "It has always troubled me, your Grace, why the Church did not think it fit to intercede on our behalf. It is perhaps understandable that the Vatican would not exert itself unduly with the *Endlösung* as it applied to the Jews, but most of the German Roma were Christian – the majority of them Catholic."

Bishop: "You will understand I cannot answer for the Church, but I am certain that at the time these barbarities were taking place, the Pope and Curia were completely unaware of them. After all, you will readily agree that Mother Church hardly makes a practice of condoning persecution."

Raklo: "You seem to have turned a blind eye remarkably well in Eastern Europe – Hungary and Romania, for example – throughout five hundred years of Roma slavery, not true, your Grace?"

Bishop: "I have no knowledge of what you are referring to but can only postulate that it must have been a case of the Church having to comply with the diktats of the ruling establishment."

Raklo: "Including owning 200,000 Gypsy slaves and literally forcing yourselves to treat them with, if anything, worse cruelty than the boyars?"

Stillwell: "The Church is not on trial here, Raklo. It is Mengele and his fellow Nazi gangsters."

Raklo: "Thank you. I was forgetting. In that case, may I now call my first witness: A Gypsy survivor of the Holocaust, Hans Braun, who remembers Mengele and his experiments at Auschwitz. I call Hans Braun."

Hans Braun: "I remember very well how he [Dr. Mengele] gave a small Gypsy boy of five or six an injection with a needle about twelve inches long. He stuck the needle in the boy's back to extract the spinal fluid. He stuck it up to the neck vertebrae. The needle broke, and it didn't take long for the child to die. Behind the building there was a kind of butcher's block with a trough for blood, like a wash basin. . . . Mengele cut the child open from neck to genitals, dissecting the body, and took out the innards to experiment with them. This was something I cannot forget."*

Raklo: "Thank you, Herr Braun. That will be all. Now let me call on another witness, this time a Jewish survivor, Vera Alexander, who had the job of supervising fifty sets of Gypsy twins in the camp. She will describe an incident which took place in 1943. I call Vera Alexander. Please take your place in the witness box."

---

* Gabrielle Tyrnauer, "'Uncle Mengele' dispensed candy, death to Gypsy children," Montreal *Gazette*, June 15, 1985.

Vera Alexander: "I remember one set of twins in particular: Guido and Nina, aged about four. One day Mengele took them away. When they returned they were in a terrible state – they had been sewn together back to back, like Siamese twins. Their wounds were infected and oozing pus.

"They screamed day and night. Then their parents – I remember their mother's name was Stella – managed to get hold of some morphine, and they killed their children in order to end their suffering. Soon after that I was taken to another camp and the Gypsies were entirely liquidated."*

Mengele: "It is an unhappy fact that despite the most stringent precautions, some of the more delicate, finely balanced experiments failed to quite measure up to original expectations. Nonetheless, I can assure you the Americans were only too glad to lay their hands on my results. I tell you, my experimental data were spirited out of Germany to Washington before you could say 'Multinational Pharmaceutical Corporation – U.S.A.'."

Stillwell: "I must object to that, Mengele. The United States appropriated your records for purely humanitarian reasons. We adopted the strictly pragmatic view that as these obscenities were a matter of history, they might as well serve mankind in the future."

Weissmann: "Can we get back to the point. Wasn't 1943 also the year Hitler decided the Gypsy camps had to be closed down?"

Raklo: "Yes. But if anything, it made the situation worse. The Roma were clubbed to death or rushed into the gas chambers or simply forced to dig their own pits and then shot, sometimes

---

* Helen Davis, 1985: 23.

two or three with the same bullet. All over Europe the brutal slaughter went on at reckless speed in an attempt to dispose as rapidly as possible of the grisly evidence."

Stillwell: "Tragic, tragic."

Raklo: "And was it not also tragic, Colonel, that throughout the Nuremberg Trials, not one Gypsy was called as a witness by the Allied prosecutors? As I remember, in the general clean-up at that time, provision was made that 'persons persecuted by reasons of nationality' should be compensated. That provision covered Jews holding German citizenship before the Nazis came to power, but didn't include us, apparently. At least the Jews had the sympathy of the world on their side. We Roma were not even accorded that. A third of all Gypsies living in Europe were anni-hilated and as many as 80 percent in those areas where Nazi control had been established the longest. How many people today are aware that the Gypsies of Europe were rounded up by the SS and sent to their death in as great if not greater proportion as the Jews? In all nearly one million people? Not one mention of this anywhere. Is it not a sad and terrible thing for a race to go to its grave unremarked by the world at large? Unmourned?"

Bishop: "I do symphathize, Raklo."

Raklo: "Yes, Your Grace, I'm sure you do. It would have been more practical and to the point if the Church had seen fit to offer a compassionate hand to assist us at the time. The one million of us Rom who perished can certainly do without your 'sympathy' now.

(turning to Colonel Stillwell): "A matter of deep regret too, I am sure, to the War Crimes Tribunal that it never attempted to dignify our loss of life in the Holocaust: subconsciously implying the same view as our persecutors that we Roma were beneath consideration.

(turning to Anton Weissmann): "And a matter of deep regret also to the Jewish nation that it allowed itself to be recognized as the one and only victim of the Holocaust. No so? Unwilling even to throw us a few scraps of recognition. Strange. After all, were we not comrades in adversity?"

Weissmann: "Look at it this way, Raklo, when you're haemorrhaging yourself, it can slip your mind about getting the other guy to hospital."

Raklo (turning to Dr. Mengele) : "And you, Mengele, foul Angel of Death, what is your regret? Surely you must have one? Just one tiny one?"

Mengele: "Perhaps. Yes, yes, actually I do, now that you mention it. And it is about time the world got to know of it. Now, as is common knowledge, I joined the Brown Shirts in 1934. Later I became aware of the possibilities that Auschwitz offered as a laboratory for experimentation in pursuit of genetic information for the benefit of the Third Reich and to improve my credentials in respect of a postwar career in eugenics. A unique opportunity. Medical experiments at Auschwitz could be followed by any number of fatal outcomes without fear of condemnation or reprisal. It would have been criminal not to take advantage of the situation. In the matter of research into twins alone, it was a veritable cornucopia of opportunities. Did you know that three thousand twins passed through my hands? I admit less than a third survived the experiments but the results were truly astonishing as evidenced by the records and human remains:

eyes, organs, even heads which I sent back to Dr. Verschuer in Berlin, the person responsible for assessing my research work.

"To get back to this business of legitimate grievance, after the war, would you believe it, Verschuer was rehabilitated and restored to a university post while I, who had done all the hard work, was stripped of my medical certificate and doctorate by the University of Frankfurt. Do you call that justice?"

Raklo: "Justice! Justice! Do you call stitching twelve-year-old children together justice? Did you show justice? You took people who lived like birds and caged them. And they went mad. They needed freedom like other people need air. You put them in striped prison uniforms with a brown triangle sewn on the left breast and then you stripped them of those clothes to torture them. Medical experiments? Bah! It was nothing more than depraved, perverted psychotic sadism."

Stillwell (intervening) : "What beats the hell out of me, I admit, is why our government didn't crack down before. Washington must have known what was going on in the Nazi Germany of the thirties. Why didn't we do something about it, for God's sake?"

Weissmann: "Didn't they tell you, Colonel? Governments only do the right thing when all other possible avenues have been exhausted."

Raklo (musingly) : "Before they died they had to take off their striped uniforms and fold them neatly. They were happy to do so. You see, the clothes were the prison. It was almost worth dying to get out of them."

Epilogue

Budapest, March 1994

I was in Hungary as an observer at a conference on minority groups organized by the Cultural Ministry. The Budapest Spring Festival was on and despite the rain there was a sunny feeling of brightness and optimism in the air of a people reborn after fifty years of Communism. There was also a downside. As an official remarked: "Too few people have jobs now. That was the case in the old days as well, of course, but at least everybody had a place of work to report to in the morning."

Outside of conference hours, I was drawn to one or other of the three main railway stations where thousands of Gypsies from Poland and Romania were seeking warmth and begging opportunities. Despite severe under-nourishment and skimpy clothing, they seemed to be bearing up stoically on a blend of cigarettes and boiled water. No one was interested in them. They had nowhere to go. Sooner or later when their presence at the railway stations became too disruptive, the authorities would take the decision to round them up and ship them somewhere. Until that time they could only beg for alms and hope for the best.

Not for the first time, I had the vision of a race doomed to struggle eternally between its internal dream world and the harsh reality of its day-to-day existence as society's fringe-dwellers.

Without consciously meaning to, I kept looking for that one

face in the crowd that I knew I would never find, would never see again. Seelya's face.

She'd left Istanbul four months ago. I'd received a letter shortly before Christmas from Fatima – in Turkish, of course. It had been a year since I'd had any news of them and I waited impatiently at the Translation Bureau while the translation was being typed up.

After hoping I was maintaining the same excellent health as she was, Fatima's letter went on: "Shortly after you left I started a catering business, preparing meals for American and foreign companies in their boardrooms. It grew and I expanded into private functions at the homes of the executives. Some time ago I thought to sell – a good offer was made – but I decided no. What else would I do? Acting the prosperous widow is not a fulltime occupation for an intelligent woman, I told myself. But now I have changed my mind. I will find a little place in the country and grow my own flowers and vegetables and search for my roots. It seems these past months that I have lost my purpose in life. Life can be very sad.

"Yes, you have no doubt guessed, Seelya is no longer with me. Oh, and I had such high hopes for her: finishing high school and then maybe the university. She is such a bright child. I could see the next few years in my mind's eye: school dances, picnics on the Bosphorus, the theater, films and all the exciting things I never had the opportunity of doing when I was her age – Turkish society was very strict then. Watching her with a mother's eyes as she fell in and out of love. Oh, it was such a good feeling! To be able to live again in the body of a beautiful young girl who every day I grew closer to. I could not have loved her more had she been my own daughter.

"And then, one morning when I brought a glass of orange juice to her bed, she was gone. No note, no explanation, no destination. He school books and school clothes arranged tidily on the bed. She left wearing nothing but a simple dress. No suitcase. Maybe some money, I don't know."

I could see it clearly: the bourgeois, comfortably off Fatima wishing to play mother, and the Gypsy girl, quick, restless, easily bored, unwilling to be fettered. As if in confirmation, the next phrase read: "I tried to put a collar around her neck, make her behave the way I thought she should. It can't be done. O, how I miss her."

There was a translator's note to the effect that there were stains on the notepaper and the next phrase couldn't be deciphered. Tears?

Then her news of Patsi. I could hardly see him staying in Istanbul forever. Well, it seems I was right.

She wrote: "As to Patsi, now that is a different story. No, the same one, really. For me. In the beginning he helped me in the business . . . odd jobs . . . carrying things. Delivering the metal containers of food. Very simple activities. He was not good. He could not speak the language and would not try to get on with people. After a while he worked only on those days when he had no money for drink. But still I persevered until I saw he was harming the business.

"He got his old job back at the *Tchingéné* nightclub but one night he argued with an important man, a member of Parliament, who said he had put the fingers of his left hand in his drink. We Moslems take these things seriously.

"As you know, Patsi doesn't have a left hand, which is why he became so angry. He drew his knife so fast they said it was like magic. Of course they made silent the affair because the man should not have been there. He had lost his wife the week before in an automobile accident and was in mourning. Two days later, very politely, the police called here at the house but

Patsi had already left for Greece. Something about a circus, he said. He was very vague. I gave him the money you left with me. I have not heard from him since. He was a good person really. At heart. I think it is that when a man is born a wolf he can never become a dog."

Then another note from the translator saying the next block of text was illegible. Then: "I suppose he is dead by now. No one could live long the way he did."

Personally I thought Patsi would live to be a hundred. He was blessed with psychosomatic good health brought on by living just the way he wanted to and not giving a damn about anything or anybody. Above all, that particular Gypsy man was buoyed up by the sense of the heroic. That aura he communicated to the world of being sovereign, unique, part of the most important drama that ever was: his very own life.

"Foolish, foolish woman," Fatima went on. "No husband, too old for children and so what is there in this world for her? She must try to tame a Gypsy. There is no rope strong enough to hold them. They do not . . . Seelya . . . Patsi they do not have a part in our world. But, Mister Roger, I tell you, I would not have missed the experiences of happiness with them for all the money in the world. They taught me to see life in their way. That it was to be enjoyed to the very most. Sometimes I think I am very lucky . . . privileged, is a better word, to have loved them, even though for so short a time."

How like history, I thought to myself. A unifying bond, my presence, I suppose, had held them together, but once gone they had to go their separate ways. It was in the blood. I had no idea whether I would ever see them again. I hoped so. But it would not be the same, I knew that.

It wasn't until toward the end of the letter that Fatima gave me news of Gopi Lal. Apparently he'd been the first one to leave.

After only six months at the Embassy, he had given notice and gone back to India. He was homesick, Fatima wrote, and besides through a friend of a friend he had been recommended for a position in some ministry or other in New Delhi. A snatch of conversation we'd once had came back to me. He thought he'd take the Indian Civil Service exam when he got back to India after the trip and to improve his chances he wanted to concentrate on some off-the-beaten-track specialty like the Tibetan dialect of the Golog nomads of Qinghai Province in Western China or . . . well, his head was full of weird and wonderful ideas. In a pantomime of Indian resignation, he had commented: "For every Public Service position in India there is one lakh [100,000] applicants sitting the exam. Per se, Uncle, one has to have an IQ of 170ish to stand a chance. Tell me, Uncle, if the people in control are so intelligent, why does India always make such an awful botch of things?"

Dear old Gopi Lal. Whatever happened, I was sure he'd succeed in life. He and the Civil Service were just born for each other.

As I finished reading the letter, the awful thought occurred that I had now lost contact with all three of them and would probably never see or hear from them again.

And that is why, in a fruitless attempt to prove myself wrong, I couldn't help turning up at Budapest's Nyugati Central Station every evening. Deep down I would not have been in the least bit surprised to have seen Seelya running toward me crying out, "*Misterji, Misterji*, Gopi Lal's being horrid again."

No, not unlikely at all. The entire quest had been full – jam packed – with fateful coincidences and lucky breaks, as if it were absolutely predestined that the saga of the Rom emerge at this time. That whatever I or anyone else did, the weirdest happenings and concurrences and coincidences would conspire to

make the truth shine through. It had been throughout a saga of
one stroke of good fortune after another. So why should I quibble
at another totally unsolicited miracle like Seelya racing along
the platform toward me? But this time it didn't happen.

Still in a bit of a reverie, I came out of the railway station.
Standing on the curbside I automatically looked right (as one
would in England) and got the fright of my life as an army bus
passed by my nose at a rattling rate from the other way. I'd been
a bare inch from leaving an ugly red blotch on Padmaniczky
Street. Somewhat shaken, I walked on and passed in front of
St. Istvan's (Stephen's) Basilica on Bajcsy-Zsilinszky Street. On
impulse I went in. It seemed a good idea to thank someone up
there for my deliverance – ironic after having spent an age charging around parts of the globe where angels fear to tread that a
bus should nearly flatten me in Budapest.

As I entered its cloistered gloom, she emerged, ghost-like,
from behind a pillar. (Shades of the Lost City, I thought.)
Although the temperature was but a few degrees above freezing, she was wearing only a high-necked – circa 1940s – thread-
bare coat. A dark brown, wrinkle-cheeked Romni. Maybe
mid-forties, it was hard to tell, there was so much pain and depri-
vation written on her face. She came at me, hands out and sup-
plicating in a way forcefully reminiscent of the Kanjar maids all
that time ago in Balotra.

I dug into my pocket and gave her a few coins and within
seconds she had my hands in hers and was kissing them warmly.
I felt very embarrassed but that was superseded by the deepest
pity. For the past few days, all I had been hearing at the conference were tales of gloom and doom for Hungary's Gypsy population (circa 750,000) now, of course, reinforced by thousands
of refugees flooding in. It was all highly dispiriting and very
much in line with the current prognosis that, given a few bad

winters, in ten years' time the Rom would cease to be a threat or burden to anyone any more. Finally, I managed to tear myself away from her and, abandoning my original intention to offer up a prayer of thanks for my salvation, walked back to the hotel situated by the Opera House.

Throughout the evening my thoughts dwelt on the enchantment of that time when I had followed the Gypsies halfway across the world. Learned to recognize their ups and downs (quite a few of the latter) and nuances of feeling and character; the way they reacted in basic "feeling" terms as opposed to the *Gaujo*'s systematic, logical, instinctively thinking approach to life and its problems.

"I was whipped," says the *Gaujo*. (That's mental/passive.)

"I ate blows," says the Gypsy. (That's physical/active.)

But there were times when I could never follow them. When they retreated to a corner of the Gypsy psyche where no one could enter. One manifestation of this was their attitude toward pain that, whether mental or physical, was a very real, ever-present thing for them, a part of their lives, and in a strange way they seemed to almost welcome it, rolling it around and sinking deep into it.

The only way to explain it is to say that the Gypsy experiences, in the most vital way imaginable, every single thing that proves to him he is alive. And that includes things the *Gaujo* wouldn't understand like anguish, pain and despair.

I have always felt, too, that somehow through the pain, but also in states of extreme joy and great but fleeting happiness, they manage to touch a corner of the universe, unroll it just a fraction to perceive the grand design in a way no other human being could or ever has save maybe the Prophets.

I first heard it put into words in "Patsi's Joint" in Istanbul's Gypsy quarter. Two *Tchingéné* women combined in a duet, a hauntingly eastern, erotic melody that made the hairs at the back of the neck stand up. They followed the song by dancing together: a long, low, melancholy dance called the Lassan, which Gopi Lal had described as "sad thoughts set to music."

I couldn't help but notice that although they both had very good voices and combined well together, the shorter, plainer one affected the audience so much more than her taller, more beautiful partner. You knew she was alive inside the rhythm and the lyrics – organically part of them – and that when they came out from her larynx you could feel your own heart hurt with the pain and misery and the joy that came from seeing the world right at this moment in that way: the ecstasy that came from riding the music, all that it meant to be a Gypsy in a *Gaujo* world. I say it once more: riding the music again and again . . . being with the music . . . above the music . . . part of the music.

The nightclub manager (himself a *Tchingéné*) was at the bar supervising an order of cocktails being prepared for a group of visiting firemen from Turin. I asked him about her. Why was it she was so much better than her partner? After he had supervised the Napoleon Brandy and Old Grandad bottles replenished with the local rot-gut mixed with a little retsina and caramel to lend maturity to the taste, he turned to answer my question in a mutilated mélange of French and English. Tidied up, it came to this:

"The plain one has lived. She sees the world through the sweat of pain, of sadness. Nothing will ever be bright again as it was with her first man. There is black in her heart and she wrings it out in the dance, in the song. Without that love for the black, the craving to squeeze it out from your body, you will never be a good singer or dancer of the *Tchingéné*."

I left it at that and said goodnight. I remember turning a corner into a narrow street that was already three centuries old when Charlemagne was born and seeing the lights of the Pelas Hotel before me. It struck me for the first time how true Miklos's words had been about how they could burn you, these people. You never really escaped from them. They scraped a raw sensitivity in you that reacted to them and thoughts of them with extraordinary awareness and sensitivity. You'd break away from anything or anyone just to be with them and to hear their spark crackle.

I couldn't help feeling as I went to bed that night that although I had answered all the questions I'd set out to — and then some — my spiritual pilgrimage was only just beginning. I had learned to think and act like a Gypsy and adopt as a matter of course a view of the world that — reduced to its simplest — lays down that the "high times" — marriage and death and other important milestones — are pretty much set out from birth and that all we, who have the blessed good fortune to be alive, have to do is to fill in the intervening spaces with love of life and passionate involvement and sense of awareness of ourselves as the greatest story that ever was. As much as we possibly can. That it doesn't much matter what chances we take in this very short existence because the next lodestar point in our life is pretty much determined anyway so there's no point in worrying about it. In fact the contrary: that determination provides security really.

And their view of happiness, too, I like. For the Rom, happiness is not a "have" thing but a "not have" thing. It's not having to go to sleep on an open, rainy heath, with your child running a fever, and not even a bit of bread in you to still the stomach cramps. It's not being without your loved ones. It's not being told to move on just when you've found a grassy spot to lay your head at the end of the day.

Two days later, turning a corner, I found myself anew in

front of St. Istvan's Basilica. A crowd had gathered around a half dozen Gypsy children who with scant regard for the temperature, clad only in trousers and shirt, were dancing and tumbling to the music of a tin whistle while a young girl of about the same age and size as I remembered Seelya being when we first picked her up was passing around an old trilby hat. Nothing exceptional about that and I, too, dug in my pocket for a few coins.

I heard a cheery "hello" and there, some thirty yards opposite, was Klara, my very helpful lady from the Department of Ethnic and National Minorities (which looks after Hungary's Gypsy population), and beside her a face I recognized but couldn't quite place. As I walked around the edge of the crowd to join them, it came to me that the other woman was the Romni who had accosted me in the church, although now she was sporting what looked like a good quality quilted jacket and fur boots.

"You know each other?" said Klara as the woman broke into an excited babble as I came up to them.

"We met in church. I gave her a few coins, that's all."

"Oh, so you're the one. Well, they were enough for her to buy a loaf of bread to give her strength to take the bus to come and see me at the department."

"Oh? So what's the story?"

"I found her children for her. Three boys and three girls. She'd become separated from them. We had them safe in the Juvenile Center."

"Are those all hers?" I asked, pointing to the young buskers just finishing their act.

"Yes, all except the little girl collecting the money. She was at the Center, too – no family or anything. Simply attached herself to them and just refuses to go back."

I cast a quick glance at the child as she came over, carefully holding the trilby to her chest and containing an amount, I found out later, equivalent to a whole week's salary for Klara.

"I don't suppose you know anyone who would like to take her in or adopt her?" Klara asked hopefully.

The little girl looked up at me with the biggest, gravest, darkest eyes in the world. In a flash I saw with crystal clarity exactly what was going to happen. She was going to stretch out her arms and tears would come to her eyes and run down that little face and. . . .

Oh, no! Not again!

"So what did you do?" asked Meredith later.

"I took the only humanitarian decision a man could in the circumstance."

"And what was that?" she asked, looking behind me.

"Bolted for dear life, darling."

Bibliography

✻ ✻ ✻

BATAILLARD, P.   1849   Nouvelles recherches sur l'apparition
et la dispersion des Bohémiens en
Europe
Frank & Cie, Paris

1884   "Les Tsiganes appelés Chimbres en
Grèce, d'après un voyageur français du
XVe siècle," *Revue critique*, 18 : 158 - 163

BERCOVICI, Konrad   1928   The story of the Gypsies
Jonathan Cape, London

BORROW, George   1841   The Zincali (Gypsies of Spain)
London

1874   Romano Lavo-Lil (A Book of the Gypsy)
Alan Sutton Publishing Ltd, Great Britain

BOSWELL, S.G.   1970   The Book of Boswell,
ed. John Seymour, London

CLEBERT, John Paul   1963   The Gypsies   .
Vista Books, London

COLSON, Félix   1839   De l'état présent et de l'avenir des
principautés de Moldavie et de Valachie
Paris

CROWTHER, Geoff   1990   Lonely Planet Travel Survival Kit — India
FINLAY, Hugh   4th edition
PRAKASH, A Raj   Lonely Planet Publications, Victoria,
WHEELER, Tony   Australia

DAVENPORT, Hugh   1975   The Trials and Triumphs of the Mewar
Kingdom, prepared for and approved
by the Maharana of Mewar Charitable
Foundation, Udaipur, Rajasthan, India

DAVIS, Helen   1985   "Angels of Life," *Hadassah Magazine*,
November: 21-25

FITZGERALD, Edward 1948   The Rubáiyát of Omar Khayyám
(Translation)   Jaico Publishing House, India

GASCOIGNE, Bamber 1971   The Great Moghuls
                                        Jonathan Cape, London

GRELLMAN, H.M.S.   1783   Die Zigeuner
                                        Dessau and Leipzig

                    1807   Dissertation on the Gipseys
                                        Wm Ballantine, London

HANCOCK, Ian   1987   The Pariah Syndrome
                                        Karoma Publishers, Inc,
                                        Ann Arbor

HAYES, Richard   n.d.   Old Irish Links with France

HOLDICH, Col. Sir   1910   Gates of India
    Thomas   Macmillan & Co Ltd, London

KENDRICK, Donald   1972   The Destiny of Europe's Gypsies
PUXTON, Grattan   Heinemann, London and New York

KINNEY, Arthur F.   1973   Rogues, Vagabonds and Sturdy
                                        Beggars
                                        The Imprint Society, Barre

KOCHANOWSKI, J.   1963   Gypsy Studies (Parts I & II)
                                        International Academy of Indian
                                        Culture, New Delhi

                    1984   L'Identité des Romane Chave
                                        (Tsiganes d'Europe)

LAL, Chaman   1962   Gypsies: Forgotten Children of India
                                        The Publications Division, Ministry of
                                        Information and Broadcasting,
                                        Government of India

MACRITCHIE, David   1886   Gypsies of India
                                        New Society Publications,
                                        Delhi, India

MAJUMDAR, R.C.   1927   Ancient India
                                             Motilal Banarisidass, Delhi, India,
                                             revised edition 1964

MASTERS, Brian   1990   Maharana
                                             Mapin Publishers Pvt Ltd,
                                             Ahmedabad, India

MIKLOSICH, Franz   1872   Über die Mundarten und die Wan-
                                             derungen der Zigeuner Europa's
                                             Karl Gerold, Vienna

OZANNE, J.W.   1878   Three years in Rumania
                                             Chapman & Hall, London

PASPATI, Alexander G. 1861   "Memoir on the language of the
                                             Gypsies as now used in the Turkish
                                             Empire," *Journal of the American
                                             Oriental Society*, 7:143-270

                        1870   Etudes sur les Tchinghianes ou
                                             Bohémiens de l'Empire Ottoman
                                             Kordmela, Constantinople

POTT, A.F.   1844   Die Zigeuner in Europa und Asien
                                             (I & II), Heynemann Verlag, Halle

RISHI, W.R.   1974   Multilingual Romany Dictionary
                                             Roma Publications, Chandigarh, India

                        1976   Roma
                                             Registrar Punjabi University, Patiara, India

                        1982   India and Russia Linguistic and
                                             Cultural Affinity
                                             Roma Publications, Chandigarh, India

ROLEINE, Robert   1978   Le prince d'un été
                                             Tallandier, Paris

                        1979   "Esclaves, les Tsiganes,"
                                             Historia, 397: 108-114

ROWNEY, Horatio Bickerstaffe   1882   The Wild Tribes of India
Low Price Publications,
Delhi, India

RUDIGER, J.C.   1782   Neuster Zuwachs der teutschen,
fremden und allegemeinen
Sprachkunde
Leipzig und Halle

RUHELA, Satya Pal   1984   The Children of Indian Nomads
Sterling Publishers Private Ltd,
India

SACHAU, Edward C.   1910   Alberuni's India (I & II)
Low Price Publications, Delhi, India

SHARMA, N.K.   1991   Camel Safari in Jaisalmer
Smt Madhuv Sharma, Jodhpur, India

SHASHI, S.S.   1990   Roma, The Gypsy World
Sundeep Prakashan, Delhi, India

SINGHAL, D.P.   1982   Gypsies: Indians in Exile
Archana Publications, India

SOULIS, George C.   1961   "Gypsies in the Byzantine Empire and
the Balkans in the late Middle Ages,"
Dumbarton Oaks Papers, 15:142-165

  1980   Historical Studies: Byzantina,
Balcanica, Neohellenica, 1927-1966
Athens

TOD, James   1829   Annals & Antiquities of Rajasthan
(I & II)
Oriental Books Reprint
Corporation, New Delhi, India

TOPSFIELD, Andrew   1990   The City Palace Museum, Udaipur
Paintings of Mewar Court Life
Madin Publishing Pvt Ltd,
Ahmedabad, India

TRIGG, Elwood B.   1973   Gypsy Demons and Divinities
Secaucus, NJ

VALLIANT, J.A.   1857   Les Romes: Histoire vraie des vrais
Bohémiens
Dentu & Cie, Paris

VESEY-FITZGERALD,   1944   Gypsies of Britain
B.   London (new enlarged edition 1973)

WAYMAN, Alex   1973   The Buddhist Tantras
Motilal Bawarsidass Publishers Pvt
Ltd, Delhi

YATES, Dora   1953   My Gypsy Days
London

YOORS, Jan   1971   Crossings: A Journal of Survival and
Resistance in World War II
Simon & Schuster, New York

JOURNALS

BANJARA, Bombay, October 1983 and other issues
JOURNAL OF THE GYPSY LORE SOCIETY:
     July-October 1955; 1957
     January-April 1960; 1962; 1964; and other numbers